The Center for South and Southeast Asia Studies of the University of California is the coordinating center for research, teaching programs, and special projects relating to the South and Southeast Asia areas on the nine campuses of the University. The Center is the largest such research and teaching organization in the United States, with more than 150 related faculty representing all disciplines within the social sciences, languages, and humanities.

The Center publishes a Monograph series, an Occasional Papers series, and sponsors a series published by the University of California Press. Manuscripts for these publications have been selected with the highest standards of academic excellence, with emphasis on those studies and literary works that are pioneers in their fields, and that provide fresh insights into the life and culture of the great civilizations of South and Southeast Asia.

RECENT PUBLICATIONS OF THE CENTER FOR SOUTH AND SOUTHEAST ASIA STUDIES:

Richard I. Cashman
The Myth of the LOKAMANYA:
Tilak and Mass Politics in Maharashtra

Edward Conze
The Large Sutra on Perfect Wisdom

Ronald Inden
Marriage and Rank in Bengali Culture

Tom G. Kessinger
Vilyatpur, 1848-1968:
Social and Economic Change in a North Indian Village

Robert Lingat
The Classical Law of India (translated by J. Duncan M. Derrett)

THE POEMS OF ANCIENT TAMIL

This volume is sponsored by the
Center for South and Southeast Asia Studies,
University of California, Berkeley

THE POEMS OF ANCIENT TAMIL

THEIR MILIEU AND THEIR SANSKRIT COUNTERPARTS

GEORGE L. HART III

UNIVERSITY OF CALIFORNIA PRESS
BERKELEY LOS ANGELES LONDON

UNIVERSITY OF CALIFORNIA PRESS
Berkeley and Los Angeles, California

University of California Press, Ltd.
London, England

ISBN: 0-520-02672-1
Library of Congress Catalog Card Number: 73-91667

Printed in the United States of America

For my wife, Kausalya

உலகெலா முள்ளடி யடக்கி யோரடிக்
கலகிலா தவ்வடிக் கன்பன் மெய்யதாழ்
இலைகுலாந் துழாய்முடி யேக நாயகன்
சிலைகுலாந் தோளினாய் சிறியன் சாலவே

-கம்பராமாயணம்

(In which Viśvāmitra relates to the boy Rāma the story of the demon Bali, who ruled the universe and who, though he knew well what it would cost him, gave to Vāmana, the dwarf incarnation of Vishnu, all that He could measure in three steps):

After He had contained all worlds inside His feet,
He had no place for His next step,
but placed it on the body of him who loved Him.
That sole Lord whose head shines with tulsi leaves,
O You whose arms appear resplendent with Your bow,
was very small indeed.

— Kamparāmāyaṇa *1.448*

सा तत्र ददृशे विश्वं जगत्स्थास्नु च खं दिशः ।
साद्रिद्वीपाब्धिभूगोलं सवाय्वग्नीन्दुतारकम् ॥
ज्योतिष्चक्रं जलं तेजो नभस्वान्वियदेव च ।
वैकारिकाणीन्द्रियाणि मनो मात्रा गुणास्त्रयः ॥
एतद्विचित्रं सह जीवकालस्वभावकर्माशयलिङ्गभेदम् ।
सूनोस्तनौ वीक्ष्य विदारितास्ये व्रजं सहात्मानमवाप शङ्काम् ॥

(In which Yaśodā inspects the mouth of her son, Krishna, to see whether He has eaten mud):

There she saw the universe with all that moves and does not,
and the sky, and the directions,
with mountains, continents, oceans, and the globe of earth,
the wind and lightning, the moon and stars, the zodiac,
water, fire, wind, and ether,
the manas, *elementary matter, and the three strands.*
This wondrous sight she beheld in the body of her son
as she looked into His open mouth
together with the distinctions
of souls, times, natures, actions, desires, and gender.
And she saw there the village with herself,
and she could not believe her eyes.

— Bhāgavatapurāṇa *10.8.37–39*

CONTENTS

PREFACE

Almost 2,000 years ago, there took place an extraordinary flowering of literature in Tamilnad, the southernmost part of India. Strangely, this literature, which includes what I believe is among the finest poetry ever written, has been neglected in the West and even in India, where it arose. In fact, much of the classical Tamil literature we possess today would certainly have perished were it not for the efforts of U. V. Swaminathaier (1855–1942), perhaps the greatest of all modern Indologists, who devoted his life to recovering and editing as many Tamil manuscripts as he could, often undergoing unbelievable hardships. In this book, I have attempted to discover some of the ways in which the earliest Tamil literature sheds light on the culture and literature of ancient India. I have tried to give some understanding of the techniques of ancient Tamil poetry and to compare them with their Indo-Aryan counterparts. I am well aware of the inadequacy of what I have done; I can only hope that it represents at least a sound beginning for what must be done in the future.

I would like to express my appreciation to all who have helped me in writing this book: to A. K. Ramanujan, my first Tamil teacher, whose wonderful translations and insights first led me to realize the profundity and importance of the Tamil anthologies; to Ramasubramaniam, my patient and understanding Tamil teacher in India; to K. V. Seshadrinathan, my Sanskrit teacher in India; to Miss Saudamini Bahulikar, with whom I had many fruitful conversations; and to my wife, Kausalya, who made many valuable suggestions and who helped in many other ways. Most of all, I am indebted to my Sanskrit teacher and guru, Daniel Ingalls. There is not a page that has not been greatly influenced for the better by his suggestions. Even before he had seen any translations of the Tamil poems, he had the insight to suspect that Sanskrit literature might have been influenced by a Southern tradition. Later, his suggestions were of great value even in those sections that lie outside the ken of Indo-Aryan and Sanskrit; I can only say that I often suspected that he had inferred more about ancient Tamil India without having been exposed to any of the primary sources than I was able to ferret out even with the help of exhaustive indices of the anthologies. In the sections that touch on Indo-Aryan, I am indebted to him not only for suggestions, but also for references too numerous to acknowledge individually. Beyond this, I can only suggest the extent to which I am indebted to him for first introducing me to India and for teaching me most of what I know about it.

ABBREVIATIONS

The actual texts followed are given in the references, at the back of the book.

Aiñ., the *Aiñkuṟunūṟu.*
Ak., the *Akanāṉūṟu.*
Bu., the *Buddhacarita.*
Cil., the *Cilappatikāram.*
D.E.D., *A Dravidian Etymological Dictionary.* See under Burrow, T., in the references.
Kali., the *Kalittokai.*
Kum., the *Kumārasaṃbhava.*
Kuṟ., the *Kuṟuntokai.*
Maṇi., the *Maṇimēkalai.*
Mbh., the *Mahābhārata.*
Megh., the *Meghadūta.* See under Edgerton, *Kalidasa, the Cloud Messenger*, in the references.
Naṟ., the *Naṟṟiṇai.*
Pari., the *Paripāṭal.*
Patiṟ., the *Patiṟṟuppattu.*
Puṟ., the *Puṟanāṉūṟu.*
R., the *Raghuvaṃśa.*
Sa., the *Sattasaī.* See under *Gāthāsaptaśatī* in the references.
Su., the *Sundarakāṇḍa*, a part of the *Vālmīki-Rāmāyaṇa.*
Subh., the *Subhāṣitaratnakośa.* See also under Ingalls, *An Anthology of Sanskrit Court Poetry*, in the references.

INTRODUCTION

In a famous passage in his *Oxford History of India*, Vincent Smith wrote, "Some day, perhaps, the history of Dravidian civilization may be written by a competent scholar skilled in all the lore and languages required for the study of the subject, but at present the literature concerned with it is too fragmentary, defective, and controversial to permit of condensation. Early Indian history, as a whole, cannot be viewed in true perspective until the non-Aryan institutions of the south receive adequate treatment. Hitherto most historians of ancient India have written as if the south did not exist."[1] When I started to write this book, it was as an attempt to begin to remedy this situation in the area of the history of ancient Indian literature. I found that there is an extremely large body of Tamil literature, the extent of which was quite unknown to Vincent Smith and the historians of Sanskrit literature, that was written between the first and third centuries A.D., before Aryan influence became strong enough in Tamilnad to change fundamentally the older Dravidian society there. Clearly, then, a comparison of the similarities between ancient Tamil and Indo-Aryan poetry, similarities that are evident to anyone who has even a brief acquaintance with those literatures, should reveal something of the history of both literary traditions. A detailed study showing just when the shared themes appeared in Indo-Aryan should lead to important conclusions concerning the source of those themes: if they first appear in the northern tradition only after they are attested in Tamil, a good case can be made that they originated in the southern tradition.

It soon became apparent, however, that a study of only shared literary themes would be inadequate for a proper understanding of the relationship between ancient Tamil and Indo-Aryan literature. For several reasons it was necessary to give a detailed description of the society that produced the Tamil anthologies. First, it was important to determine the exact extent of northern influence on that society. If such influence was as great as some

[1] (London, 1958), p. 43.

writers have claimed, the shared themes might well be of Aryan origin in spite of their anterior appearance in Tamil. Secondly, it became apparent that the literary themes of ancient Tamil could not be separated from the beliefs and culture of the men who used them. In order to understand properly the significance of the shared themes, it was necessary to acquire an understanding of ancient Tamil society and its religion, neither of which has been satisfactorily described to date. Thirdly, if in fact there was an influx of South Indian poetic elements into Aryan literature, it is to be expected that other cultural elements would also be making their way into North India. In order to determine whether in fact there were such common cultural elements that originated in the South and, if so, just when they first appeared in the North, it was necessary to describe ancient Tamil society in detail and to compare it with relevant aspects of northern society. Finally, and most importantly, it soon became apparent that the poems contain cultural information of great importance that throws light on such vital issues as the development of caste, the institution of kingship in India, and the origins of and reasons for many customs concerning women that today are pan-Indian. Thus the first part of this book, which primarily concerns the culture and religious beliefs and practices of the ancient Tamils, came to be written.

For the second part of the book, which is devoted to the study of literary elements and techniques common to ancient Tamil and Indo-Aryan, it was necessary to pick Indo-Aryan works that would represent the most important phases in the development of ancient North Indian literature. Clearly a good starting place was the *Mahābhārata*, which for the most part dates from before ancient Tamil literature. The poetic elements in that epic have been well described by Ram Karan Sharma in *Elements of Poetry in the Mahābhārata*, on which I have depended for the occurrence of themes in that epic. The next important source was the *Rāmāyaṇa*, in which the poetic approach is very different from the *Mahābhārata* and which also antedates the Tamil poems. For themes in that epic, I have indexed the *Sundarakāṇḍa*, commonly considered its most beautiful and poetic section. Between the epics and the full-blown classical poetry of Kālidāsa, there is only one Sanskrit poet whose works have survived to any extent

—Aśvaghoṣa, who lived in the first century A.D., and who thus antedates by a few years the Tamil poems. I have indexed the first nine books of his *Buddhacarita*. For Kālidāsa, who certainly wrote after the first half of the fourth century A.D.,[2] I have indexed the *Raghuvaṃśa*, the first eight books of the *Kumārasaṃbhava*, and the *Meghadūta*. For post-Kālidāsan Sanskrit poetry I have depended on Ingalls's excellent translation of the *Subhāṣitaratnakośa*.

It was evident from the first that there is an extremely large number of themes shared by the *Sattasaī* and the Tamil tradition. All the poems of that work have therefore been indexed for this study. Unfortunately, the date of that work is somewhat dubious; nevertheless, it appears to me that Keith is right when he writes:

> Of the date of Hāla it is impossible to be certain. The mechanical method of assuming that he is to be looked for in the list of Sātavāhana kings and placing him in the first or second century A.D., because he ought to come about the middle of the list, and the dynasty extended on one view from c. 240 or 230 B.C. to A.D. 225 is clearly fallacious. What is more important is that, to judge from the evidence of the Prakrits of Aśvaghoṣa and the inscriptions, the weakening of consonants which is the dominant feature of Māhārāṣṭrī cannot have set in as we find it in Hāla until about A.D. 200. This makes it likely that the poetry was produced in the period from A.D. 200 to 450, though we have no assurance of the date. Moreover, only 430 stanzas have a place in all the recensions, so that we must admit that there has been extensive interpolation. It is possible, even probable, that in its origin the *Sattasaī* was no mere anthology, but a careful collection of verses largely his own or refashioned by himself—much as Burns refashioned some of his material—on the basis of older verses, and that in course of time by interpolation and change the collection lost much of its individuality.[3]

Thus for all intents and purposes the *Sattasaī* may be placed between Aśvaghoṣa and Kālidāsa. It is certain that Kālidāsa knew of the Maharashtrian poetic tradition, for in his plays he

[2] See M. Winternitz, *A History of Indian Literature*, trans. S. Ketkar (Calcutta, 1959), III:23–25.

[3] Arthur Berriedale Keith, *A History of Sanskrit Literature* (London, 1920), pp. 223–224.

has composed verses in Māhārāṣṭrī that are similar to those of the *Sattasaī*.

For Tamil sources, I have indexed the whole of the *Puṟanāṉūṟu*, the *Kuṟuntokai*, the *Aiṅkuṟunūṟu*, and the first 234 poems of the *Akanāṉūṟu*. Occasionally I have found relevant passages in other works of ancient Tamil, by indices, and utilized them. It should be borne in mind that the common poetic elements analyzed in the second part of this book represent only a small number of the actual shared elements that exist. I have here tried to give an accurate account of the relationship between ancient Tamil and Indo-Aryan literature. I am quite aware that all aspects of that relationship cannot be understood without a more comprehensive study many times the length of this one; nevertheless, I believe that the conclusions I have made are fully warranted and substantiated by the selected material treated.

All translations are mine except those from the *Subhāṣitaratnakośa*, which are by Ingalls, those from the *Meghadūta*, which are by Edgerton, those from the *Buddhacarita*, which are by Johnston, and those from the first seven books of the *Raghuvaṃśa*, which are by Moreshwar Ramchandra Kale. I have checked all translations except Ingalls' and Johnston's against the texts and made revisions where necessary.

Part I

THE MILIEU OF THE ANCIENT TAMIL POEMS

1

THE POEMS, THEIR NATURE AND THEIR DATE

The earliest poems in Tamil that have survived to the present comprise eight anthologies and ten songs, a total of 2,381 poems by 473 poets and including 102 poems by anonymous authors. A work on grammar and poetic technique entitled the *Tolkāppiyam* and eighteen minor works, which are somewhat later than the other writings, have also survived.

The anthologies consist of poems divided into two broad categories, called *akam*, or interior, and *puṟam*, or exterior. The former poems concern all the phases of love between man and woman; that is, their subject is life viewed from inside the family. The other category, puṟam, contains many different kinds of poems—poems of war, of kings' praise, of suppliants' requests, of mourning, of ethics—all of which have in common the fact that they deal with men's interactions in society, outside the family.

Five anthologies contain akam poems exclusively. The *Aiṅkuṟunūṟu*, or five hundred short poems, contains stanzas of from three to five lines by five different poets, each of whom has written one hundred poems on one of the akam themes. The *Kuṟuntokai*, or short anthology, contains 401 poems of from six to eight lines by 205 poets; the *Naṟṟiṇai* has four hundred poems of from nine to twelve lines by 192 poets; the *Akanāṉūṟu*, or four hundred on akam, contains poems of from thirteen to thirty-one lines by 142 poets; and finally the *Kalittokai* has 150 poems, in the *kali* meter, of twelve to eighty lines by five poets, each of whom has treated a different akam theme.

Two anthologies contain only puṟam poems: the *Puṟanāṉūṟu* contains four hundred puṟam poems of four to forty lines by 156 poets, and the *Patiṟṟuppattu* has eighty poems of between five and fifty-seven lines, ten by each poet on one Chera king (two sets of ten poems have been lost; originally the work contained one hundred poems). Finally, there is one anthology, the *Paripāṭal*, containing mixed poems of thirty-two to one hundred forty lines by thirteen poets. Only twenty-two of the original seventy poems are extant. The *Pattuppāṭṭu*, or ten songs, are much longer poems, of from 103 to 782 lines by ten different poets. These are poems of description and of praise of gods, and they do not fit well into the category of either akam or puṟam.

Of the early Tamil works described, the *Pattuppāṭṭu*, the *Paripāṭal*, and the *Kalittokai* seem slightly later than the others on stylistic and linguistic grounds. As for the date of the main corpus of poems, it has been shown recently by Iravatham Mahadevan that the inscription at Pukalūr, which can be dated by paleographic methods to about 200 A.D., mentions the names of Chera kings and other chieftains who appear in the *Patiṟṟuppattu* and other anthologies.[1] This evidence agrees with the fact that the *Cilappatikāram*, an epic that must have been written several hundred years after most of the early literature described above, judging by its language and style, mentions King Gajabāhu I of Ceylon, who is known to have reigned from 173 to 195 A.D., as the contemporary of the Chera king Ceṅkuṭṭuvaṉ, who appears in the early anthologies. Many historical references in the poems seem to fit this period as well. Thus the poems describe trade with the Yavanas, or westerners, a trade whose date is indicated by the fact that hoards of Roman coins of the emperors of the first and second centuries A.D. have been found in Tamilnad.

[1] Iravatham Mahadevan, "Tamil Brahmi Inscriptions of the Sangam Age," *Proceedings of the Second International Conference Seminar of Tamil Studies* (Madras, 1971), I:94–95.

It is clear that, in the six earliest anthologies, few if any poems were written outside the period of the first to third centuries A.D.: the language is too consistent and does not contain forms and words that Mahadevan has shown occur in the earliest inscriptions of the second and first centuries B.C.,[2] or that occur later in such literature as the *Cilappatikāram.* The people mentioned in these anthologies, moreover, seem all to have lived within about ten generations. It is almost certain, then, that the six earliest Tamil anthologies were written in the first, second, and third centuries A.D., after the use of the old Brāhmī script, which was probably first adapted for Tamil during the reign of Aśoka (272–232 B.C.), had become standardized and after literacy in it had spread widely. It is significant that about the same period elapsed between the time the Greeks first adapted Phoenician letters to their language and the appearance of their written lyric poetry as between the two corresponding events for Tamil.

There is a strange legend concerning three Tamil literary academies, called *cañkams* (Sanskrit *saṃgha*), first mentioned in the ninth century by the commentator Nakkīrar in his commentary on the *Iṟaiyaṉār Akapporuḷ.* It is said that the first cañkam flourished for 4040 years in southern Maturai with 549 members, the second for 3700 years in Kapāṭapuram with 59 members, and the last for 1800 years in northern Maturai (presumably after the southern one had been swallowed up in the deluge) with 49 members. This legend, which has generally been thought to be based ultimately on history, has influenced most accounts of Tamil literature. There is, however, no reference to this legend in all of early Tamil literature, in spite of the fact that if any of the academies had existed it would have been of great importance. Indeed, it is almost unthinkable that none of the poets who glorified the Pandyan kings would have mentioned an academy in Maturai, since such an institution would have redounded greatly to that monarch's credit. Nor do any of the poems mention a large body of written literature that preceded the anthologies. On the other hand, there was a permanent Jaina assembly called a Saṃgha established about 604 A.D. in Maturai.[3] It seems likely

[2] Ibid., p. 92.

[3] Jyoti Prasad Jain, *The Jain Sources of the History of Ancient India* (Delhi, 1964), pp. 160–161.

that this assembly was the model upon which tradition fabricated the cañkam legend. In any case, the first telling of the cañkams is at least six hundred years after the anthologies; even if the legend contains some truth (and in my opinion it is unlikely that it does), it is certain that the truth has been so altered through the centuries that the legend is useless as a historical source.

The *Tolkāppiyam*, a treatise on grammar and poetic convention, is generally said to have been written even before the anthologies. This claim, if true, would make that work of great importance in this investigation. However, Mahadevan has shown that the writing system described by the *Tolkāppiyam*, and specifically the part that calls for putting a dot (*puḷḷi*) over a letter to indicate that it is not followed by the vowel *a* (as a *virāma* in Sanskrit), was not used until several centuries after the period of the anthologies. In other words, parts of the *Tolkāppiyam* are quite late, though some parts may be as early as has been generally claimed. Unfortunately, since it is quite impossible to separate the early parts of the *Tolkāppiyam* from the later parts, that work cannot be relied upon for historical data on the period of the anthologies.

To what extent were the Tamil anthologies and the culture they describe influenced by elements from North India? This problem will be treated in detail in chapter 4; here, I offer what others have said regarding the issue of northern influence in ancient Tamilnad.

K. A. Nilakantasastri, the most frequently cited authority for early South Indian history, is of the opinion that, in the early Tamil anthologies, Sanskrit ideas and institutions are so intermixed with Dravidian ones that the two are virtually inseparable. He says, "none can miss the significance of the fact that early Tamil literature, the earliest to which we have access, is already fully charged with words, conceptions, and institutions of Sanskritic and northern origin";[4] "all these literatures [Tamil, Kannada, Telugu, and Malayalam] owed a great deal to Sanskrit, the magic wand whose touch alone raised each of the Dravidian languages from the level of a patois to that of a literary idiom";[5] and "the most striking feature in the pictures is its composite character;

[4] K. A. Nilakantasastri, *A History of South India from Prehistoric Times to the Fall of Vijayanagar*, 3rd ed. (London, 1966), p. 22.

[5] Ibid., p. 340.

it is the unmistakable result of the blend of two originally distinct cultures, best described as Tamilian and Aryan; but it is by no means easy to distinguish the original elements in their purity."[6] Clearly, if what Nilakantasastri writes is correct, it will be necessary to look to the North for the explanation and source not only of many of the institutions of ancient Tamilnad, but of most of its literary forms as well. However, as I view the evidence, though there certainly was northern influence, Nilakantasastri has exaggerated its extent.

His statements stress the notion that old Tamil was full of Sanskrit words, especially the earliest inscriptions: "The language of the short Brāhmī inscriptions of the second century B.C. was Tamil, still in its [formative] stages, with an admixture of words of clearly Sanskritic origin."[7] It is from this stepping stone, I believe, that he has derived many of his notions concerning the later Tamil anthologies: clearly if the language was first written under Sanskritic influence, with many northern words, it is reasonable to expect that its later literature would be fully charged with northern conceptions and words, as is in fact the case with other Dravidian literatures, especially Telugu. It is true that the earliest Tamil inscriptions were originally believed to be full of Prakrit (not Sanskrit) words; however, Mahadevan has recently shown that in fact they contain few such words and that they are in relatively pure Tamil, though with a slightly greater number of northern words than the anthologies.[8]

It is difficult indeed to see how Nilakantasastri can state that early Tamil literature is full of northern words. Any reader who knows which words are of Sanskritic origin can see that they are few and far between. J. V. Chelliah has estimated that the *Tirumurikāṟṟuppaṭai*, one of the ten poems of the *Pattuppāṭṭu*, which is later than most of the poems of the anthologies, contains only two percent Sanskritic words, even when such words as *mīṉ*, *tāmarai*, and *muttu*, which are now known to be of Dravidian origin, are counted as Sanskritic.[9] A survey of the *Mahābhārata* would, I believe, show a much higher percentage of Dravidian

6 Ibid., p. 129.

7 Ibid., p. 117.

8 Mahadevan, "Tamil Brahmi Inscriptions," p. 93.

9 *Pattuppāṭṭu*, trans. J. V. Chelliah (Madras, 1962), p. 337.

words. Nilakantasastri's contention that early Tamil is full of Sanskritic words is, then, mistaken. Indeed, the purity of the vocabulary of early Tamil should, I believe, occasion doubts about the degree of mixture of northern institutions in ancient Tamil society. There can be no doubt that there were many institutions in the Tamilnad described in the anthologies that had their origin in Aryan India; yet on the whole, I believe, these had not yet mixed with the indigenous ones to such an extent that the different elements are no longer identifiable, as will become clear when they are considered below.

One final fact regarding the vocabulary of early Tamil should be indicated. When Sanskritic words do appear, they are wholly adapted to Tamil pronunciations. For example, Sanskrit *rūpa* ("form") becomes *uruvam.* Usually, however, the Sanskrit word is simply translated into Tamil: *śruti* becomes *kēḷvi*; *veda* becomes *maṟai.* So strongly was this dislike of Sanskrit sounds felt that even the gods are rarely given their Sanskrit names, but are denoted by Tamil equivalents or by descriptive epithets. Kubera, for example, is *mā niti kiḻavaṉ.* This must mean that, unlike the other Dravidian languages, whose earliest works were written when Sanskrit influence was strong and are full of unchanged words from that language, Tamil literature goes back to a period before northern literature had enough prestige in the South to be imitated there and to a time before northern institutions were so strong that they brought with them northern words.

2

THE KING AND HIS KINGDOM

In ancient Tamil society, the king was the central embodiment of the sacred powers that had to be present and under control for the proper functioning of society. The poems indicate that before the advent of the Brahmins there was no priestly class of higher status than the king; indeed, those members of society who dealt closely with sacred powers were of low status, as will be seen. The king's position is suggested by the fact that words that meant king in ancient Tamil now denote God. For example, *iṟaivaṉ* ("he who is highest") used to mean king but is now generally applied to the supreme deity, while *kōyil* ("king's house" or "palace") now means temple. The position of the king is described by Puṟ. 186:

Paddy is not life,
water is not life.
The life of this broad world
is the king,
and to know
"I am life"
is the duty of the king
with his many-speared army.

The position of the king in the Tamil social structure contrasted with the king's role in North India, where the sacred was largely in the care of the Brahmins. It is significant that in the North, the word for god, *deva*, came to mean king, whereas in Tamil the process was reversed.

There were three preeminent kings in Tamilnad, the Chera, Chola, and Pandyan kings,[1] with capitals respectively at Vañci, Uṟaiyūr, and Maturai (usually spelled Madurai in English). Puṟ. 50 calls these monarchs "the three kings of Tamil," while Puṟ. 357 mentions "the world which is held in common by the three kings." Each of these kings had his own special emblem, his own festival, and his own flower, as will be seen. Besides these three great monarchs, there were many smaller kings or chieftains, many of whom gave tribute to one of the three great kings.

The arena in which these Tamil kings acted was Tamilnad, that area of South India bounded by the Vēṅkaṭa hills on the north, the ocean on east and west, and Cape Comorin on the south. Indeed, for the most part, the horizons of the Tamils were limited to this land, and Tamilnad was for them "the world, encircled by the ocean" (Puṟ. 19, 35–38, 168, 175, 357). An important example is Puṟ. 175:

Hail, lord Ataṉuṅkaṉ!
All who open my heart
will find you there,
and if I forget you
it will be
only when my life is leaving my body
and I forget myself.
Only then will I forget you
whose just demeanor
means that you care for many
every day
like the broad-rayed orb of the sun
abiding in the entrance to the world
cut for the passage of strong-spoked wheels
by the Maurians
with bannered chariots,

[1] I have used the usual English forms of these names. In Tamil, the three kings are Cēraṉ, Cōḻaṉ, and Pāṇṭiyaṉ.

lofty parasols touching the sky,
and victorious spears.

It appears that the entrance alluded to in this poem is in the Vēṅkaṭa mountains, which border Tamilnad on the north, for in Ak. 69, the hero, who conventionally journeys into Telugu country, is said to have gone "following the ways which the golden wheels of the Maurians' chariots cut in tall mountains which touch the sky." The Maurians must have made expeditions into Tamilnad in about the third century B.C.

The various emblems and accoutrements of authority that the Tamil kings possessed lend insight into the position of the king. First, as agent of the sacred, the king held a staff symbolizing both the connection between this profane world and the sacred world above and the king's role as the guardian of that connection. If a king ruled unjustly, his staff was said to have bent, the implication being that the king's connection with the sacred was broken (Cil. 16.216); if he ruled justly, then his staff was said to be straight or in an auspicious condition (*ceṅkōl*). Staffs were also held by bards (Puṟ. 152, 399), by the village elders at marriage ceremonies (Kuṟ. 148), and by the priest of Murugan,[2] all people who had a special connection with the sacred.

As symbol of his power, the king had a royal drum, called a *muracu.* The sacred status that this drum possessed is well described in Puṟ. 50, where the poet, after traveling, comes to the palace and mistakenly lies down on the table of the drum, which has been taken out to be given a bath:

Before they brought back from its bath
the fearful drum, which thirsts for blood,
its black sides lined by leather straps
and adorned with a sapphirelike garland
of the bright eyes of long peacock feathers
and with golden-shooted *uḻiñai,*
unknowing I climbed upon its bed,
which was covered with soft flowers
as if the froth of oil had been poured upon it.
Yet you stayed the edge of your sword, which cuts in half.
Just that was sufficient for all of Tamil land to know of it.

[2] N. Subrahmanian, *Pre-Pallavan Tamil Index* (Madras, 1966), p. 797.

But you were not satisfied with only that.
You approached me,
and, raising your mighty arm, which resembles a concert drum,
you fanned me and made me cool.
Did you do that act, mighty lord,
because you have heard and understood
that, except for those whose fame here spreads over the broad earth,
no one can stay there in the world of high estate?

In war, a victorious king would at once take his enemy's drum (Pur̲. 26), by which act he received the right to his kingdom (Pur̲. 70). If a muracu broke, it was an extremely bad omen (Pur̲. 238). The muracu was made of the skin of a bull that had vanquished a rival in a bullfight (Pur̲. 288) and of wood taken from an enemy's tutelary tree.[3]

In many ways, the muracu resembles the drums used by Siberian shamans, which also received sacrifices with blood, also were made of wood from a special tree, and also were covered with special skins whose history would be recounted at certain ceremonies. Eliade states that, by playing the drum, the shaman is projected into the vicinity of the cosmic tree, from which the drum was made, and can thus ascend into the sky.[4] It seems certain that when the muracu was beaten in the morning to awaken the king and bring him back from the other world (Pur̲. 397) and when it was beaten during battle (Pur̲. 288), its function, like the drum of the Siberian shaman, was to create sacred space and time.

Also sacred to the monarch was the tutelary tree (*kaṭimaram* or *kāvalmaram*), which, as its name's literal translation ("guarded tree") indicates, was carefully guarded so that enemies could not approach it. When a king was victorious, he would cut down his foe's tutelary tree (Ak. 46; Pur̲. 23, 57; Kur̲. 73), sometimes using its wood to make a muracu. Enemy kings might tie their elephants to a foe's tutelary tree to show how they scorned him (Pur̲. 57, 347). In Pur̲. 162, a bard to whom a king has refused to give anything

[3] Ibid., p. 694.

[4] Mircea Eliade, *Shamanism: Archaic Techniques of Ecstasy* (New York, 1964), pp. 170–176.

goes to another king, receives from him an elephant, brings the elephant back to the first king, and ties it to his tutelary tree to make him feel remorse.

In Kuṟ. 292, the poet describes how a girl's mother gives her no chance to meet her lover, invoking king Naṉṉaṉ's tutelary tree in a simile:

A bright-faced girl went to bathe
and ate a green fruit
brought by the water.
For that crime
Naṉṉaṉ refused nine times nine elephants
and a doll her weight in gold,
but had her killed.
May mother go to unending hell
like him
who killed a woman,
for remembering how a guest came one day
with a smiling face,
she does not sleep
like a city under attack
by its enemies.[5]

It appears that no one kind of tree was invariably adopted as the tutelary tree, for Kuṟ. 45 states that the tree of Titiyaṉ was a *puṉṉai*.

The function of the king's tree was to represent the cosmic tree, joining heaven and earth. It, like the cosmic tree that the Siberian shamans used for their drums, was used to make the muracu. It was in order to break the king's connection with the sacred that an enemy would attempt to cut down his tree and take his drum. The seriousness with which a desecration of either of those objects was punished shows how important to the king was the connection with the sacred that they effected for him.

Another emblem of royal authority was the royal umbrella. Unlike the drum and tutelary tree, this emblem was used in North

[5] Although Kuṟ. 292 does not specify that the mango was Naṉṉaṉ's tutelary tree, it is evident that it was from Kuṟ. 73, which describes how Kōcars entered the country of Naṉṉaṉ after cutting down his mango. Only the tutelary tree was cut down in this manner by enemies. It does not seem likely that a different tree is meant in the two poems: in both instances, it is simply called "Naṉṉaṉ's mango tree," a name that shows it was so infamous that it needed no other description.

India as well as in Tamilnad; indeed, it was even used in the ancient Near East. The royal umbrella had partly, at least, the symbolism of the cosmic tree; that is, it was thought to be a link between heaven and earth. Thus in Puṟ. 229, it is a bad omen for the kingdom when the royal umbrella snaps at the base. The umbrella was conceived as shielding those in the king's realm from the heat of the sun of misfortune (Puṟ. 35, 60). Perhaps its symbolism was that it shielded the king's subjects from actual, profane time represented by the sun and allowed them to live in sacred time.

The three great kings had several other emblems. Each had a distinctive flower: the Chola, a chaplet of *ātti*; the Chera, a chaplet of the cut leaves of palmyra; and the Pandya, a chaplet of margosa (Puṟ. 5). In addition, the Chola king's emblem was a tiger; the Chera's a carp fish; and the Pandya's a bow. These emblems were carved in enemy land (Puṟ. 33, 39, 58) and put on forts (Puṟ. 174). Then, as now, flags were used in many places: on war elephants (Puṟ. 9, 38; Ak. 111, 162), in camps (Puṟ. 69), on forts (Puṟ. 31; Ak. 114), on chariots (Puṟ. 377), on bazaar streets (Ak. 83, 126), on boats (Ak. 110), and at temples or during festivals (Ak. 149, where Murugan's banner carries a peacock). Unfortunately, the device on the flags is not described in most of these instances.

The nature of Tamil kingdoms in periods subsequent to the one under discussion here has been analyzed by Burton Stein in a recent article. He traces three episodes of integration of the agrarian order of South India between the nine and nineteenth centuries.[6] The first of these is the Pallava-Chola period, during which the nuclear areas of South India were dominated by the Brahmins and the high-caste landlords, to whom the warriors were subordinate. Such nuclear areas had only the lightest links to the great warrior families of Kanchi and Tanjore, their chief duty being the payment of taxes. In the fourteenth and fifteenth centuries, the Brahmin-landlord hegemony of the nuclear areas broke down, according to Stein because of a new need for self-defense caused by the intrusion of Muslim warriors. The control

[6] Burton Stein, "Integration of the Agrarian System of South India," in *Land Control and Social Structure in Indian History*, ed. Robert E. Frykenberg (Madison, Wis., 1969), pp. 175–216.

of the nuclear areas passed to warriors who could command enough troops to control the Muslims. Thus, Stein writes, "Warriors whose private jurisdiction had been forged by the warriors themselves were recognized by and submitted to the overlordship of the great warriors of Vijayanagar."[7] The third episode resulted from the coming of the Europeans and is not relevant here.

The poems of ancient Tamil provide enough data to analyze their period using Stein's concepts. The poems describe clearly the agricultural organization that preceded the Pallava-Chola period. The land was divided between *men̲pulam*, which was paddy land, and *van̲pulam*, mountainous or forested territory on which only such inferior crops as millet could be grown. Cultivable land was further divided into mountainous (*kur̲iñci*), forested (*mullai*), ocean (*neytal*), and riverine (*marutam*) tracts. Most kings and chieftains had control of only one kind of land, and the poets sometimes describe the different tracts ruled by a particularly great monarch in order to praise him by demonstrating that he ruled a greater area than was common (Pur̲. 49, 58, 377, 384, 386, 395). The riverine tracts, on which paddy is grown, are less prominent than in the periods Stein has described, but it is clear that the strongest kings governed such areas.

The period of early Tamil literature is analogous to the warlike Vijayanagar period. The country was divided among small kings, most of whom controlled one nuclear area. The poems describe dramatically how such small kings would be reduced to the worst poverty when there was famine in their area. Pur̲. 127, for example, describes how a king would give to bards even if he had only a pitifully small amount of rice, while in Pur̲. 327, a chieftain is reduced to giving all of his tiny millet yield to creditors and then borrowing enough to eat. Sometimes, if a chieftain did not have enough to give to bards and other suppliants, he would order his soldiers to go out on a looting expedition (Pur̲. 180).

As in the later periods described by Stein, in this early period the administrative authority of the Tamil kings—even of the three great kings—extended only within the small area constituting the capital city and the land surrounding it. In order to increase their wealth, and, what is more important, their glory, kings who were

[7] Ibid., p. 191.

strong enough would demand tribute from the warrior kings of other nuclear areas (Pur̲. 22, 97, 156). For example, in Pur̲. 51, the poet describes the Pandyan monarch in the following words:

If he [the Pandyan king], not bearing men who say,
"Cool Tamil land is shared in common,"
opposes in battle wishing tribute,
then those kings who say, "Take!" are without trembling.
But pitiful, pitiful are those who lose his favor.
Like the winged drones issuing from red mounds
laboriously raised by myriads of tiny termites,
they suffer to live even one day.

Stein writes that in the Vijayanagar period, traditions of personal loyalty such as were found in feudal Europe were absent.[8] Perhaps so, but the poems indicate that such traditions existed when they were composed. Thus, in Pur̲. 139, the poet tells his patron to give at once, for he might have to die at any time for his king. In Pur̲. 287, the poet describes how kings would reward their warriors by giving them conquered lands. In Pur̲. 166, the poet approaches a Brahmin to whom a king has granted land and begs him to give. The Brahmin is treated as a king would be: he has personal authority over his area.

It is clear that in the period of the poems, the Brahmin-landlord hegemony of nuclear areas that characterized the Pallava-Chola period had not yet begun. Rather, each nuclear area was in the hands of a warrior king, who might render tribute to a stronger king or exact tribute himself. If he could cause others to give him tribute, it seems certain that he would also require that they give him men for his army. In many cases, the chieftains of nuclear areas were personally loyal to the king of another area and were willing to die in battle for him.

[8] Ibid., p. 190.

3

SOME INDIGENOUS ELEMENTS IN THE RELIGION OF THE ANCIENT TAMILS

Gods and Goddesses

The gods of the ancient Tamils were frightful beings indeed. Of the words used to denote deity, one is from a root meaning to fear (*cūr*), one from a root meaning to afflict (*aṇaṅku*), and one, as will be shown later in this chapter, from a root meaning debt or sacrifice (*kaṭavuḷ*). Their activities accurately mirror their etymologies. For example, Puṟ. 362 says that a gathered army terrifies like a god (*aṇaṅku uruttaṉṉa*); Kuṟ. 87 says, "the god [kaṭavuḷ] of the pipal tree in the courtyard terrifies and strikes down the wicked"; and in Ak. 166, the hero swears, "May I be tormented by a terrifying god [*uru keḻu teyvam*] if I made love [with the courtesan]." Anything that causes pain or suffering or is threatening is said to have a god within it. Thus, in Kuṟ. 308, an elephant rubs his head on plantain leaves that have a spirit (aṇaṅku) in them and then sleeps fitfully in pain; in Ak. 7, a girl who has reached puberty is warned not to go about the city, for it has gods that attack (*tākkaṇaṅku*); in Aiṅ. 363, the hero says to his beloved, "You think that there are spots [a sign of puberty] on your afflicting [aṇaṅku] breasts, but my heart thinks they contain a god [aṇaṅku]"; and, in Ak. 20, girls of the city, possessed by a noisy god (aṇaṅku), gossip. A curious extension of the meaning of the word kaṭavuḷ is found in Kuṟ. 203: "Like people who live near ascetics [kaṭavuḷ], my man lives avoiding me."

Very few deities in ancient Tamil actually have names—I have found only three indigenous deities who are named: Murukaṉ, Koṟṟavai, and Kūṟṟuvaṉ. Of these, Murukaṉ is by far the most prominent. His name means tenderness, tender age, youth, beauty.[1] He is said to have killed the demon (cūr) and his tribe (Puṟ. 23; Ak. 59), but he appears to have been no less malevolent on account of that. Thus, in Kuṟ. 1, the girl's friend refuses the love token offered by the lover, a bunch of red *kāntaḷ* flowers, sacred to Murukaṉ, in these words:

Murukaṉ,
the red one,
his elephant red-tusked,
his arrows red-shafted,
crushes demons
as he kills
so the field grows red
and his anklets whirl.
This is his hill
and it is thick
with blood bunches
of your kāntaḷ.

Ak. 22 says of Murukaṉ, "His hands have the fame of wiping out those who do not bow to him." In Ak. 118 and 158, he is compared to a hunter with dogs. In Puṟ. 56, Murukaṉ is said to have the peacock on his banner and to use this bird as his vehicle, a notion that may have been borrowed from the North through identification of Murukaṉ with Skanda, as this poem also mentions several Aryan gods and their vehicles and banners. Murukaṉ carries a long spear, through whose metonymy he receives the name Neṭuvēl ("long spear"); he wears a garland of *kaṭampu*, which blooms in the monsoon (Puṟ. 23). He is especially worshipped by hill folk (Ak. 13), and his special place was Tirupparaṅkuṉṟam near Maturai (Ak. 149), as it is even today. His sacred places were not only in the hills, however, for Puṟ. 55 mentions the sands at Centil (modern Tiruccentūr) as a place where he was established (as he still is).

[1] D.E.D. 4081.

Murukan̲ takes possession of people and makes them sick. One of the most common themes in the akam poems is that a girl's despondency at being in love with an unsuitable man is mistaken for possession by the god. In order to heal her, a priest, called a Vēlan̲ ("one with a spear"), is called to perform various rites to Murukan̲. The god was thought to be very beautiful, as the meaning of his name implies; in Ak. 120, a flock of herons in the sky is compared to the pearl necklace on his breast.

Another class of divinity is the celestial woman, called variously Cūraramakaḷir (from *cūr*, "vexing," and *aramakaḷ*, "goddess"), Varaiyaramakaḷir (*varai* means mountain), and Vān̲aramakaḷir (*vān̲* means sky). All except the last inhabit mountains in the poems surveyed. Promises are made before them (Kur̲. 53), and the heroine is said to be as inaccessible as they (Ak. 162), to be like them in her chastity (Ak. 198), or to resemble them in her beauty and tenderness (Aiṅ. 255, 418).

In Kur̲. 218, a goddess is mentioned named Cūli, "she who [holds] a trident," from Sanskrit *śūla*; from her name, she appears to be identified with the northern goddess Durgā, also called Śūladharā, "the trident holder." She inhabits a mountain slope and is offered a sacrifice by a woman whose lover has left on a journey (Kur̲. 218). According to Swaminathaier in his commentary on Kur̲. 218, she is the same as Kor̲r̲avai, the goddess of war and victory (*kor̲r̲am*), who was also identified with Durgā in the *Cilappatikāram*, where, like that goddess, she is said to have killed the demon Mahiśāsura.[2]

In Ak. 345, Kor̲r̲avai is said to live in a forest (*kān̲ amar celvi*), and to have given a horse to a certain bard. In Kali. 89, she is called the victory goddess of the great forest (*peruṅkāṭṭu kor̲r̲i*) who knows all, and the efforts of the hero to deceive the heroine about his affair with his courtesan are likened to the demon's (*pēy*) efforts to set riddles to the goddess. In line 459 of the *Perumpāṇār̲r̲uppaṭai*, one of the songs of the *Pattuppāṭṭu*, she is called "the lovely goddess of the *tuṇaṅkai* dance" (*tuṇaṅkai am celvi*), and the vain effort of the demon (*aṇaṅku*) to deceive her with riddles is again described.

[2] N. Subrahmanian, *Pre-Pallavan Tamil Index* (Madras, 1966), p. 330; Cil. 12.68, 12.88, 23.111, 23.181.

It seems to me that Kor̲r̲avai must have been an indigenous goddess, at least in her character as a goddess of war and victory who lives in a forest and dances the tuṇaṅkai. Certainly the northern goddess Durgā is not associated with victory, and none of her names has that meaning. Yet even at the time of the anthologies, Kor̲r̲avai and Durgā had been identified to such an extent that it is somewhat difficult to determine the original character of Kor̲r̲avai. Thus the epithet *celvi*, elsewhere used only of northern gods (in its masculine form, *celvan*—see below, chapter 4), is applied to her quite often.

Another kind of supernatural creature was the demon or ghost who haunted places of death, especially the burning ground and the battlefield. These creatures, like the Piśācas and Rākṣasas of the northern tradition, ate corpses, and many gruesome poems describe their cannabalism in scenes that might have been taken from Bhavabhūti's *Mālatīmādhava*. These demons, called *pēy*, *kal̲utu*, and *pal̲u*, are to be distinguished from the malevolent deities, called *avuṇar* and *cūr*, whom Murukan̲ killed and who are identified with the northern *asuras* in Pur̲. 174, where the avuṇars are said to have taken the sun and Krishna is said to have gotten it back. These demons were sacrificed to, and Nar̲. 73 describes the "dim evening when demons with strong jaws and unclean fingers like clusters growing on a *murukku* tree in the summer approach the courtyard to eat the sacrifice of flowers." This may be compared to the last verse of act three of Kālidāsa's *Abhijñāna-śākuntala*, where demons flit about the altar on which the evening rites are being performed.

The final indigenous Dravidian deity to be considered is Death, Kūr̲r̲uvan̲. He is said to carry an axe (Pur̲. 145) or a club (Pur̲. 42), but never a noose as in the North, and to take people at the appointed time (Kur̲. 267). Many poems compare the king on the battlefield to Death (Pur̲. 3, 23, 41, 42), or scold Death for being so stupid as to take the king, who is doing his work for him by killing in battle (Pur̲. 210, 227, 230). The point of such poems is that the sacred power of the king can be enhanced by likening him to the most terrible deity in battle.

The Tamil gods haunted mountains (Kur̲. 218), bodies of water (*tur̲ai*, which may be a reservoir, a bay, a harbor, or a similar body; Ak. 156; Aiñ. 53, 174), and, as today at Śrīraṅgam, river islets (Kuṟ. 263). As today, they also haunted trees: Puṟ. 198 and 199 speak of the god in the banyan tree (identified as Vishnu in the old commentary on 198); Kuṟ. 87 speaks of the terror-inflicting god of the *marā* (pipal) tree in the courtyard, in front of whom the hero has sworn to return from his journey; and Puṟ. 260 speaks of a bard who sees a bad omen and salutes the god who lives in the shade of the *kaḷḷi*, a desert plant.

Temples were erected to Murukaṉ (Ak. 138), and it was dangerous for impure people to enter them. Thus Puṟ. 299 speaks of defeated horses "which stand terrified like [menstruous] girls, who cannot touch dishes, in the temple of Murukaṉ." There were also temples to Śiva: Puṟ. 6 mentions a temple to the three-eyed god worshipped by sages (*muṉivar*), which the king circumambulates. Often mentioned is the god of Kolli hillside, where a figure drawn by the god was reputed to kill any who looked upon it, first making them confused at heart, then distressing them, and finally making them fall lifeless.[3] The heroine is described sarcastically by the hero as "mild-mannered like the good-natured doll drawn by a black-eyed god [*teyvam*] on the west slope of Kolli" (Kuṟ. 89; see also Kuṟ. 100; Ak. 62, 209). There were other pictures of gods, for Ak. 167 mentions a house in a deserted village with a veranda "not smeared with dung, where sacrifices formerly constant have been forgotten, empty because the lovely god drawn there has departed." This practice is probably related to the present-day custom of making designs called *kōlam* with powder in front of the threshold of houses in South India, a practice found also in parts of the North. Images were used in ancient Tamilnad. Aiṅ. 245 and 247 mention a small image called a *kaṉṉam*, used by the priest of Murukaṉ to effect a cure, while in Ak. 149, an image (*paṭimam*; Prakrit *paṭima*; Sanskrit *pratimā*) is said to be taken by a king who conquers a city.

Another place thought to be haunted was the *naṭukal*, or memorial stone, erected to an eminent man who had died. The spirit of the dead person was thought actually to reside in the stone, for again and again it is said that a man has become a memorial stone (Puṟ. 221, 264, 265). These stones were set up by roads, sometimes under pandals roofed with cloth (Puṟ. 260).

[3] *Kuṟuntokai*, comm. U. V. Swaminathaier (Madras, 1962), p. 361. See also Aṭiyārkkunallār on Cil. 6.61.

Garlands were put on them (Pur̲. 264), and invariably they were decorated with peacock feathers (Pur̲. 232, 329; Ak. 35). The names and deeds of the man memorialized were often inscribed in the stone (Ak. 131, 179; Aiñ. 352). The spear and shield of the dead man were placed beside it, and, since Ak. 365 describes how elephants mistake one for a real soldier, it may have been made in the likeness of the dead man.[4] The stone is often said to have a god in it: "To honor the god in the memorial stone, play the *tuṭi* drum, and give it a lamb sacrifice with rice and toddy" (Ak. 35). "God" here evidently means only the spirit of the man commemorated by the stone, for Pur̲. 263 says, "Do not fail to bow when you pass the rock that belongs to that man," and Pur̲. 335 states that in a certain land (presumably a wilderness —part of the poem is lost), the only gods are stones, worshipped with offerings of paddy, erected because men killed elephants and died. The concept of divinity actually residing in the stone was transferred later to the *śivaliñgam*, which seems to have taken over many of the functions of the naṭukal.

It is clear from the foregoing, I believe, that the gods of the ancient Tamils were not transcendent beings, but rather immanent powers, present in objects encountered every day and involved in every aspect of ordinary life. They are to be distinguished from the gods of the early Aryans in that their potential danger was stressed more than their benevolent aspect, and their transcendent character is far less important. Thus they were thought to reside in any object that was potentially threatening or dangerous, such as a woman's breast, a king's drum, or a column set up in a Brahminic ritual (Pur̲. 52). There seems to be no word to denote a chiefly beneficent and transcendent deity. Aṇañku, kaṭavuḷ, and even teyvam, from Sanskrit deva, were all used interchangeably to signify the sort of dangerous immanent deity described above, although there did also exist even more malevolent deities denoted by such words as pēy and cūr.

The most often encountered etymology of the word kaṭavuḷ is *kaṭa* ("to cross over") and *uḷ* ("mind" or "soul"). Originally the word is generally said to have meant "that which transcends mind."[5] If this is so, then a good case can be made that the an-

[4] Subrahmanian, *Tamil Index*, p. 476.
[5] D.E.D. 929.

cient Tamils did in fact have a notion of a transcendent, benevolent deity that corresponds to the descriptions of Śiva and Vishnu in the *Dēvāram* and *Divyaprabandham*. However, this etymology appears unlikely to me. First, I know of few valid etymologies in any language that are comparable to this in its imaginativeness and profundity. Secondly, it does not correspond to the notion of divinity found in the old Tamil poems, none of which mentions anything that would indicate that the Tamils worshipped such a god. If they did have a transcendent deity, he was not called kaṭavuḷ, a name applied to dangerous immanent deities, and he must have been so remote and unimportant that he had become a *deus otiosus*, playing small part in the culture and receiving little worship, a situation often found in archaic religions.[6] Thirdly, and most importantly, there is an alternate etymology that is more reasonable. Kuṟ. 218 speaks of a goddess to whom there is made no *kaṭaṉ*, a word whose primary meaning is debt but is here used to mean sacrifice. The syllable *uḷ* is often used as a suffix to make a noun from a root: *aruḷ*, grace, from *ār*, to be full; *poruḷ*, object, from *poru*, to put together. Thus kaṭavuḷ would mean that to which sacrifice or debt pertains, a meaning well in accord with the character of the ancient Tamil deities.

The nature of the indigenous Tamil gods will become even clearer when the treatment of the borrowed Aryan gods in the poems is considered (see chapter 4 below). The nature of the indigenous deities is of great importance in the consideration of pollution and the role of woman. But first it is necessary to consider the kinds of worship and sacrifice described in ancient Tamil literature.

Ancient Tamil Worship and Sacrifice

Obeisance was performed by bowing before a sacred object with folded hands, as today. Thus, Puṟ. 306 says: "The woman . . . clasped her hands in obeisance to the great rock [the memorial stone] without fail and prayed to it, 'May guests come to me, and may a great war come to my husband.'" (See also Ak. 115, 125,

[6] Mircea Eliade, *Patterns in Comparative Religion*, 4th ed. (New York, 1967), pp. 46ff.

138.) Objects thus venerated included the crescent moon (Kuṟ. 178, 307), which seems to have been revered especially by women in the evening (Ak. 239), the bard's lute (Ak. 115), which was thought to contain a god (aṇañku), and gods wherever they might be, whether in a temple (Ak. 138), a tree (Puṟ. 260), or a memorial stone (Puṟ. 306).

When a girl was thought to be possessed by Murukaṉ, that god was worshiped with frenzied dancing and ecstatic rites, as described in the following excerpts:

Women skilled in ancient truths
said as if it were a fact,
"She will recover
if we worship the long-speared one
whose mighty hands
have the universal fame
of crushing his foes."
They arranged well the worshiping ground,
put the garland on the spear,
sang so the prosperous town resounded,
offered sacrifice,
spread lovely red millet and blood,
and worshiped Murukaṉ. (Ak. 22.)

Women who utter ancient truths, skilled at lying,
spread out rice in a winnowing fan to discover the truth
and say, "It is the presence of Murukaṉ, hard to bear."
Mother believes them,
and in a house so well made it could be a picture,
she prays:
"May my daughter's loveliness, as lovely as a doll's, return."
The sweet instruments are played together,
the floor is prepared,
a large pandal is decorated with ornaments for the dance,
they put on kaṭampu and white pieces of palmyra leaves,
the sweet drone sounds behind a compelling beat,
they cry out the great name of the god
throwing up their hands,
and the priest makes the large floor resplendent
with his frenzied dancing,

moving like a puppet
manipulated by a skillful puppeteer. (Ak. 98.)

They put on *nīlam*
and the fragrant green leaves of margosa,
bring me to the house of Murukan̲
fearful in his preeminence,
bowing as sweet instruments play
behind a swelling drone . . .
and they sing of his kaṭampu tree and of his elephant
and, shaking, take palmyra leaves
and katampu garlands
and dance all night. (Ak. 138.)

In Aiñ. 245 and 247, the priest of Murukan̲ comes to the girl's house and raises a small image called a kan̲n̲am to cure her. In later times, according to the *Tamil Lexicon*, the kan̲n̲am was presented to the temple in order to cure someone. The Vēlan̲, or priest of Murukan̲, might also roll molucca beans at the girl's house, presumably to confirm his diagnosis that Murukan̲ was the cause of her condition (Aiñ. 245, 249, 250).

Ecstatic dancing was common in Tamil worship. Pur̲. 22 mentions a place near which men with palmyra leaves on their heads dance the *ver̲ikkuravai* (frenzied *kuravai*) "boiling like water in flood"; Pur̲. 129 describes hill men who get drunk and dance in frenzy; Pur̲. 259 speaks of a bull that dances and frolics like a Pulaitti (a low-caste woman) whose body has been possessed by Murukan̲; Kur̲. 105 describes a peacock that eats a ripe ear of millet put for a god to eat and gets feverish and shakes as gracefully as a frenzied dancing girl; and Kur̲. 366 mentions frenzied dancing as goats are sacrificed. The custom of ecstasy in worship survived in Tamilnad to produce the Nāyan̲mārs and Āḻvārs, who went about Tamilnad singing ecstatic songs about Śiva and Vishnu, and were largely responsible in later times for the position of preeminence those gods attained as well as for the Bhakti movement, which produced the *Bhāgavata Purāṇa* and spread all over India.

Flowers played an important part in ancient Tamil worship. Ak. 99 mentions flowers in the temple of a god (aṇañku); in Aiñ. 259, the daughter of a hill man worships the family god with flowers from the *vēṅkai* tree in the courtyard; and in Pur̲. 106, the poet says, "though the *erukkam* flower is neither good nor bad, gods [*kaṭavuḷ*] do not fail to desire it." (The erukkam flower was not worn by women in their hair, as it had a bad smell, but it was nevertheless used for worship.) In Ak. 152, it is said that on the slopes that belong to King Nalli there are kāntaḷ flowers sacred to a god, spread for the bees to taste. In order to worship Murukan̲, men wore palmyra leaves and kaṭampu (Ak. 58), which was also his special tree (Ak. 138). In Nar̲. 73, flower sacrifices are put out for demons to come and eat in the evening.

Flowers were also important in other connections. It has been seen that each of the three kings used a flower or plant as his special emblem. Victorious kings were supposed to wear the white flower of *tumpai* (Pur̲. 21, 22, 96, 97, 283, 347). Women who were widowed or whose husbands were away could not wear flowers in their hair (Pur̲. 242; Kur̲. 9, 191), while women who were married and whose husbands were at home were supposed to wear flowers in their hair (Pur̲. 44). Indeed, as a sign of fertility, flowers played an important role in the culture of the Tamils, as they still do. It seems likely that, since the Vedas, Brāhmaṇas, and Upaniṣads scarcely mention flowers, the universal Indian custom of offering *pūjā* or *upahāras* of blossoms to gods must have had its origin in Dravidian India.

Many different kinds of sacrifices are mentioned in the poems. It has already been seen how paddy, toddy, and rams were offered to the memorial stones and how the king's drum was anointed with blood. The only animals whose sacrifice is mentioned in the poems surveyed are the lamb and the goat. In Pur̲. 366, a whole flock of sheep is slaughtered during frenzied dancing, and it is said that if any of them escape it is a bad omen; in Kur̲. 263, the throats of goats are cut on river islets; and in Kur̲. 362, the Vēlan̲, to cure the heroine of her disease, kills a kid, rubs the girl's forehead, and offers the sacrifice along with many-colored rice to Murukan̲. In Ak. 156, the mother of the distressed girl takes to Murukan̲ an offering consisting of a chaplet and a ram. In Ak. 166, the hero swears to his wife, "If I made love [to the courtesan], . . . may I be tormented by the dreadful god who receives sacrifices that make swarms of bees . . . cease drinking at the garland of fragrant flowers at the entrance of Vēlūr city [to go instead to the meat]." In Pur̲. 146, men offer a sacrifice for rain and then, when it comes in too much abundance, pray for it to stop (a good instance of the capricious and dangerous nature of the Tamil gods); in Aiṅ. 251, men make loud noise (in worship?) so that it rains. In Kur̲. 105, an ignorant peacock on a mountain eats a ripe ear of millet set out for the gods and gets feverish and shakes like a frenzied dancing girl. The most bizarre of the ancient Tamil sacrifices was the war sacrifice, which is described below.

The Ancient Tamils in War

Much light is shed on the religious beliefs of the ancient Tamils by their conduct in battle, which, like that of other archaic peoples, was dictated to a large extent by their religion. In Pur̲. 293, when battle is about to commence, a huge war drum, called a *taṇṇumai*, is beaten to assemble the soldiers, and is then carried around the city on an elephant and beaten to call any who are hesitant to join the battle. The man who beats the taṇṇumai is a Pāṇan̲, a low-caste bard (Ak. 106). Pur̲. 293 also describes a flower girl who has sold flowers to the soldiers (evidently because their sacred properties were thought to be important in battle), but who can sell nothing after the soldiers have departed (since women were not supposed to wear flowers when their men were away). In Pur̲. 284 the messengers of the king call everywhere, "Come at once!" and the hero puts on a garland and goes to battle. In Pur̲. 89 the king hears the voice of the taṇṇumai drum in the courtyard as the wind blows it against the tree on which it hangs, and he thinks war has come. In Pur̲. 289 the voice of the taṇṇumai of the low-born one (that is, of the Pāṇan̲), its mouth covered, says, "Now is the time to take flowers [for battle]." In Pur̲. 34, the king prepares for war by bathing in a tank and commanding his men to take flowers. Pur̲. 98 says that warriors inhale the smoke of mustard seed before fighting (for its prophylactic qualities). In Pur̲. 79, the king bathes before battle and then puts on a shoot of margosa from his courtyard. In Pur̲. 332, before battle a warrior's sword is taken in procession around the streets and the tanks with a garland on it while the sweet voices of women mix with the sound of lutes. In Pur̲. 354, a spear is plunged up to its full shaft in water before battle, and, when the warriors are gathered, the king goes to bathe. There seems to have been a custom by which the king gave to the best of his warriors a cup of liquor before battle (Pu<u>r</u>. 289), but the exact procedure is not clear. Pu<u>r</u>. 336 says, "Warriors, taking their swords, have shut their mouths," indicating perhaps that men would not talk as they went into battle.

As battle was joined, the taṇṇumai drums would roar out, urging the men on; the royal muracu would be beaten (Pu<u>r</u>. 288), invoking the sacred power present in it; and the tuṭi, a small drum shaped like an hourglass, would be beaten (Pu<u>r</u>. 287). The importance accorded to the playing of these drums in battle is indicated by Pu<u>r</u>. 260, which states that the king crossed over the flood of arrows on the raft of the tuṭi drum, and by Pati<u>r</u>. 75, which says that the players of the *pa<u>r</u>ai* drum caused the enemy's defeat.

The battlefield itself was metamorphosed into another world for the participants, a place where everything was charged with sacred power to the highest degree. Thus the poems describe over and over the metamorphosis of the gruesome objects of battle into beautiful or productive things associated with peace, especially things connected with agriculture. A warrior hindered by guts around his feet is like an elephant whose legs are chained (Pu<u>r</u>. 275). Elephants' heads are cut off and roll on the ground, so they resemble plows, the tusks being like handles and the hollow severed trunk being like the plowshare (Pu<u>r</u>. 19). Kings on the field beautiful with the *karantai* creeper bring down elephants with trunks like black palmyra trunks (Pu<u>r</u>. 340). Dead horses with wounds covering their bodies lie in lovely pools of blood and are like ships when there is no wind (Pu<u>r</u>. 368). In Pu<u>r</u>. 4, swords have become like the red sky; legs, their anklets polished down, are like the horns of murderous bulls; shields, pierced by arrows, are like targets not fixed to the ground; horses with mouths bloodied from the bit are like tigers that have seized the neck of prey; the king on his golden chariot is like the sun rising from the black sea. Also described are the feasts of various demons and demonesses, whose actions, like those of the participants in battle, are compared to nonfearful pastimes. Thus, in Pu<u>r</u>. 370, demon girls get stuck in their intestines on the field and weep because they cannot dance. In Pu<u>r</u>. 371, a demon girl makes a garland of intestines, puts it on, and dances, singing, "May the king live longer than there are stars in the sky!"

The most striking example of this identification of gruesome things with benign objects is the war sacrifice. This is described by Pur̲. 26:

Like a ship propelled by the wind
on the black deep of the vast sea,
you pushed through the field on your elephant.
And in the wide space where you had pushed battle aside
you brandished your bright-bladed spear,
stirring up the fight and seizing the drums of fallen kings
to spread your fame.
Then, making a hearth of crowned heads,
putting on it a pot with blood instead of water,
and stirring up that food with a bangled arm for a stick,
you made sacrifice on the field of carnage,
Cel̲iyan̲ of murderous battle!
You completed the ancient sacrifice
with a retinue of sages of the four Vedas [Brahmins]
who had vows of restraint and great learning
and with kings who did their bidding.
O monarch whose sword brings success,
your foes must have done great acts of mortification
to receive the name
of being your enemies,
for even though they cannot prevail,
they will live in the next world.

In Pur̲. 372, the same sacrifice is described:

The whole reason I came praising you,
beating loudly my tightly bound drum [*kiṇai*],
was to take your necklace,
shining as if it were moonlight,
O you who have celebrated the war sacrifice,
making the field of carnage resplendent
while arrow-drops rained down
and shining swords were lightning
in your camp
as you gained victory!

Kūviḷam wood was fuel
for an oven made of severed heads.
Lined intestines were cooked and boiled up,
stirred with *vaṉṉi* sticks stuck in skulls
by a barren sacrificial priestess
who scooped and stirred,
cooking a ball of food
that animals avoided
and that the male cook offered,
saying,
"May the fresh water
poured from a little spout
be enough
for the guests
at the marriage festival."

Even today, the pouring of water, which seals a contractual agreement, takes place at the marriage celebrations of certain castes. The imagery of the war sacrifice is based upon an identification of the process of waging war with the process of harvesting. Such imagery occurs often in the poems (Puṟ. 352, 369, 370, 372, 373). For example, in Puṟ. 370, on the field of battle ripe fruits have been felled by a rain of shining weapons; bent heads of corpses have been cut to the stem; and elephants have trampled the field just as buffaloes thresh the paddy. Nacciṉārkkiṉiyar, perhaps the greatest of the medieval commentators on the *Tolkāppiyam*, expounds the meaning of the sacrifice in his commentary on *sūtra* 21 of *Puṟattiṇai*. He says that just as men cut grain, heap it on fields, scatter the heaps, thresh it with buffaloes, and then, before eating it themselves with their relatives, offer it to God and give some to suppliants, just so a king cuts down the enemy army, heaps up corpses in piles on the field, threshes, using elephants as his buffaloes and swords as whips, puts fat and blood in a large pot, offers for sacrifice the food cooked by a barren sacrificial priestess, and then gives the horses and elephants that remain to him, and much that he won in battle, to suppliants to take away.

To the ancient Tamil, there were two events in common life that had to turn out well for the continued survival and prosperity of the kingdom: the harvest and war. The poems make it clear that the primary function of the king was to carry out these two endeavors successfully by properly controlling and directing his sacred power. Should the power of the king fail, then there would be drought in his land, and his kingdom would be overrun and ruined by the armies of his enemies (Patiṟ. 13). Of the two primary activities, it is the harvest that is the more basic to an agricultural people. It is not strange, therefore, that the Tamils endowed war with the elements of harvesting, and felt that, just as the newly harvested crop had to be consecrated by sacrifice and distribution to suppliants, so the newly won booty had to be consecrated. Moreover, it is common among archaic peoples that warriors must be purified after killing enemies lest the spirits of the dead haunt them. Frazier writes, "Among the Basutos, 'Warriors who have killed an enemy are purified. The chief has to wash them, sacrificing an ox in the presence of the whole army.'"[7] It is also common for archaic peoples to eat some part of their slain enemies to absorb their qualities of valor[8]—a motive that clearly can be attributed to the Tamils who celebrated the war sacrifice, identifying their slain foes with the harvested paddy (though it should be pointed out that in none of the poems is there mention of the victor's actually consuming the "food" prepared at the war sacrifice). The reference to marriage in Puṟ. 372 might be explained by the fact that marriage is distinguished by the food given away at it and by its auspicious character.

Yet there is another element that can be discerned in the war sacrifice. Crawley writes, "Manslayers inoculate their dead foe with themselves or themselves with their dead foe, to secure immunity from his ghost."[9] Looked at from this perspective, the war sacrifice can be seen as an attempt to create a bond of relationship between the killer and his victim. It will be seen below in chapter 5 that in certain situations—and perhaps universally—when a Tamil king died, those close to him took their own lives, just as many widows committed suttee. In other words, when a

[7] James George Frazer, *The New Golden Bough*, ed. Theodore Gaster (New York, 1969), p. 217.

[8] Ibid., pp. 540–543.

[9] Ernest Crawley, *The Mystic Rose*, ed. Theodore Besterman (New York, 1927), I:294.

king, who possessed great sacred power, died, those close to him were infected to such an extent that they were supposed to take their own lives. It is hardly surprising that the power that went out of control at the death of a king was deemed especially menacing to the slayer of the king and that it was even more dangerous if the man responsible for the death was himself a king and possessed of power that had to be kept carefully under control. It seems to me that the war sacrifice can be interpreted as an attempt to create a relationship between the king and his royal victim so that the unleashed power of the dead king would not destroy the victor.

The nature of this relationship is suggested by the end of Pur̠. 372, in which the war sacrifice is homologized to a marriage. In Tamil marriage, two people are joined together in such a way that they become identical in certain respects (see chapter 5 below). They cannot harm one another without harming themselves, and their contact is carefully regulated lest they harm each other. Similarly, in the war sacrifice a relationship of identity is established between the slayer and the slain in such a way that they cannot injure one another. In marriage, moreover, the husband benefits from his wife's sacred power, which protects him as long as she is alive and chaste. Likewise, in the relationship established by the war sacrifice, the power of the slain king accrues to the victor. It might be objected that, in the marriage relationship, the woman's power goes out of control at the death of her husband in such a way that she must either kill herself or undertake severe ascetic measures; yet, for two reasons, I believe that that situation is not germane to the bond created by the war sacrifice. For one thing, the king with whom the relationship is being established is already dead; he cannot die again and thereby compromise the power of the victor. For another, the dead king would seem to be homologized to the woman in marriage. The death of a wife in no way hurt the husband among the ancient Tamils.

When a man was wounded in battle, potent measures had to be taken to insulate him from the dangerous forces that threatened the gravely ill (and, presumably, were augmented by the dangerous forces unleashed in battle). In all the poems on this theme, the low-caste men who made music played a prominent role in protecting the wounded hero. Pur̠. 285 describes a Tuṭiyan̠ (who plays the tuṭi drum) and a Pāṇaṉ (who plays the lute and sings) who stand over a wounded king, while in Puṟ. 291, the Pāṇaṉ exclaims:

Children!
Tuṭiyaṉs!
People skilled in singing [Pāṇaṉs],
come near the black man
whose garments are of pure white.
Keep away the sound of birds.
I,
making *viḷari* [a *rāga* of mourning] go round
will keep away
white foxes.

Birds and, presumably, white foxes were animals of ritual portent; they were evidently considered to be carriers of dangerous forces. In Puṟ. 281, measures are taken to keep away dangerous forces as a man lies wounded in his house. The speaker appears to be his wife, addressing one of her friends:

Margosa has been put in the house
with sweet-fruited *iravam*.
Many instruments sound
with the curved-sided lute.
Come, friend,
we will smear collyrium [on his forehead]
with gentle hands,
we will spread mustard,
blow the flute,
strike musical bells,
sing *kāñci* [songs of disenchantment with the world],
spread the smoke of incense
all over the house,
and protect his wounds
whose feet wear anklets marked with flowers,
who repulsed
the danger to the king.

Since elsewhere the lute played only by Pāṇaṉs, it is virtually certain that it is played by them here also.

After battle, the war sacrifice might be celebrated, as has been seen above. Another practice was to destroy ritually the enemy's land. Thus, in Puṟ. 15, donkeys with mouths white with froth are yoked to plows and used to plow up the roads, chariots are driven in the fields, and watering places are ruined by driving elephants into them. In Puṟ. 392, the king is described as being covered with blood and fat as he yokes donkeys, plows the ground, and plants white millet (*varaku*) and thorns (*koḷ*). In Puṟ. 78, the kiṇai drum is beaten while a victorious king has his enemies executed in their homeland.

All through the poems are found conventions whose purpose is to glorify war. One of the most dreadful of these is the mother in Puṟ. 278 who rejoices to discover that her son died a hero:

Many said,
"The son of the old woman
on whose soft dry arms flesh hangs and veins are raised,
and whose stomach is like a full lotus leaf
has failed in battle and fled."
At that, enraged, she said,
"If he has been routed in the thick of battle,
I will cut off these breasts from which he sucked,"
and, sword in hand, she turned over fallen corpses,
groping her way on the red field.
Then she saw her fallen son lying, cut in pieces,
and she rejoiced more than the day she bore him.

(See also Puṟ. 279, 19.)

There are many other passages that show people reacting with enthusiasm to war. In Puṟ. 68, "Because [the king] does not order his men against an enemy . . . , those men of uncontrollable valor say, 'We will die!' and strike their great arms to the beat of a drum that calms them." In Puṟ. 287 the poet addresses the drummer who is summoning men to battle and describes how great men fight, not running "even if arrows pierce like monsoon showers, if spears leap like carp fish in a tank, if elephants . . . gore. What is it to them if they receive farming villages [as a reward for their having fought]? . . . If they die, they will delight in the world of high estate, marrying faultless women [there]. . . . Stand here and look for the army of a new king [to fight with]."

Part of the glorification of war consisted in the veneration of wounds. In Puṟ. 93, warriors who die in bed are cut with swords so that they will seem like soldiers who died in battle and be able to enter paradise. In Pur̲. 167, the poet addresses a king, saying, "Your body full of sword scars, you have good fame but are ugly to look at. They [your enemies], because when they see you they turn their backs [and flee], are good to look at, their unmarred bodies untouched by affliction, but they are ugly to hear of." In Pur̲. 180, the king is as full of scars as a tree whose bark is used for medicine; all of his scars have come together so that he appears scarless. In Pur̲. 373, Koṅku soldiers rejoice at the affliction of being cloven in two by raised swords dripping with blood, and women do not go to the courtyard to burn themselves (because they are widowed) but are thrilled at the wounds of their husbands. It was shameful to flee the enemy; for a warrior to have a wound in his back was considered so heinous that when Cēramān̲ Peruñcēralātan̲ was pierced by a spear in his back, he faced north and starved himself to death (Pur̲. 65; Ak. 55).

Weapons as well as men were supposed to bear scars from frequent use. In Pur̲. 95, the poetess Auvaiyār addresses an enemy king:

These spears
kept in a large guarded palace
are adorned with peacock feathers
and with garlands.
Their strong, thick shafts
are handsome,
anointed with ghee.
But those spears
have tips and joints broken
from spearing enemies.
They are in the blacksmith's hut,
those sharp-tipped spears
of our great king
who surrounds himself
with the destitute,
who gives
if there is food enough
and shares
if there is not.

Through all of the examples given above, there runs the theme of glorification of war, a notion found among all martial nations.

Certain ideas, however, distinguish the Tamil notion of war from that of most other peoples. The most important is that for the Tamils the battlefield changed its character entirely, its dreadful and gruesome aspects becoming benign. Thus, again and again, images are used in which elements of war are likened to elements of agriculture, especially of the harvest. It seems to me that the Tamils' view of war relates to their concept of the sacred as dangerous and threatening. It was natural for them to consider the battlefield—filled as it is with horror, death, and danger—as one of the most important manifestations of the sacred. Eliade has pointed out that the cannibalism, collective orgies, and other violent conduct of archaic peoples are for them a return to the chaos that preceded original Creation and without which other creation cannot take place.[10] For the Tamils, it was battle that best met the requirements of a return to chaos, a situation in which all the elements of the sacred were present, but in uncontrolled form. Thus the battle was like the process leading up to a harvest; the end of the battle, with the war sacrifice, when the sacred was finally brought under control again, was like the harvest: the process of creation was complete.

In later times, the disposition of the Tamils to see the return to the chaos that precedes creation in situations of danger and death led them to give great importance to the Tāṇḍava, Śiva's dance of destruction at the end of the world. Indeed, the Tāṇḍava dance is of Dravidian (though not Tamil) origin.[11]

The identification of the horrors of war with benign objects has come into Sanskrit and appears in Kālidāsa, though it is absent in the parts of the two epics I surveyed. In R. 4.62, the severed heads of bearded enemies lie strewn on the earth like honeycombs covered with bees; in R. 7.49, the battlefield looks like a place of death's carousing, rich in fruits in the form of severed heads, with helmets for drinking cups and blood for wine; and in R. 10.44, Vishnu says of Rāvaṇa that he will make a mound of his lotus heads on the battlefield (according to Mallinātha, in order to offer *pūjā*).

[10] Mircea Eliade, *Cosmos and History: The Myth of the Eternal Return*, trans. Willard R. Trask (New York, 1959).

[11] D.E.D. 2528.

The Afterworld

It is now necessary to consider the beliefs of the ancient Tamils regarding life after death. Those beliefs are ill-defined, like those of the Ṛg-Vedic Aryans and the Homeric Greeks. The Tamils did believe in a Valhalla to which warriors who died in battle would go; indeed, so strong was their belief that a warrior should die in battle that they would cut with swords men who had died in bed before burying them, as in Pu̱r. 93:

Who is left to defeat in battle
advancing as the strong-thonged drum roars out?
Those who came could not prevail before your vanguard,
but scattered and ran.
The mean kings there died
and so escaped the rite
that would have rid them of their infamy:
when they had died in bed,
their bodies would have been taken,
and, all love for them forgotten,
to purge them of their evil,
Brahmins of the four Vedas and just principles
would have laid them out on green grass
prepared according to ritual,
would have said,
"Go to where warriors with renowned anklets go
who have died in battle
with manliness their support,"
and would have cut them
with the sword.
They died there, great one,
while you received a fine wound
as you attacked, making battle scatter
and bringing down on the field of killing
elephants whose rut hummed with striped bees
as it trickled into their mouths.

In Pu̱r. 287, the poet says that if men fall in war, they will delight in the world of high estate and marry faultless women there. In Pu̱r. 362, men who die heroically or who gain fame are actually said to rise to paradise in their bodies, a result that, according to Pur̲. 231, seems to be gained by exposure of the corpse. Even if a man did not die in battle, he might go to paradise if he possessed sufficient fame. Thus Pur̲. 50 says, "Except for those who have fame so that it spreads, there is no abiding there in the world of high estate."

Side by side with this conception of paradise is the animistic belief that the spirit of a man who has died heroically somehow remains in his memorial stone, as has been seen. Even today the Nāyāḍis of Kerala believe that their ancestors actually inhabit the stones erected to them.[12] The ancient Tamil belief in animism has survived among the Par̲aiyan̲s, whose "conception of life after death is merely a vague belief that the departed soul continues its existence somewhere [and who] have no ordered eschatology."[13]

While the poems do not mention the practice, it was common in South India to erect stones to *satīs*, women who cremated themselves upon the death of their husbands.[14] It seems quite certain that these stones were worshiped in much the same way that the memorial stones erected to fallen heroes were. It is curious that the souls of famous men and of men who fell in battle are said in the poems to go to paradise or to inhabit memorial stones, and that the souls of satīs inhabit stones, while the souls of ordinary people suffer at death a fate that is passed over in silence. This fact is explained, I believe, by the consideration that the souls that are mentioned are those that have accumulated the most sacred power in life and are therefore the most threatening in death. That is why stones are erected to house those souls and why the stones are propitiated lest the spirits do harm. The nature of the forces inhabiting the stones is suggested by the fact that a man was supposed to bathe and burn incense after worshiping a naṭukal (Pur̲. 329), and that one of those who worshiped the naṭukal was the player of the tuṭi drum,

[12] A. Aiyappan, "Social and Physical Anthropology of the Nayadis of Malabar," *Madras Government Museum Bulletin*, general section 2 (1930–37), pp. 13–85.

[13] Edgar T. Thurston, *Castes and Tribes of Southern India* (Madras, 1909), VI:108.

[14] For example, in the *Cilappatikāram*, a stone is brought from the Himālayas and erected to Kaṇṇaki. See also Pandurang Vaman Kane, *The History of Dharmaśāstra* (Poona, 1930–62), II:629.

a man of low caste whose office was to help control dangerous forces, especially those surrounding death (Ak. 35).

Omens

The most frequently invoked omens are birds, which are divided into good and bad kinds and signify a good or an evil outcome of an undertaking by their presence (Pu<u>r</u>. 20, 68). It has been seen that in Pu<u>r</u>. 291, the Pāṇa<u>n</u> tells the tuṭi player and others to keep birds away from a wounded man while he keeps white foxes away. To me, this indicates that birds were ominous because they were thought to be impregnated with sacred power, which could do harm if someone in a weakened condition came into contact with it. Thus in Ak. 19, the hero crosses "a lofty hill where cruel-voiced owls [*kuṭiñai*] hoot so that their meaning is apparent, like tuṭi drums on which sticks are rolled." Like the tuṭi drum, which was used to control the forces unleashed at death, the owl was thought to contain sacred power. In Ak. 88, 356, and 362 also, the hooting of the owl is said to be a bad omen, especially in the day.

A theme commonly encountered is the crow whose calling means that guests are coming. In Ku<u>r</u>. 210, the heroine's friend hears the crow calling, consoles the heroine, saying that her lover will surely return, and then praises the crow: "Even if I took hot boiled rice . . . and put it in seven pots with butter . . . it would be small *bali* [sacrificial offering] for the crow, which called for guests to come so that my friend's arms would not grow thin." A similar use of this theme is found in Ak. 391, where the mother of the eloped daughter says to the crow, "I will give you food with fresh fat and fresh meat in a golden dish. Call so that my girl . . . will come with her man."

In the North, birds were also used as omens. In the *Sundarakāṇḍa*, 25.38, a bird on a branch singing out a welcome is said to be a good omen for Sītā, while in Subh. 1449 a sweet-voiced crow in a fig tree is called a good omen for suppliants. Almost exactly the same use of the notion of the crow's calling that is found in Tamil occurs in a famous passage of the *Jñāneśvarī* of the Marathi poet and saint Jñānadeva written in about 1290 A.D. There, the heroine says, "The crow is foretelling something auspicious. Fly, fly, crow! I will put gold on your feet. Viṭṭhala [Krishna] is coming as a guest. I will give you yogurt and rice."[15] Just as the Tamil word for bird, *puḷ*, means omen (Pur̲. 124; Kur̲. 140; Ak. 151), the Sanskrit word for bird, *śakuna*, also has that meaning.

It seems to me that there is a difference in the use of birds as omens in the northern and the Tamil traditions, however. In the North, the notion fits the English word omen: birds indicate that something will happen by their presence or their acts. In Tamil, it seems that birds not only indicate that something will happen but also, in some sense, cause it to happen. Thus, in Ak. 391, the mother tells the crow to "call so that my girl . . . will come." It seems to me that this concept is connected with the idea that certain birds are impregnated with sacred power.

It will be seen in chapter 4 how astronomical phenomena were used as omens. Many miscellaneous bad omens are mentioned. In Pur̲. 41, bad omens include a leafless branch withering on a tree, teeth falling out, the pouring of oil (in one's hair), clothes coming off (curiously, a good omen in Su. 27.5, when Sītā's garment comes off a bit as it is blown by the wind), and the overturning of a table with weapons on it. In Pur̲. 229, the bad omens enumerated include elephants sleeping as they lie on their trunks, the king's muracus (royal drums) bursting their eyes (black spots put on their skin) and rolling on the ground (also in Pur̲. 238), the king's umbrella snapping at the base, and wind-swift horses losing their speed. In Pur̲. 238, it is a bad omen for a driverless elephant to lose its tusks. In Pur̲. 260, it is a bad omen for one to see a woman with her hair drying and for a bard's lute to play *viḷari*, the rāga of mourning, against his will. And finally, in Pur̲. 280, it is a bad omen for lamps not to stay lit, for bees to swarm in the middle of the day, and for the words of the old woman who tells the future "not to be full" (perhaps meaning that she foresees calamity, but refrains from telling what she has foreseen with the result that her prophetic words are short and not to the point). For the most part, these omens can be reduced to the case of an object filled with some sort of sacred power behaving in an unnatural way, indicating that the sacred power

[15] I am grateful to Saudamini Bahulikar for quoting this verse to me. I have been unable to discover the number of this verse in the works of Jñānadeva.

has gone out of control. It has already been seen that sacred power that is not controlled is thought to be dangerous and threatening.

The good omens mentioned are a lizard calling (Kuṟ. 140; Ak. 351) and *vēṅkai* flowers, said to portend a good day (according to the commentary, the marriage day; Ak. 133). Both good omens (Ak. 141) and bad omens (Puṟ. 41) could be seen in dreams.

Festivals

Festivals were a time of rejoicing and renewal, and everywhere prosperous things are compared to them: "Though it is no festival, in dishes of plowmen the meat of *keṭiṟu* fish is mixed with flowers" (Puṟ. 384); "[A courtyard] like a broad field in festival redolent with flowers" (Puṟ. 390); "If my beloved is near, then . . . I will rejoice like a city in festival" (Kuṟ. 41); "[A king] who has rich meat as if it were for a festival" (Ak. 113); "The black girl whose hair is as luxuriant as a festival" (Aiṅ. 306). The absence or passing of a festival is often invoked to signify the loss of prosperity or beauty: "[Now that the king has died], the village with wide streets has forgotten its festivals" (Puṟ. 65); "When he did not leave me . . . I knew evening as a time for making festival ornaments for girls with spotless bangles. . . . Now I know it as full of loneliness" (Kuṟ. 386); "Your forehead is desolate like the field with fireless ovens . . . the day after the festival" (Ak. 137).

Puṟ. 29 indicates that at many festivals there were costumed players: "In this world whose players come and go in regular succession like the costumes of Kōṭiyaṉs [concert givers] at a festival." There were also dancers at many festivals, for in Kuṟ. 31 the heroine says, "At the festival where warriors [*maḷḷar*] have assembled, or at the *tuṇaṅkai* dance where girls clasp one another, nowhere do I see him. I am a dancing girl [*āṭu kaḷa makaḷ*; literally "girl of the dancing platform"] and he is a dancing man." Swaminathaier in his commentary on this poem suggests that in this festival, fighting men would stage a mock battle on village streets. In Ak. 222, a man named Āṭṭaṉ Atti, "shining with beauty, danced at the festival in the great harbor of Kaḻār, a place of ecstasy where concert drums [*muḻavu*] never cease."

Several festivals are mentioned by name. Ak. 137 speaks of the festival of the month of Paṅkuṉi (Sanskrit Phalguni): "Your forehead is desolate like the field with fireless ovens in the little forest thick with trees . . . the day after the assembly [*muyakkam*] of Pañkuṉi, by the cool grove fragrant with pollen, by the lovely white sand of the great river . . . in Uṟantai." According to the modern commentary by Kāci Vicvanātaṉ Cēṭṭiyār, this festival would be held on the day of the conjunction of the full moon and the constellation *uttaram* (also called Phalguni in Sanskrit), and was celebrated only in Uṟantai, the Chola capital. Each of the other two great Tamil kings also seems to have had his special festival also, for in his commentary on the *Kaḷaviyal* of the *Iraiyaṉār Akapporuḷ*, Sūtra 16, Iṟaiyaṉār mentions the Avaṉiyaviṭṭam festival as celebrated in Maturai, the Pandyan capital, and the Uḷḷi festival as held in Karuvūr, the Chera capital, and remarks that people do not sleep at night when those festivals are being celebrated. The Uḷḷi festival is also mentioned in Ak. 368, where during its celebration men of Koñku land (a part of Chera country) are said to have danced in the streets with bells hanging from their waists. Naṟ. 234 makes the national character of these festivals clear when the foster mother of the heroine asks her real mother, "if you consider . . . Uṟantai with its Pañkuṉi festival and Vañci [Karuvūr] with its Uḷḷi festival are too little to get [as brideprice] for [our daughter's] growing breasts." Ak. 187 speaks of the Pūntoṭai festival of cruel warriors (*maḻavaṉs*), a festival that Subrahmanian says marked the ceremony of formally putting trained archers into the field for the first time.[16] Aiṅ. 62 says that a festival to Indra was celebrated in the *marutam* tract (the riverine tract).

The most often mentioned festival is that of Kārttikai, celebrated on the night of the full moon in that month (November-December): "The world's tasks have stopped, plows sleep. Clouds have ceased raining in the sky. The moon is full, and its blemish, a little hare, has appeared. It has joined with the Pleiades [*aṟu mīṉ*, "the six stars"; Sanskrit *kārtikeya*]. In the middle of the dark-filled night, they have put out lamps in the streets and hung garlands. May he come to celebrate the festival with us, as many join together in the ancient city of victories" (Ak. 141). In other references, the lamps lit at the festival are compared to the red

[16] Subrahmanian, *Tamil Index*, p. 592.

flowers of *ilavam* trees: "[A wasteland] where many old ilavam flowers dwindle on long stems as the wind blows, like lamps fed with ghee in an ancient city of victories celebrating the festival [of Kārttikai]" (Ak. 17; see also Ak. 11, 185). This festival is celebrated in much the same way even today. It was also celebrated in North India, for in Mbh. 3.80.52 and 57, whoever goes to the holy place of Puṣkara on Kārtikī is said to receive eternal merit, while Mbh. 3.179.16 says, "The most auspicious night for [the Pāṇḍavas] was the full moon night [*parvasandhi*] of Kārtikī in autumn."

For special occasions such as festivals, houses would be decorated in a way described by Ak. 195: "[Because the couple is coming], his mother has put red clay on her decorated wall, has put sand in her house, has hung up garlands, and is happily drawing [designs called *kōlams*, according to the commentary]." Especially common is the mention of spreading sand on the floor, which was done before the priest of Murukaṉ came to try to cure the heroine (Aiṅ. 248) and on occasions of celebration and rejoicing (Puṟ. 262). Other elements associated with festivals are ornaments put on by women (Kuṟ. 386), *muḷḷi* flowers (Ak. 26) and leaf skirts of *neytal* (blue waterlilies) (Ak. 70), which women would wear, and meat-eating (Puṟ. 384; Ak. 113).

Of the festivals described above, only one, the festival to Indra, involves a god. Most seem to involve special times when the sacred powers that fill the world are in an auspicious state, and one may rejoice by eating and dancing. Since the sacred is controlled, there is promise of prosperity and fertility, which must be celebrated. The festival is the opposite of those times of danger, such as a battle, when the sacred is in a threatening state and must be controlled very carefully. It is like a woman in an auspicious state, happily married and not in an impure condition, who is a sign of fertility and auspiciousness, unlike the widow or the menstruous woman, who must be avoided and is a bringer of bad luck.

Marriage

In spite of the fact that many of the poems concern love between two strangers not sanctioned by the girl's parents, it seems certain that the majority of marriages in ancient Tamilnad, as today, were arranged and were between cross-cousins, or at least relatives. One custom was to invite suitors, sometimes from out of town, to the house of the prospective bride so that they could look at the girl (Kuṟ. 171, 385), a practice still followed today, though it appears that in ancient times many men would come at once. In several poems, the hero asks the girl's parents for their permission to marry her (Aiṅ. 228, 230; Kuṟ. 350). In Kuṟ. 374 the heroine's friend says, "After [I] told the news that we had hidden to mother and father . . . and that man . . . came and asked them, . . . this city, deluded, accepted."

There is no mention of dowry, which almost certainly was not given; however, several poems mention a bride price. Thus in Naṟ. 234, the foster mother tells the real mother, "Considering the trouble being taken by good men [to bring valuables from the hero to you as part of the brideprice], and having in mind the excellence of your family, so lofty it seems to touch the sky, it would be right to accept his hill, where lovely jewels are gathered, and give [to him] her maturing breasts. For, if you do not do that and consider [what would really be right for him to give], . . . even Uṟantai and Vañci would be too little." Similarly in Puṟ. 343, the poet says that the father will not give his daughter in marriage even if he receives wealth equal to the city of Muciri (see also Puṟ. 352). Even today, there is a bride price among the Paṟaiyaṉs and other low-caste communities.[17]

In Kuṟ. 276, the hero, who has evidently tried to make his beloved's parents agree to give her to him in marriage, says, "I made her lovely rising breasts bright by painting sandal marks on them [that is, I am her lover]. The people who look after her do not know that. If I ask for her in the court of the king who is just and whose rule is righteous, how will it be?" This indicates how essential the consent of the girl's parents was if a marriage was to take place. In many poems, the couple have no recourse other than to elope. They have become lovers, and the girl cannot hope to marry anyone else (for in ancient Tamilnad, a girl's virginity and unsullied reputation were as important to a prospective bridegroom as they are today); nor have they been able

[17] Thurston, *Castes and Tribes*, VI:96.

to gain the consent of her parents. Therefore they run off, traversing the wilderness (Kuṟ. 262, 297, and others), sometimes with her relatives in pursuit (Aiñ. 312; Ak. 7). In Aiñ. 379, the mother asks, "Is going and embracing him who has a white conquering spear in the grove where a herd of elephants wanders . . . sweeter for her than enjoying good marriage here [where she can be with] her friends?" It seems certain that eloping was an expedient rarely if ever adopted in real life and that almost all marriages were arranged.

The marriage ceremony is described well in Ak. 136, where, according to the colophon, the hero, who has just quarreled with his wife, remembers their wedding day:

With unrestrained generosity
they honored eminent guests,
giving them white rice flowing with ghee
and full of faultless meat.
As omens fell together favorably,
as the vast sky shone with clear light,
and as there was an unjeopardized conjunction
of the moon and *cakaṭam* [the wagon, a constellation],
they readied the marriage house
and worshiped the god.
Then, as the great kettle drum
roared with the loud marriage drum
and the girls who had washed her for marriage
looked unwinking with their flower eyes
and then quickly hid themselves,
her relatives put on her a white thread
with fragrant cool buds
brought forth in the first rain by roaring clouds
from *aṟukai*,
a tuber with black petals like polished sapphires
spread in valleys
where almost-grown calves
graze on the forked, dull-backed leaves
of soft-flowered *vākai*.
And they made her resplendent with pure garments.
Then they came
arousing my desire,

and they gave her to me lovely with ornaments
and wiped off her sweat
in that pandal where the sound of marriage was like rain.
That night she, her chastity perfect,
as close to me as my body to my life,
covered herself entirely with her still fresh garment.
I said,
"Open it just a little
so the strong wind can dispel the sweat
breaking out on your hot, crescent-moon forehead,"
and, my heart full of desire,
I ripped off her garment.
Her form exposed shone like an unsheathed sword,
and she, not knowing how to hide herself,
took off the colorful garland of lilies holding her hair
and hid the private parts of her body
with the darkness of her thick black tresses
full of flowers and humming with bees,
and, ashamed, begged and pleaded with me.

In Ak. 86, the marriage ceremony is also described in detail: "[At dawn], when the curved white moon was not affected by inauspicious planets, . . . four girls with pure bangles, whose spotted stomachs have given birth to sons, said together, 'May you have love so that you care for the man you receive [as husband], and so that you, not slipping from chastity, are a help to him.'" After that, the guests take flowers and rice, dip them in water (according to the modern commentary, turmeric water), and throw them at the bride so that they adhere to her hair. The poem ends like Ak. 136 with a description of her modesty on that night.

A somewhat different picture of the ceremony is given in Kuṟ. 146: "Today they gathered to unite the [couple] who had been separated; sticks in hand, *citaval* cloths on their white hair, the elders said, 'It is good,' in the assembly." It appears from Aiṅ. 399 that before the marriage there would be a ceremony in which the girl's anklet was taken off. There the girl's mother tells the mother of the boy: "Even though [the ceremony] of taking off [her] anklet was done in your house, let the marriage take place in ours."

4

NORTHERN ELEMENTS IN TAMILNAD AT THE TIME OF THE ANTHOLOGIES

Brahmins

Some of the Brahmins who lived in Tamilnad at the time of the anthologies were not very much like their northern counterparts. Brahmins were called *antaṇaṉs*, a word whose folk etymology is "those who are lovely [*am*] and cool [*taṇ*]"[1] and *pārppāṉs*, "the seers," from *pār*, to see.[2] It has already been seen in chapter 3 how Brahmins would surround the king at the war sacrifice (Puṟ. 26), and how they officiated at the rite in which men who died in bed were cut with swords and buried (Puṟ. 93). Some of the Brahmins accepted the Tamil language and its culture wholeheartedly, for many of the finest Tamil poets were Brahmins, and their poems do not mention Aryan or Sanskritic ideas or customs any more than those of non-Brahmin authorship. Thus it is clear that some of the Brahmins of ancient Tamilnad had so accommodated themselves to the customs and beliefs indigenous to Tamilnad that they bore little resemblance to the northern ideal of a Brahmin.

At the same time, some Brahmins retained much of their Northern outlook and way of life: they introduced Vedic sacrifices

[1] D.E.D. 126.
[2] D.E.D. 3366.

(Pur̲. 166) with sacrificial posts (Pur̲. 224, 400), and they kept the three fires (Pur̲. 2). Kur̲. 156 describes an orthodox Brahmin who is addressed by a man (according to the commentary, a king) annoyed at the Brahmin's attempts to explain to him why he should not suffer at being separated from his beloved:

Brahmin's son, Brahmin's son,
your water vessel
hangs
from a stick
cut from the red-flowered palas tree
and stripped of its bark;
you eat
only to break your fasts.
Brahmin's son,
what remedy is there
in your words so learned in writing
to unite the separated?
No, this is nothing but delusion.

Pur̲. 166 describes an orthodox Brahmin: he performs without omission the twenty-one sacrifices; he knows the ancient book with six *aṅgas* of four parts that never leaves the mouth of Śiva; he wears the skin of the *pulvāy* deer over his thread; his wife wears a *valai* (an ornament worn on the forehead by the wife of the chief sacrificer, according to the *Tamil Lexicon*); he uses so much ghee in his sacrifices that water feels shame; and he has realized the lie of those who would quarrel with the ancient book (the four Vedas). As in the North, the orthodox Brahmin performs six acts: reciting, sacrificing, making others do those two things, giving, and accepting (Patir̲. 24), an account that agrees exactly with *Manusmṛti* 10.75.

Pur̲. 305 makes it clear that Brahmins sometimes acted as advisers and envoys, as they did in North India:

A young Brahmin,
his withered waist like a *vayalai* creeper,
creeping sadly along,
came at night,
entered the camp without pausing,
and said a few words.

At that they gave up their ladders and bolts
and bells were taken from the elephants of many wars.

Brahmins were treated with respect. In Pur̲. 9, the poet advises women, cows, and Brahmins to leave a city before it becomes a battleground. In Pur̲. 43, the Brahmin poet, overcome by anger when the king accuses him of cheating in a gambling session, calls the king a bastard. Then, when his anger has cooled, he praises the king for not killing him, adding that the king's ancestors never harmed Brahmins. Brahmins had the reputation of being moral, for in Pur̲. 200 and 201 when Kapilar tries to give Pāri's daughters in marriage to kings after the death of their father, he makes the point that he is a Brahmin and a Pulavan̲ (poet), and that there need be no fear that he might have spoiled them. Even in the most ancient times, it was common for kings to give land to Brahmins (Pur̲. 122).

As today, Brahmins lived apart and refused to keep dogs or chickens lest they become polluted. Thus Kur̲. 277 mentions a "sinless street, where there are no dogs in the wide doorways," and *Perumpāṇār̲r̲uppaṭai*, one of the *Pattuppāṭṭu*, speaks of a village of Brahmins where chickens and dogs are banned (297ff.). Several times the poet Kapilar, who was a Brahmin, mentions feasts full of meat in which he participated (Pur̲. 14, 113); however, these descriptions may be simply rhetorical, taken from the oral models provided by the Pāṇan̲s and others. At least some Brahmins appear to have been vegetarians, for the *Perumpāṇār̲r̲uppaṭai* describes the food a bard may expect to receive at a Brahmin's house, and it does not include meat even though the ancient Tamil poets usually included that staple in their descriptions of excellent food (304–310). In Kur̲. 167, where a wife's cooking for her husband is described, the family that the poem concerns is Brahmin according to the medieval commentator Naccin̲ārkkin̲iyar, since no meat is mentioned.[3]

Brahmins seem to have been associated with gentleness and with the orthodox North Indian religion penetrating Tamilnad. Thus, in Pur̲. 362, the poet addresses Brahmins, telling them of how kings die in battle: "Hear the voice of attack [the drums]! It has nothing to do with the four Vedas, for it is not concerned

3 In his commentary on *Tolkāppiyam*, *Akattiṇai* 24.

with kindness [*aruḷ*]. It has nothing to do with *dharma* [Tamil *aṟam*], for it is concerned with *artha* [*poruḷ*]." This poem makes the point well that the Brahmins set themselves apart from the indigenous religion and its sacred objects, such as the drum. Unlike indigenous sacred power, things associated with Brahmins appear from this poem to be beneficent; thus the four Vedas are said to be concerned with kindness. The lengths to which the Brahmins went to isolate themselves from polluting sacred power is suggested by Ak. 220, where the hero says that his beloved's breasts are as hard to gaze on as the sacrificial post used by Paraśurāma found at Cellūr (and presumably in a temple).

In Puṟ. 6, the king is told to "circle the temple of the three-eyed god [worshiped by] sages [*muṉivar*, from Sanskrit *muni*). Bow down your head, great one, while sages of the four Vedas raise their hands [in blessing]." Since Puṟ. 166 describes a Brahmin as adhering to the Vedas, "which never leave the mouth of the one with matted hair [Śiva]," it seems certain that the muṉivaṉs in the temple of Śiva are Brahmins. It is significant that nowhere in the poems surveyed are Brahmins mentioned in Vaishnava temples—indeed, Vaishnava temples themselves are not mentioned. Moreover, Brahmins were not present in the temples to Murukaṉ or at the rites of the common people, such as marriages, which they conducted as early as the *Cilappatikāram*.[4] Rather, Brahmins seem to have identified themselves closely with the kings, as is evident from most of the references given in this section. One king proudly called himself Irāyacūyavēṭṭa Perunaṟkiḷḷi, "Perunaṟkiḷḷi who sacrificed the Rājasūya [coronation]," a northern rite at which Brahmins officiated. It takes little imagination to see that it must have been the urging of the Brahmins that made the king wish to distinguish himself among the Tamil kings by this sacrifice.

From the above account, it may be concluded that some Brahmins in ancient Tamilnad resembled their northern counterparts very little, while others were very much like them. There are two explanations, it seems to me, that may account for this fact. It may be that some Brahmins were of indigenous origin, going back to a class of priests called Antaṇaṉs, while others were of

[4] Cil., canto 1.

Northern origin. When Brahmins from the North appeared, the indigenous Brahmins found it expedient to adopt the four Vedas as their own. Yet I believe that this explanation is almost certainly wrong. For one thing, the Brahmins did not concern themselves with the indigenous idea of the sacred, but rather strove to isolate themselves from it and to keep themselves unpolluted by it. There is no discernible place in the indigenous religion where a priestly class called Antaṇaṉs might fit, for the sacred was manipulated by men of low status such as the Pāṇaṉs. Moreover, in almost every reference to Brahmins, they are qualified by the description "of the four Vedas." If the Antaṇaṉs were in fact of indigenous origin, one would expect to find them at least occasionally not yet assimilated with the Brahmins of the North; yet even in those poems where Brahmins have the seemingly unbrahminical tasks of presiding at the war sacrifice (Puṟ. 26) or cutting the bodies of those who died in bed (Puṟ. 93), they are called *nāṉ muṟai mutalvar*, "those eminent ones of the four Vedas."

There is, I believe, a much more satisfactory explanation for the various types of Brahmins in ancient Tamilnad. Brahmins must have been coming from North India for a long time. Three or four hundred years before the anthologies, Buddhism and Jainism existed in Tamilnad, and there is no reason to suppose that Brahmins were not present as well. Now, the first Brahmins who came to Tamilnad must have found a society utterly alien to them and their way of life. The priests were of low caste, and were thought to contaminate others by their presence. There was no complex mythology, no plethora of gods, and what gods there were failed in almost every respect to resemble the Aryan gods. Rather than being transcendent beings who were summoned to help mankind, the sacred forces of the Tamils were immanent, were capricious, and had to be kept carefully under control lest they wreak havoc. The earliest Brahmins did the only thing they could do if they were to stay in Tamilnad: they associated themselves with the kings, who were considered by the people to be the representatives of the sacred on earth, and they attempted to gain their backing. Thus they had to participate in such unbrahminical activities as the war sacrifice and cutting the bodies of those who had died in bed. They also served as envoys for kings and as advisers; many of them became Pulavaṉs, or poets, who advised kings and were very much respected by the people. Through these activities, the earliest Brahmins made themselves a place in the society of ancient Tamilnad. As other Brahmins came to Tamilnad, they found that they were accepted and did not need to change their accustomed way of life—not, at least, as much as the earliest arrivals. Thus there came to be many kinds of Brahmins. Some were very much Tamilized, while others resembled in most respects their northern counterparts.

Even today this distinction is found among Tamil Brahmins. Thus the Teṉkalai Aiyaṅkārs use the Tamil *Divyaprabandham* along with Sanskrit scriptures in their worship and consider the *Tiruvāymoḻi* of Nammāḻvār, a non-Brahmin, of equal sanctity with the Vedas; the Vaṭakalai Aiyaṅkārs and many Śaiva Smārta Brahmins, on the other hand, identify themselves much more closely with the North and dissociate themselves from most non-Brahmin Tamil tradition. Among the numerous endogamous groups of Tamil Brahmins, almost every position between these two extremes is represented.

Mythological Elements from the North

It has been seen that Śaivism had already penetrated Tamilnad at the time of the anthologies, that there were temples to that god where Brahmins worshiped, and that the Vedas were identified with Śiva. Aiṅ. 181 says that tanks were constructed "to beautify Ālamuṟṟam, [a place] of the three-eyed god of the ancient four Vedas, whose good fame has spread over the earth." In Puṟ. 55 the king is said to be life itself, like the eye of Śiva next to the crescent moon. Puṟ. 55 says that Śiva has a black throat (see also Puṟ. 56) and that he gave the gods victory over the three-walled cities, using a mountain for his bow, a snake for its string, and one arrow, an account that does not tally exactly with the standard Sanskritic version, where no mention is made of the mountain as the bow, and where Vishnu is the arrow.[5] In Puṟ. 56,

[5] Daniel H. H. Ingalls, *An Anthology of Sanskrit Court Poetry: Vidyākara's "Subhāṣitaraṭnakośa"* (Cambridge, Mass., 1965), 4.14.

Śiva's flag is a bull, his matted hair is like fire, he carries a mace (*kaṇicci*), and he is called the destroyer.

In Pu<u>r</u>. 56, Krishna is invoked for his fame, Balarāma for his strength. Krishna is described as having a body like blue sapphire, having a bird (presumably the *garuḍa*) on his flag, and being accompanied by Balarāma, who has a body the color of a conch, a plow for his weapon, and a palmyra on his banner. In Pu<u>r</u>. 58, where Krishna is said to wield the discus, the color of the two brothers is again contrasted, Krishna's body being black, Balarāma's like milk. In Pu<u>r</u>. 174, Krishna, his body like collyrium, is said to have retrieved the sun when the demons (Avuṇa<u>n</u>s) took it, perhaps a transferral of the myth in which Indra was originally the hero. Ak. 59 describes "an elephant who bends down tall *yā* trees so his mate can eat, like Krishna [Māl], who bent [branches] down by treading on them [*miti*—after climbing?] so that the cowherd girls on the wide sandy shore of the To<u>l</u>u<u>n</u>ai [Yamunā] in the North could [make and] wear cool dresses." This is one of the earliest references to the story of Krishna and the Gopīs in Indian literature; it must be about contemporary with the or only a bit later than *Harivaṃśa*. In any event, its appearance in Tamil at this early date indicates that it must have been well known in many parts of India already. The theme of the hero presenting his beloved with leaves for her to make a dress (*ta<u>l</u>ai*) is one peculiar to Tamil. Moreover, the names used for both the god Krishna and the river Yamunā are Tamil terms: Māl, "the black one"; and To<u>l</u>u<u>n</u>ai, probably from the root *to<u>l</u>u*, "to worship," the only example in the poems surveyed of a pure Tamil name for a place in North India. Thus it is evident that, from the very beginning, the Tamils applied their own poetic conventions to the gods and mythological figures from North India, and that from the first they emphasized the roles of the new gods in what was for them the central and most sacred act of life, love between man and woman. In the succeeding centuries, the Vaishnava and Śaiva Tamil saints continued and developed this practice. For example, in the *Tirukkōvaiyār*, the great Śaiva poet Māṇikkavācakar uses the Tamil akam conventions to describe the relation between the soul (the hero) and God (the heroine). In a final reference to Krishna (or Vishnu), a rainbow is compared to the garland on the breast of the handsome god, masterful in battle, with a straight-rayed wheel (*nēmi*—Ak. 175). It is significant that no temples to Vishnu and no worship of him are mentioned, although, since the epithet *celvaṉ* is applied to him in Ak. 175, it appears that he was accepted as a god, as that epithet is elsewhere applied only to Śiva.

The goddess Lakṣmī, or Śrī, appears several times under her Tamil name Tiru or Tirumakaḷ (where *makaḷ* means woman). Tiru is probably a *tadbhava* of Sanskrit śrī, and, like that word, means venerable when prefixed to a noun and wealth when it stands alone. In Puṟ. 7, a king's breast keeps Tiru from the breasts of others, while in Ak. 13 the Pandyan king's breast is said to be desired by Tiru. Her connection with the king's breast in these examples would seem to be an extension of the Sanskrit notion that she reclines on the breast of Vishnu. In Puṟ. 342, a girl who is the cause of war is fit to be envied by Tirumakaḷ.

In Puṟ. 241, Indra (called Neṭiyōṉ, an epithet of Vishnu in later literature) carries his *vajra* in his hand as he stays in his heavenly palace where the drum roars out, "Antiraṉ . . . is coming!" after the death of that king. Indra is said in Aiṅ. 62 to have a festival that according to Swaminathaier, was celebrated on the marutam or riverine tract. The *Tolkāppiyam* says he was the chief deity of that tract,[6] but this claim is belied by the fact that this is the only mention in the poems examined where he may have that office. In Puṟ. 182 the name of Indra is used in the plural in the phrase "the nectar [*amiḻtam*, from *amṛta*] of *intirar*." According to Aṭiyārkkunallār, the chief commentator on the *Cilappatikāram*, the meaning of intirar here is gods.[7] However, it is possible that the form is a respectful plural meaning Indra, much as the plural celvar is used for Śiva in Puṟ. 6. It is possible that the frequency with which the name of Indra is mentioned and the respect accorded him are due to the influence of the Buddhists and Jainists, for whom he remained a major god; for among the Hindus in North India at the time of the epics, he was a god not to be taken seriously, the butt of many jokes, as in the Ahalyā story where he is cursed to be covered with a thousand vaginas.

[6] See *Tolkāppiyam, Akattiṇai* 5.

[7] In his commentary on Col. 16.172.

Paraśurāma is mentioned only once, in Ak. 220, where the breasts of the heroine are said to be as hard to get to see "as the well-guarded tall post, its middle tied with a rope, of the sacrifice completed in Cellūr, a place of undying [sacrificial] fires, by the one with an axe, who, striving, cut down the race of warriors." This shows that the story of Paraśurāma had gained enough currency for a place in South India to identify itself with him. It also suggests that the more orthodox Brahmins in the South had a strong sense that non-Brahmins would pollute their sacrifices, even in the most ancient times. Cellūr seems to have been in Tulunad, the home of the Kōcars, for Ak. 90 speaks of "Niyamam of the black-eyed Kōcars . . . bathed by the great sea, to the east of Cellūr of the god of hard strength." It is significant that Cellūr is not far from Kerala, the place with which Paraśurāma was especially connected in later times, and that the Kōcars here associated with Paraśurāma, the hero par excellence of Brahminism, are said to have formed the vanguard of the Maurian armies invading Tamilnad (Ak. 251, 261), a fact that suggests they had close connections with North India.

Kubera also is mentioned only once, in Ak. 66. There, the hero going in his chariot to see his courtesan has decorated himself with new ornaments and is said to look like Māniṭikiḻavaṉ, "[the] lord of great treasure"—according to the commentary, Kubera. It is possible, however, that only the literal meaning of the words, and not Kubera, is intended.

Arundhatī, a mythological figure who was regarded in the North as the highest pattern of conjugal excellence and wifely devotion, is invoked in the Tamil poems for her chastity. In Puṟ. 122, the chastity of the king's wife is compared to that of the star in the North (*vaṭa mīṉ*), or Arundhatī, who was thought in both the North and the South to have been made into a star. In Aiṅ. 442, the hero praises his wife as being chaste like Arundhatī in the world of high estate in the dark monsoon sky. Chastity had in ancient times as important a place as it occupies now among Tamil values. This fact probably accounts for the references to Arundhatī, a minor figure in Sanskrit, when so many more important figures are not mentioned.

The *Mahābhārata*

The great Sanskrit epic *Mahābhārata* is mentioned only once in the Tamil poems. In Pur̲. 2, the poet sings to King Cēramān̲ Peruñcōr̲r̲utiyañ Cēralātan̲, whose name indicates that he gave rice:

Great one
whose good land has wealth and ever-new prosperity,
whose country is so high
that it is bounded by the sky [i.e. by the Western Ghats],
you gave without interruption great quantities of good rice
until the hundred with golden chaplets who had appropriated the earth
perished on the field,
fighting furiously
the five
whose horses had waving manes.

The old commentary, which surely must be correct, identifies the hundred with the Kauravas and the five with the Pāṇḍavas. Here the poet can only be indulging in hyperbole; for the great war of the epic, if in fact it was ever fought (and I believe that it was not), must have taken place many hundreds of years before the Tamil poems were composed.

The *Rāmāyaṇa*

There are two references to the *Rāmāyaṇa* in the poems surveyed. In Pur̲. 378, the poet humorously describes how a bard's family puts on ornaments given by the king, comparing that act to the monkeys' putting on Sītā's ornaments after they found them lying where she had dropped them:

He [the king] gave wealth
of excellent precious stones,
letting them fall down without end,
many more than I was fit for.
When they saw that,
my large family, burnt by the sun,
put the ornaments meant for fingers on ears;
those meant for ears they squeezed on fingers;

those for waists they made fit their necks;
and those meant for necks they put on their waists,
so that,
like the red-mouthed family of monkeys
all decked out
when they took the lovely ornaments
fallen on the ground
the day the mighty demon [*arakkaṉ*, from Sanskrit *rākṣasa*]
abducted Sītā,
who had been joined to Rāma of great destruction,
we laughed happily and unceasingly.

Ak. 70, the other poem that refers to the *Rāmāyaṇa*, describes the gossip of the city, saying that now that the couple has married, it has ceased "like the banyan tree with many falling roots when Rāma, victorious in battle, made [its birds] hush for his difficult rite in the harbor while the great ocean roared in ancient Kōṭi [Dhanuṣkōṭi]."

It is instructive to compare these two accounts to those given by Vālmīki. In the episode concerning the ornaments, Vālmīki never describes the scene in which the monkeys find the ornaments; rather, in 4.6 he has Sugrīva show Rāma the bodice and ornaments, saying that they were dropped by Sītā when she saw Sugrīva and four other monkeys as she was being abducted. As far as the episode in Dhanuṣkōṭi is concerned, in Vālmīki's version (6.21), before Rāma sets out for Lañkā, he propitiates the ocean by making obeisance to it, lying down on the shore, sleeping for three days and nights on a bed of *darbha* grass, and then performing obeisance to it again. When the ocean still does not become tranquil, he threatens to dry it up, putting to his bow the weapon given by Brahmā (the *brāhman astram*). At that, the ocean appears and grants him what he wishes. In both of these instances, the Tamil account is quite different from that of Vālmīki. The Tamil accounts appear to me more poetic, especially the second one; Vālmīki simply describes Rāma's actions without imagery or ornament, while the Tamil poet makes the sacred banyan tree hush as Rāma sleeps and makes the ocean roar, emphasizing the daring and contrary nature of that element.

Given the difference of these Tamil passages from the Sanskrit accounts and given the familiarity the poets assumed on the part of the audience it appears that a widely known Tamil version of the *Rāmāyaṇa* existed even at this early date. This is not at all surprising when the number of poets of those times and the status of poetry in Tamilnad are considered. In fact, some of this ancient Tamil *Rāmāyaṇa* may have survived. Mayilai-Cīṉi Vēṅkaṭacāmi gives four passages from an ancient *Rāmāyaṇa* that have come down to us by virtue of their being included in two ancient anthologies;[8] unfortunately, however, it is not possible to determine whether this work is in fact as ancient as the Tamil anthologies.

It is interesting indeed to find Dhanuṣkōṭi (under its Tamil name, Kōṭi), the very tip of the mainland before Adams Bridge, called the place from which Rāma set out for Laṅkā as early as the ancient Tamil poems, for this shows that in the second and third centuries A.D. the historical framework of the Rāma story was accepted to an extent that, I believe, few western scholars would have expected. This reference leaves little doubt that the Laṅkā of which Vālmīki spoke was in fact Ceylon. It should be noted that nowhere in the poems is Rāma identified with Vishnu, a fact in agreement with the older middle books of the *Vālmīki-rāmāyaṇa*.

Miscellaneous Gods and Mythological Figures

The story of Śibi, the king who is prepared to sacrifice his own life for that of a dove in the Buddhist *Jātakas*, is mentioned in Puṟ. 37 and 39. It is noteworthy that the Sanskrit name is changed to Cempiyaṉ, a name that seems more natural in Tamil. There are several gods mentioned in the early Tamil works that may or may not be of northern provenance. In Puṟ. 39, a king's ancestors are said to have destroyed the hanging wall that raised fear in its (the wall's) enemies (who, according to the old commentary, were the gods). From other references, it appears that the wall was erected by the demons (*avuṇar*) and that it was destroyed by a Chola king named Cempiyaṉ, the Tamilization of Śibi.[9] Several

[8] Mayilai-Cīṉi Vēṅkaṭacāmi, *Maṟaintu Pōṉa Tamiḻ Nūlkaḷ* (Madras, 1967), pp. 90–92.

[9] *Puṟanāṉūṟu*, comm. U. V. Swaminathaier (Madras, 1963), p. 104.

times, natural forces are made into gods. In Puṟ. 27, the moon god is said to circle the world, "showing for even the most ignorant to learn that there is waning and waxing, death and birth." In Puṟ. 365, the earth goddess weeps, saying, "My face is the sky covered with storms and lightning; my eyes are the two great moving orbs. . . . Even though kings have gone, I do not go, but I live on like a whore as many praise me." The meaning seems to be that the earth cannot commit suttee and follow her husband, the king, in death. The fact that the earth is conceived of as the king's wife, an idea common in Sanskrit but found nowhere else among the ancient Tamil poems surveyed, suggests that this personification is of northern provenance. One final mention of the gods that is certainly borrowed is in Puṟ. 62, where the gods of paradise are said to have unwinking eyes and unfading garlands (compare Mbh. 3.54.23).

Foreign Gods Compared to Indigenous Ones

The foreign origin of the gods described above is clearly shown by their names. Not once are the epithets of the indigenous deities, kaṭavuḷ, aṇañku, or, strangely, teyvam (from Sanskrit deva), applied to them. Rather, they are designated by the term celvaṉ, the wealthy one, used for Vishnu in Ak. 175 and for Śiva in Puṟ. 6 and Ak. 181. Elsewhere the northern gods are referred to without being named by phrases that describe them and are used as epithets, such as *mutu mutalvaṉ*, "the ancient first one," for Śiva in Ak. 66; *nīla maṇi miṭaṟṟu oruvaṉ*, "the one whose neck is like blue sapphire," for Śiva in Puṟ. 91; and *añcaṉa uruvaṉ*, "he whose form is [like] collyrium," for Krishna in Puṟ. 174. The only god given his Sanskrit name is Indra, though Rāma, Sītā, and Arundhatī receive their northern appelations. To quite another category, apparently, belong the gods of paradise—called the world of *vāṉōr*, "the sky ones" (Puṟ. 213), or of *mēlōr*, "the high ones" (Puṟ. 299). The moon in Puṟ. 22, the one poem in which it is a god, is called a *puttēḷ*, while in Puṟ. 27, the king's land is likened to the land of the puttēḷ—presumably paradise. This word is from the root *putu* ("new") and also means stranger, strange woman, novelty; unfortunately, the application of its etymology is not at all clear.[10] The earth goddess referred to in Pur̲. 365 is called *nilamakaḷ*, from *nilam* ("earth") and *makaḷ* ("woman").

All these gods were benevolent, or at least indifferent, deities. Since they were not considered threatening, they were not called by the names used for the indigenous gods, such as kaṭavuḷ. On the other hand, the demons who took the sun, which Krishna got back in Pur̲. 174, are called "avuṇan̲s who have aṇañku." In Pur̲. 299, Murukan̲ is said to have aṇañku, and in Ak. 98 the heroine is said to be afflicted by "the hard aṇañku of Murukan̲ [*murukan̲ ār aṇañku*]." In other instances, aṇañku is clearly used to mean a god rather than the sacred power that a deity possesses; for example, Ak. 99 mentions a temple that has an aṇañku that is worshiped, and Aiñ. 28 speaks of the aṇañku of the watering place. From these examples, it appears that the primary meaning of aṇañku is sacred or dangerous power and that the term came to mean a god by metonymy. The same seems to be true of cūr, for in Kur̲. 105 a mountain where a god resides is said to be cūr. That word, however, came to denote a being even more malevolent than aṇañku. The spirit that has sacred power or aṇañku is called kaṭavuḷ, that to which one owes a debt or must make a sacrifice. It is noteworthy that ascetics, who were thought to possess power to harm people, are called kaṭavuḷ and avoided by people in Kur̲. 203.

In sum, the words used to denote gods make it clear that the new gods from the North were conceived of differently from the indigenous ones. The new gods were distant beings, the subjects of story and myth, who were not involved directly in everyday life (though Śiva appears to have been more involved than the others), while the original gods were little more than dangerous forces that resided in certain things and made them dangerous —potential causes of suffering—a quality that led the epithet aṇañku to be applied to the northern demons (avuṇan̲s) rather than to the northern gods. In time, the two sets of divine forces began to merge: even in the *Kalittokai*, which is only a little later than the anthologies surveyed, Indra is said to have aṇañku (Kali. 105), a quality that one cannot imagine being applied by

[10] D.E.D. 3511.

the northerners of the time to the god cursed by Gautama to be covered by a thousand *yonis*. Yet even to this day there is a distinction between the originally Aryan gods, who are transcendent and at least sometimes benevolent, and the village gods, fearful deities who cause smallpox and other scourges and who must be appeased.

PARADISE

There are many northern ideas concerning paradise in the poems. In Puṟ. 6, paradise is called "the world of the cows," a notion found in the *Harivaṃśa*.[11] In Puṟ. 27, a soul is said to go in a driverless vehicle in the sky after death. Puṟ. 62 states that the world that is hard to obtain fills with men killed in battle as "those who have fragrant food, unwinking eyes, and unfading garlands [the gods] celebrate feasts [given to celebrate the arrival of so many dead heroes]." In a similar vein, Puṟ. 241 states that upon the death of King Āy Antiraṉ, the drum in the palace of Indra roars out, "Antiraṉ is coming!" Puṟ. 367 says that the earth is as wonderful as Nāgaloka (the world of the Nāgas), which in Sanskrit is below the earth and is inhabited by Nāgas, beings with the faces of men and the tails of serpents. In Kuṟ. 83, the heroine says, "May my mother go to that great-named world where amṛta, hard to obtain, is food."

Many poems connect the notions of paradise and *karma*. In Puṟ. 38, for example, the poet says:

> Even those who live in sweet paradise
> with groves of gold flowers,
> though they receive reward for the good acts
> they have done,
> live incomplete lives,
> for there the rich do not give
> and the poor do not ask.

The word used for paradise in this poem is *naṉṉāṭu*, "the good land." In Puṟ. 213, the poet advises, "Do good so that you will be a guest desired at once by those who are in the hard-to-reach

[11] Daniel H. H. Ingalls, "The *Harivaṃśa* as a Mahākāvya," *Mélanges d'Indianisme à la Mémoire de Louis Rénou* (Paris, 1968), pp. 386–387.

world of the gods [vāṉōr, the sky ones]." In Puṟ. 214, the poet exclaims:

If noble men with lofty aims
attain reward
for a portion of their good acts,
they may experience delight
in the eternal world.
If they do not experience delight
in that world,
they may not have to be born again.
And if they are not born again,
it is crucial
that they die
with bodies devoid of evil,
establishing their fame
like a Himalayan peak.

In many poems, like this one, the importance of fame is stated. In Puṟ. 50, for example, the poet says, "Except for those whose fame here spreads over the broad earth, no one can stay there in the world of high estate." In Puṟ. 165, the poet says, "Rich men, because they did not give, have failed to achieve any connection with the ancients [*toṉmai mākkaḷ*]," by which he evidently means that their names have failed to pass into legend. In two poems the poet urges the king to share his wealth, giving as motive the fact that his good fame will remain; in both there is no mention of paradise. Thus in Puṟ. 359, the poet says, "There will come a day when you too [will go to the burning ground]. Ignominy and fame remain. If you give . . . , after you have gone there for all to see, you will have lofty, brilliant fame here," and in Puṟ. 360 he says, "after they have entered the mouth of fire, many people have left nothing behind, never having shared what they ate."

Hell is mentioned four times, with the Sanskrit loan *niraiya* (from Sanskrit *niraya*) used in every instance. In Puṟ. 5, the king is enjoined not to give up love and mercy, lest he join those who go to hell; in Kuṟ. 258, a king's spears are said to be "hell"; in Puṟ. 376, the poet's poverty is compared to hell; and in Kuṟ. 292, the king Naṉṉaṉ, who executed a girl for unwittingly having eaten a fruit from his tutelary tree, is said to have gone to hell.

I believe that it can be concluded with some certainty that virtually all of the mentions of paradise cited above are due to northern influence. Not only does the paradise described not accord with the indigenous religious system described in chapter 3, but also, in many of the instances cited, elements of obvious northern provenance are included: in Pur̲. 6 (which uses the loan word Nāgaloka), the notion that earth is the lowest of the three worlds; in Kur̲. 83, amṛta; in Pur̲. 62, gods with unwinking eyes and unfading garlands; in Pur̲. 241, Indra's palace; and in Pur̲. 38, 213, and 214, the doctrine of karma.

The only element described above that appears indigenous is the importance placed on fame. It has been seen that the Tamils erected memorial stones to men and women who had distinguished themselves on earth—men in battle, and women by committing suttee. Their idea seems to have been that the spirits of such people were much more strongly charged with sacred power than those of ordinary people, and that therefore a place had to be provided to house those spirits, and arrangements had to be made to propitiate those spirits, lest they bring misfortune to mankind. In the poems cited above, the idea of the importance of fame has survived: by gaining renown, a spirit charges itself with sacred power and so is strong enough to win through to paradise. It is interesting that in Pur̲. 359 and 360 fame has been desacralized and is said to be its own justification.

Karma and Reincarnation

The doctrines of karma and reincarnation are mentioned in several poems. In Pur̲. 71, a king swears, "If I do not [win] . . . , may I be reborn as the protector of the dry lands of others." Pur̲. 236 and Kur̲. 49 express the wish to be with a beloved person in the next birth. In Pur̲. 134 and 141, rebirth is spoken of with scorn, indicating perhaps that the idea was not universally accepted: "Āy is no merchant dealing in the price of virtue, thinking that what one does in this birth will be repaid in the next. No; he is generous because it is the way followed by good men [*cān̲r̄or*] and others"; and "Pēkan̲ . . . is generous for the sake of the indigence of others, not for the sake of his next birth." Pur̲. 361 considers karma from a Brahminic point of view: "O Death . . . , he [the king] is not afraid of your coming, for he poured showers of precious gems to Brahmins who sacrifice and who are wholly versed in *śruti* [Tamil *kēḷvi*], which is full of excellent things." Pur̲. 357 says that death comes even to absolute monarchs and that the only help is good deeds, which are like seeds. Wealth, it says, is of no avail to those who have forsaken that raft. Pur̲. 367 says that except for good deeds, the cause of life, there is no ship when you sink. The most eloquent poem on karma is Pur̲. 192, where that subject is considered in a manner I find quite different from any North Indian system. The poet seems to say that ultimately we are responsible for what happens to us, but that this process is so hidden and mysterious that our only rational response is to react with equanimity and compassion. This poem is a good example of the fact that, while the religious system of the ancient Tamils was less sophisticated than the systems of North India, the Tamils were imbued with a better sense of poetry than their northern counterparts; no northern account of karma is in my estimation as profound and poetically well wrought as this. This poem contrasts with the *Cilappatikāram*, which was written a few centuries later when the theory of reincarnation was well established in South India, and which is marred by the attribution of the misfortunes that befall Kōvalan̲ and Kaṇṇaki to their acts in former births.

All lands home, all men kin.
Evil and good are not from others,
nor are pain and its abating.
Death is not new,
and we do not rejoice
thinking life is sweet.
If there is something hateful,
even less do we find it cause for grief.
Through the vision of the able ones
we have come to know
that hard life takes its course
as if it were a raft upon the waters
of a mighty river
roaring as it ever flows on rocks
while cold drops pour from flashing skies,
and so

we do not wonder at those big with greatness
and still less
do we despise the small.

Jainism, Buddhism, and Hinduism

The stress on good deeds in the poems cited immediately above sounds very much as if inspired by Jainism or Buddhism. Although no explicit mention is made of those two religions in the anthologies, it is known that they had penetrated Tamilnad by then, for several Tamil inscriptions that antedate the anthologies by two or three centuries refer to monks and nuns of those religions.[12] The frequent mention of Indra as representative of the gods seems to indicate Buddhist or Jaina influence as well, for Indra had long since lost his important place in Hinduism while he continued to be the most important of the gods for the Buddhists and Jainas. The occurrence of the story of Śibi may also point to a Buddhist source.

There are many poems on the ephemeral nature of life that seem certainly to have been influenced by Buddhist and Jaina ideas (Puṟ. 27, 29, 165, 194, 195, 243, 245, 251, 252, 356–367). In keeping with the ancient Tamils' flair for the poetic, most of these poems emphasize the tragic aspects of existence more than the philosophical lessons to be learned from suffering. For example, in Puṟ. 356, the poet says:

Covered by barren soil,
thick with milkhedge,
where owls hoot in the day
and demon women
with glistening teeth
are lit up by cremation fires,
this burning ground
with its white clouds of smoke
is fearful.
Tears of lovers
with yearning hearts

[12] Iravatham Mahadevan, "Tamil Brahmi Inscriptions of the Sangam Age," *Proceedings of the Second International Conference Seminar of Tamil Studies* (Madras, 1971), I:100.

extinguish the hot ashes
on the bone-strewn earth.
It has seen the back of every man,
the only thing abiding in the world,
and it knows none
who has seen its back.

Here the poet does not state that one must do good acts to go to paradise or to obtain a good birth in the next life; rather he leaves what will happen after death unstated and dwells on the horror and tragedy of death. Occasionally, however, the poet does include philosophical ideas. In Puṟ. 194, for example, he says, "In one house beats the funeral drum; in another resound the melodious notes of the marriage drum. Women joined with their lovers are ornamented with garlands; the blackened eyes of bereaved women sorrow, flowing with cool water. Certainly he who made this creation is cruel [*paṇpilāḷaṉ*, literally "an uncouth one"]. The world is suffering; may those who have realized its nature find happiness." The Buddhist *Dhammapada* adopts a similar tone:

While eagerly man culls life's flowers,
with all his faculties intent,
of pleasures still insatiate—
Death comes and overpowers him.[13]

It is probably no coincidence that Puṟ. 366, one of the poems on this theme, is addressed to one Tarumapputtiraṉ (the tadbhava of Dharmaputra), evidently a Buddhist from his name. In Puṟ. 214, Kōpperuñcōḻaṉ, who is about to commit suicide by ritually starving himself to death,[14] speaks of "an outlook stained by impurities," and says that dying with a body free of evil is important, an attitude that suggests he was influenced by Jainism.

Most of the evidence for the presence of the orthodox Hindu religions (those religions that acknowledge the authority of the Vedas—principally Śaivism and Vaishnavism) has been given above in the section on Brahmins. Puṟ. 166 suggests that a struggle was underway between the orthodox and the nonorthodox religions: in the poem, a Brahmin is addressed "who established

[13] Henry Clarke Warren, *Buddhism in Translations* (New York, 1963), p. 264.

[14] In the rite of *vaṭakkiruttal*, or sitting facing the north. See below, chapter 5.

the truth, not agreeing with those who claim the true is false, and who realized the lie that seemed as if it were true to utterly defeat those who would quarrel with the one ancient book." In Puṟ. 251 and 252, a man is described who has become an ascetic. He lives in the forest, has long hair, and practices asceticism by sitting before a fire. It appears that he was adopting the ascetic model of the orthodox religions, for both Buddhist and Jaina ascetics did not have hair on their heads. Moreover, the practice of sitting in front of a fire to mortify the flesh is one most commonly found among orthodox ascetics. These poems are noteworthy also in that they show the influence of the indigenous value system. In Puṟ. 251, the poet writes:

We saw then
a warrior
who made loose the ornaments
of small-bangled women
like dolls
in their houses,
which seemed paintings.
Now
he bathes in a waterfall
dropping from a high bamboo-filled summit,
goes to a hot red fire
raging on logs brought by forest elephants,
and dries his curly matted hair,
which hangs low on his back.

Unlike the North Indian of those times, who would consider the ascetic a fortunate man, happier than most of mankind, the Tamil poet feels that the ascetic must be ill-fated, the victim of some terrible calamity, to give up family life, which was for the Tamils the most important manifestation of the sacred and the arena in which human fulfillment took place.

In the struggle between the orthodox and the nonorthodox religions, the Jainas and Buddhists prevailed under the Kalābhras, the shadowy rulers of Tamilnad in the period immediately after the anthologies. Ultimately, however, beginning with the Pallava dynasty in the sixth century, the Śaivas and Vaishnavas triumphed. The reasons for their ultimate victory seem clear enough: it was the Hindus, and especially the Śaivas, who built on the indigenous elements of the religion of the Tamils, making for their gods temples similar to the ones that already existed, identifying Murukaṉ with Skanda, replacing the naṭukal with the *liṅgam*, adopting the technique of ecstatic worship through the examples of the Nāyaṉmārs and Āḻvārs, and in general making Śaivism, and, to a lesser extent, Vaishnavism, natural developments of the original religion of the Tamils rather than wholly new religions as Jainism and Buddhism were. It appears from the texts that the Vaishnavas arrived later than the Śaivas and that they were less willing to absorb the native customs (though they too showed considerable flexibility, especially in the example of the Āḻvārs). That is perhaps why Vaishnavism did not fare as well in Tamilnad as its rival, Śaivism. Indeed, a perusal of the lives of the Āḻvārs and of the Nāyaṉmārs shows that while the Vaishnava saints did write in Tamil, and while several of them were of low caste, their histories are animated by sweetness and light, they lack the extremes and the violence so often found in Tamil literature, while the Śaiva saints were far more in the Tamil tradition. Thus Kaṇṇappar, one of the Nāyaṉmārs, tears out his eyes to offer them to the lingam, while Ciṟuttoṇṭar cuts up his own son and cooks him for Śiva masquerading as an ascetic. Even today the Vaishnava temples in Tamilnad are more strict than their Śaiva counterparts in observing pollution taboos, a fact that suggests they were less willing to accept the native customs than the Śaivas. The great majority of non-Brahmins today consider themselves Śaiva.[15]

Astrology

The position of the stars was used to determine the days of marriages and of festivals. Thus, in Ak. 136, the marriage took place "as omens fell together favorably, as the broad sky shone with clear light, and as there was an unjeopardized conjunction of the moon and *cakaṭam*," while in Ak. 86 the marriage cere-

[15] There is one Vaishnava work, the *Kamparāmāyaṇam*, that, like most works of the Śaiva Tamil tradition, is full of violence and emotional conduct as part of the worship of God. That work, however, is quite ignored by the orthodox Srivaishnava tradition of Tamilnad and, unlike the *Vālmīkirāmāyaṇa*, is never cited in the works of the commentators on the *Divyaprabandham*.

mony takes place "[at dawn], when the curved white moon is not affected by inauspicious planets." It has been seen above in chapter 3 that the festivals of Pañkuṉi and Kārttikai were determined by the month and the moon. There occur in the poems many other descriptions of the positions of the stars, generally in order to indicate a bad omen or an unfavorable time. In Puṟ. 24, the poet says, "May the star of your [birth]day be established and remain; and may the star of your enemies' day be fickle and leave." Often it is said that when Venus is in the south (in the summer), there is no rain (Puṟ. 35, 117, 384, 388, 389). It is a bad omen for a comet (*tūmakētu*, the tadbhava of Sanskrit *dhūmaketu*) to appear and for Saturn (Maimīṉ) to be in the wrong place (Puṟ. 117). It is also inauspicious for the sun to appear in the four directions (Puṟ. 35, 41; what is intended is uncertain) and for falling stars to be seen in the eight directions (Puṟ. 41). In Puṟ. 395 the poet gives as reasons for the impoverishment of the world the appearance of Eri (literally "fire"—according to Subrahmanian, a comet[16]), the unfavorable position of Kuḷamīṉ (literally "the tank"—Sanskrit Punarvasu), and the unfavorable position of Tāḷ (according to the *Tamil Lexicon*, a comet; but perhaps a constellation, since Eri evidently means comet in the same poem). Puṟ. 229 gives a complicated description showing that the ancient Tamils had become skilled in observing the heavens and used a complex system of astrology. I have translated most of the poem immediately below, depending on the old commentary for the meaning and using the Sanskrit equivalents of the Tamil terms that that commentary supplies; I furnish the original Tamil terms in brackets, followed by their European equivalents where available and by the number assigned them by Indian astrologers: "When Kṛttikā [Aḻal, fire; the Pleiades; the third lunar asterism] was in conjunction with Meṣa [Aṭu, the ram; Aries], at darkness-filled midnight, from the base of Anurādha [Muṭappaṉaiyam, the bent palmyra; part of Scorpio; the seventeenth lunar mansion], in the first half of Phalguni month, as the Star Uttaram [*talai nāḷ mīṉ*, the head asterism star; Denebola or Leonis; the twelfth lunar asterism] left its top place, as Mūla [*nilai nāḷ mīṉ*, the established asterism star; the nineteenth asterism] arose, and as Mṛga-

[16] N. Subrahmanian, *Pre-Pallavan Tamil Index* (Madras, 1966), p. 302.

śīrṣa [*tolai nāḷ mīṉ*, the old asterism star; the fifth asterism] descended into the water, a star fell in the sky, not going to the east or north, a light to the sea-girdled earth, spreading fire, as the whirling wind blew at it. When we saw that, I and many other suppliants thought, 'It will be a good thing if the king . . . is without disease. . . .'" Here, though the system seems identical to that used in North India and expounded by Sanskrit texts, the words are all Tamil with the exception of Paṅkuṉi (from Phalguni). The words referring to Uttaram, Mūla, and Mṛgaśīrṣa are not the Tamil names of those asterisms but rather terms denoting their positions in the first half of the month Paṅkuṉi: Uttaram is "the head" or "the top" asterism; Mūla, the "stable" one that is rising to take the place of Uttaram; and Mṛgaśīrṣa, the "old" asterism, which is sinking down, presumably after having occupied the place of the top asterism some time before. The old commentary mentions that each of these asterisms is separated by eight stars. Of the other names, one, the ram, has the same meaning as the Sanskrit term; however, the other three are quite different: "fire" for Kṛttikā, "the bent palmyra" for Anurādha, and "the tank" for Punarvasu. According to Swaminathaier's remarks on Puṟ. 229, the name fire is given to Kṛttikā because fire is the tutelary deity of that asterism, an identification that appears quite early in Sanskrit.[17] However, it seems unlikely to me that this is the case. The other two asterisms were evidently named for their shape and appearance; it is more plausible that the Pleiades should be called fire for their bright burning appearance rather than for some tutelary deity who appears nowhere else in early Tamil literature. Another constellation mentioned is Cakaṭu, the wagon (Ak. 136; the fourth lunar mansion), a *nakṣatra* that had the same name (Śakaṭa) in the North but is now known by the name Rohiṇī.

Besides Paṅkuṉi (March-April), the only months mentioned are Tai (January-February) in Puṟ. 70 and Kuṟ. 196; and Māci (February-March) in Patiṟ. 59. The Sanskrit sources of all three of these terms cannot be doubted. Paṅkuṉi is from Phalguni, by way of Prakrit Phagguṇi according to the *Tamil Lexicon* (though if the *Lexicon* is correct, the absence of the retroflex *ṇ* in

[17] Pandurang Vaman Kane, *The History of Dharmaśāstra* (Poona, 1930–62), V:501.

Tamil is puzzling, since that language differentiates strongly between retroflex and nonretroflex sounds). Tai is from Sanskrit Taiṣya, which in turn is from Tiṣya, a personage who appears in the *Ṛg Veda* (5.54.3, 10.64.8). Māci is from Māgha, a month that appears in the *Śatapathabrāhmaṇa* (13.8.1.4). The other Tamil months, though none appears in the anthologies, seem to have been borrowed at an early date because their Tamil forms are so changed from the Sanskrit ones. By the time of the *Tolkāppiyam*, the rules for adapting Sanskrit words to Tamil had been standardized, and these are followed for the most part in the anthologies, especially when Sanskrit proper names are used. However, none of the Tamil months, with the exception of Cittirai, conforms to these rules. The months are Cittirai from Citrā (earliest occurrence, *Cilappatikāram* 5.64); Vaikāci from Vaiśākha; Āṉi, which has no known northern source; Āṭi from Āṣāḍha (or Āṣāḍhī); Āvaṇi from Śrāvaṇa; Puraṭṭāci from Proṣṭhapadā; Aippaci from Āśvayuj; Kārttikai from Kārttika (earliest occurrence *Paripāṭal Tiraṭṭu* 11.1); Mārkaḻi from Mārgaśīrṣa; Tai from Taiṣī; Māci from Māgha; and Paṅkuṉi from Phalguni. Occasionally Tamil equivalents are used for the months: in Pari. 11.76, Kuḷam, "the tank," means the month of Mārkaḻi, while in Ak. 141, the poet shows that the month is Kārttikai by his description of the Pleiades (which he calls Aṟu mīṉ, "the six stars"; the constellation is called Kārtikeya in Sanskrit).

It would seem a logical hypothesis that the Tamil forms are so different from the Sanskrit ones because they were borrowed by way of Prakrit. Unfortunately, a consideration of the Prakrit forms of the months shows that they have even less in common with most of the Tamil forms than do the Sanskrit ones. Thus, in Prakrit, Cittirai is Cittā; Vaikāci is Vēsākha; Āṭi is Āsādha (Āsāḷha in Pāli); Āvaṇi is Sāvaṇa; Puraṭṭāci and Aippaci have no equivalents that I could locate; Kārttikai is Kattiya; Mārkaḻi is Maggasira; Tai has no equivalent I could discover; Māci is Māha; and Paṅkuṉi is Phagguṇa (Phagguna in Pāli).[18] Of the above months, the Prakrit names for Cittirai, Vaikāci, Kārttikai, Mārkaḻi, and Paṅkuṉi (the *Tamil Lexicon* notwithstanding, because of the lack of the retroflex) are even farther from their Tamil

[18] These are given in Ralph Lilley Turner, *A Comparative Dictionary of the Indo-Aryan Languages* (London, 1962).

equivalents than the Sanskrit names. Only Āvaṇi seems a bit closer to the Prakrit word than the Sanskrit one. Indeed, because the Prakrit names for Cittirai and Kārttikai lack an *r*, it seems certain that the Tamil names for those months were not borrowed from Prakrit; and because in general the names for the months are closer to the Sanskrit names than the Prakrit ones, I believe that all of them must have been borrowed from Sanskrit, not from Prakrit. It seems unlikely that one was borrowed from Prakrit while all the rest came from Sanskrit. One of the Tamil months, Āvaṇi, appears also in Kannada, a fact that suggests that the names of the months could conceivably have been borrowed by the South Dravidians before the separation of Tamil and Kannada, which Zvelebil says took place between 400 and 300 B.C.[19] Of course, it is quite possible that Kannada simply borrowed the Tamil name. Not only were the names of months borrowed by the Tamils and distorted in the process, but some of the asterisms also underwent that process. For example, Sanskrit Āśleṣa has given Tamil Ayiliyam.

Planets are also mentioned in some of the poems, under the general name *kōḷ* (from the root *koḷ*, "take"), evidently a translation of Sanskrit *graha*. In Ak. 86 a marriage is said to take place on a day when the moon is without kōḷ, which the commentary takes as designating unfavorable planets. *Ci̱rupāṇāṟṟuppaṭai*, one of the *Pattuppāṭṭu*, mentions in line 242 "golden vessels whose appearance puts to shame the shining-rayed sun, surrounded by kōḷ in the bright sky." Puṟ. 392 compares a golden vessel to kōḷ. Some of the planets are named. In Puṟ. 60, Cemmīṉ, "the red star" and according to the old commentary, Mars, is likened to a light in a fishing boat at night; however, the star called Arundhatī in Sanskrit was also called Cemmīṉ (Patiṟ. 4.1, 9.9; *Perumpāṇāṟruppaṭai* 302–304), and it seems possible that that star is meant in Puṟ. 60 also. Arundhatī was also called Vaṭamīṉ, "the north star." Puṟ. 117 mentions Maimīṉ, "the dark star," a name of Saturn, which was considered inauspicious then as it is now.

Lunar eclipses are mentioned several times; unlike the Sanskrit explanation, a serpent (*aravu*) is said to swallow the moon (Kuṟ.

[19] Kamil Zvelebil, "From Proto-South Dravidian to Old Tamil and Malayalam," *Proceedings of the Second International Conference Seminar of Tamil Studies* (Madras, 1971), I:69.

395; Ak. 114, 313). It seems possible to me that by using the word aravu, the Tamils were imitating the sound of Rāhu, the demon who is supposed to swallow the moon during an eclipse in Sanskrit. It should be pointed out, however, that in Kali. 14.17, the word used for the snake that swallows the moon is *pāmpu*. In later times aravu came to denote the constellation Āśleṣa, also called Sarpa (snake) in Sanskrit.

The bases of ancient Tamil astrology were the lunar asterisms and the months, which were determined by them and, for the most part, named after them. There is incontrovertible evidence that this system was borrowed from the North: all the months but one have names borrowed from Sanskrit; the term for planet is a translation of the Sanskrit term graha; and the system itself is almost identical to the system used in the North. The use of terms quite unrelated to the northern ones for many of the asterisms and the planets suggests, on the other hand, that the Tamils had their own names for some constellations and planets before they imported the northern system. The northern system must have been imported long before the time of the anthologies, for the Sanskrit terms have been changed radically to conform to Tamil phonetics (and changed in ways quite at odds with the rules for such changes given in the *Tolkāppiyam*), and the system had been so completely assimilated in Tamilnad that it was used to determine the dates of most festivals and marriages. It seems most likely that the Tamils had a simple system of astrology based on the position of certain planets, the occurrence of falling stars, and similar phenomena. When they heard of the system being used in the North, which was more complex and systematic—and hence more reliable—than their own, they must have made attempts at once to get it, so that they could tell the future with greater accuracy. Northern astrologers must have been brought by kings and others at a very early date, perhaps before Kannada and Tamil split apart, but in any case probably before the Brāhmī writing system was adopted, which would explain why when the names of the months were first written they had changed so much from their original Sanskrit forms. In support of this view, it should be pointed out that the astrological system used by the North Indians came originally from Babylon and that that system was so superior to any used by people of the ancient world that it spread all over Europe and the Middle East as well as India. It is not surprising, therefore, that the ancient Tamils made such efforts to acquaint themselves with that system at such an early time, and that it came so soon to influence virtually every area of life.

Chariot Driving and Elephant Training

The word *nūl*, thread, is used as a translation of Sanskrit *sūtra* to denote books concerning horses and chariot driving several times (Ak. 114, 234, 314, 400). In Ak. 234 the hero tells his driver, "Drive very swiftly the high chariot . . . according to the nūl," while, in Ak. 400, horses are mentioned whose "stock [is recommended by the] nūl." It is notable that the famous inscription of the Mitanni in the Middle East, which contains the first recorded Indo-Aryan words, uses those words in the context of horse training. It is known that chariots were introduced to India by the Aryans; it is therefore not surprising to find the ancient Tamils using their books as texts for chariot driving and horse training.

Improbable as it may appear, elephant training seems also to have been an Aryan science borrowed by the Tamils. In Ak. 276, the courtesan swears that she will take the hero by the hair and bring him to her street "like a great [wild] male elephant brought by a cow elephant of the Aryans, practiced in her craft." The *Mullaippāṭṭu*, one of the poems of the *Pattuppāṭṭu*, describes how elephant keepers, "though unlearned, repeat northern [that is, Sanskrit] words and with their goads urge the beasts to eat" (35), and in line 327, the *Malaippaṭukaṭām*, another poem of the *Pattuppāṭṭu*, mentions "mixed words"—presumably Tamil mixed with Sanskrit—which drivers shout to angry elephants.

Grammar

There can be little question that the grammatical system expounded by the *Tolkāppiyam* owes much to Sanskrit grammar. For example, that treatise uses the Sanskrit system of seven cases to describe the Tamil noun, while in fact the Tamil noun is agglutinative and is best considered as taking many suffixes rather than having an arbitrary number of cases. It has been seen in chapter 1 that at least part of the *Tolkāppiyam* is several centuries later than the anthologies. There are three references in the poems surveyed that indicate that the science of grammar was widely known at the time of their composition. In Kuṟ. 224, the heroine says, "Like an *uyartiṇai* dumb person who sees the agony of a tawny cow fallen into a well at night, I cannot bear to see my friend's grief for me." In Tamil grammar, uyartiṇai, "the high division," is comprised of men and women and is contrasted to *akṟiṇai*, "the division that is not [high]," which includes animals and inanimate things. According to Swaminathaier, the point of calling the dumb person (*ūmaṉ*) uyartiṇai is to show that the ūmaṉ that means owl is not intended; however, it seems to me that the poet also wishes to compare the heroine's suffering to that of a rational human being and that of her friend to that of a nonrational cow, thus implying that her suffering is crueler than her friend's. Another reference to grammar occurs in Puṟ. 92, where children's words are said to be sweet to their father, even though they have the wrong tenses (*poḻutoṭum puraiyā*). Finally in Patiṟ. 21, a king is mentioned "whose resolve never involves afflicting others because he has learned the five: morphology [*col*; literally "word"], poetics [*peyar*; literally, "name" or "meaning"], astrology [*nāṭṭam*], the Vedas [*kēḷvi*; the Vedas, according to the old commentary; however, the word could also refer to technical treatises], and heart [according to the old commentary, how to have a heart unaffected by the senses]." Two of these categories, morphology and poetics, have divisions of the *Tolkāppiyam* devoted to them, though for the latter the word *poruḷ* ("meaning") is used instead of peyar.

Omens

In Aiṅ. 218, the quivering of a woman's eye is said to be a good omen: "Friend, my lovely-browed eye quivers; the bangles on my wrist have become tight; he will come." Swaminathaier explains that her left eye is meant; if so, that omen is the same as the belief found in Sanskrit that if a woman's limb on the left quivers it means good luck, but if one on the right does so, it is ominous, while for a man it is the other way about. This notion is found as early as the *Rāmāyaṇa* in Sanskrit (Su. 27.2, 27.3, 25.35; Ragh. 6.68, 14.49; Sa. 137). Since this omen appears only once in Tamil in juxtaposition with a word borrowed from Sanskrit for brow (*puruvam*, from *bhrū*, genitive *bhruvaḥ*), it seems likely that it was borrowed from the North.

Miscellaneous Ideas from the North

The *trivarga* of *dharma*, *artha*, and *kāma* (using the Tamil equivalents *aṟam*, *poruḷ*, and *iṉpam*) appears in Puṟ. 31, addressed to the Chola king: "Just as . . . wealth [poruḷ] and pleasure [iṉpam] give way to dharma [aṟam], the two umbrellas [of the Pandyan and Chera kings] go behind your resplendent parasol." The trivarga also appears in Puṟ. 362, where Brahmins are identified with aṟam, and warriors with poruḷ. In Puṟ. 2, the five great elements, or *mahābhūtas*, are mentioned. In Puṟ. 6, the three worlds, earth, atmosphere, and sky, are mentioned, and the ocean is said to have been dug, evidently a reference to the story of Sagara and his sons. In Puṟ. 377, the army of four parts is described. In Puṟ. 9, children are said to do their duty to (dead) parents who are in the southern land, while in Puṟ. 58, the king's race is compared to the trunk of a banyan tree supported by aerial roots, which are its descendents.

The theme of respect for cows is found only twice. In Puṟ. 9, cows, Brahmins, women, the sick, and the childless are warned to leave before the city is besieged. In Puṟ. 34, wicked men are said to cut the udders of cows (but not to actually kill the cows—it would seem that their wickedness consists of destroying the productivity of the cows). Some men in ancient Tamilnad ate beef, for in Ak. 129 a wasteland is mentioned "where there are battles so grievous that villagers put their hands to their heads, and where warriors [*maḻavaṉs*] who have eaten cows, bearing sharp weapons and wearing sandals on their feet, drink from the cool spring." Today the beef-eating taboo is weaker in the South than in the North.

5

THE ROLE OF SACRED POWER IN ANCIENT TAMIL CULTURE

Throughout the preceding chapters, the importance of sacred power, or aṇaṅku, has been suggested. It has been seen that for the Tamils, the sacred was primarily manifested not through a number of discrete deities, each of which had an extensive mythology associated with it, as in North India, but rather through a power thought to inhere in certain objects and persons and to be activated in certain situations. Moreover, this aṇaṅku, as the Tamils called it, was not a force that worked for human welfare, but rather was capricious and potentially malevolent; therefore, it had to be carefully controlled lest, like fire, it bring destruction. It is now necessary to investigate this subject in an organized manner, considering its role in the events and people for which it was most important: death, the king, woman, and certain castes. It will then be possible to draw conclusions regarding its nature, and to incorporate what has been said regarding sacred power into one system. Such an understanding of sacred power is of paramount importance if one is to understand ancient South India (or, indeed, modern South India).

Death and Funeral Ceremonies

There are two ways mentioned of disposing of the dead: cremation and exposure with subsequent interment in pots. Cremation is well described in Puṟ. 363:

Benevolent kings who have ruled this vast earth
surrounded by the black sea
so that not even a part of the center of one *uṭai* leaf
belonged to another—
even they have gone to the ground of burned corpses
as their final home,
more of them than there is sand heaped by the waves.
All have gone,
others taking their land,
and perished.
Therefore you too hear:
there is no life that stays with an undying body.
Death is true, no illusion.
Before the ugly day
when on the wide burning ground
spread with milkhedge and thorns
and marked with rising biers,
a man of despised birth takes boiled, saltless rice
and gives it, not looking around,
so you eat a sacrifice undesired
whose vessel is the earth,
do the things you intend
and utterly renounce the place whose limit is the sea [the earth].

In Puṟ. 360, where the same rite is described, the dead man is said to eat "a few grains of rice on some grass with liquor as the Pulaiyaṉ orders." The Pulaiyaṉ is a man of very low caste; his name is from the root *pulai*, which means pollution.[1] It is significant that the same substances, rice and wine, are offered at the funeral ceremony to the memorial stone.

Before interring a dead man in a pot, it was the custom to expose him. Thus, in Puṟ. 231, the poet says, "Let [his body] shrink if it will in the shining cremation fire burning on wood

[1] D.E.D. 3714.

whose ends are blackened, like pieces [of wood] cut by a hill man on a burned-out field; or let it expand until it touches the sky. It is all the same. The fame will never die of that man who was like the shining sun and whose white umbrella resembled the cool-rayed moon." The old commentary explains that here the choice is between burning the body and exposing it. Although it is nowhere stated that the bones were collected after excarnation and placed in urns, it may be inferred that such in fact was the case from the large number of such burials found in the eastern coastal plains of South India by archaeologists.[2] In any case, Pur̲. 228 shows that it was common to inter the dead in pots:

Potter who make vessels
in a large ancient town,
your kiln spewing into the broad sky
dense smoke
whose color is as if darkness
were gathered together,
listen.
You are to be pitied.
What will you do?
Great Vaḷavan̲
whose elephants have swaying banners,
Cempiyan̲'s scion
whose greatness shines far
like the broad-rayed sun spread in the sky,
its unfailing fame
praised by royal poets
whose long, tall armies
cover the earth,
has gone to the world of the gods,
and you would make an urn
wide enough to cover him.
Somehow,
with the broad earth for your wheel
and the great mountain for your clay,
can you fashion it?

[2] J. M. Casal and G. Casal, *Site Urbain et Sites Funéraires* (Paris, 1956).

The pot was left in a "forest" (*kāṭu*; Puṟ. 238), where it is described as being surrounded by owls, crows, and demons.

Puṟ. 231, quoted above, suggests that at the time of the anthologies there were at least two ways of disposing the dead, and that there was often controversy concerning which way was to be followed in a given case. Similarly, in Puṟ. 239, the poet says that, since the king was so great, it does not matter whether his head is (cut off and) exposed or whether it is burnt. Several other ways of disposing of the dead are given in a passage from the *Maṇimēkalai* (6.66–67): cremation (*cuṭuvōr*), exposure (*iṭuvōr*), laying in pots dug in the ground (*toṭukuḻippaṭuppōr*), interment in subterranean cellars in vaults (*tāḻvayiṉaṭaippōr*), and placing in a burial urn and inverting a lid over it (*tāḻiyiṟkavippōr*).

The Allchins point out five different kinds of graves found in the iron age (the megalithic culture) of South India: large urns containing collected bones previously excarnated; legged urns and legged pottery sarcophagi; pit circle graves; cist urns; and rock-cut chambers in the Malabar coastal laterites. They point out that the centuries after the introduction of iron "saw an enormous proliferation of varied practices of disposing of the dead, and as modern observation has revealed a corresponding variety still in vogue in South India, it seems reasonable to infer that the burial complex has continued as a part of South Indian culture for a very long time."[3] It should be noted that nowhere in the poems surveyed are any burial practices described that correspond to the megalithic graves that have been found, though the practice of erecting a memorial stone is clearly related to such burial customs.

Before the funeral, the dead man would be placed on a "bed without legs" and covered with a white cloth (Puṟ. 286), a practice showing that, then as now, white was the color of mourning. A soldier would be carried on his shield (Puṟ. 310), as in ancient Greece. At the house of the dead man, drums would beat out a rhythm called *neytal*, which is also the name of the division of akam poems in which the heroine despairs.

After a man's death, his widow would smear a place the size of an elephant's footprint with cowdung, put grass over it, and

[3] Bridget Allchin and Raymond Allchin, *The Birth of Indian Civilization: India and Pakistan before 500* B.C. (Baltimore, Md., 1968), pp. 224–225.

offer to him what was called a *piṇṭam*, evidently a ball of unsalted rice (Puṟ. 234, 246), the same as was offered to the dead man before he was cremated. Among the Aryans a similar rite was performed for ten days after a man's death, in which a *piṇḍa* (which is probably the source of the Tamil word piṇṭam) was offered to the dead man. The Aryan rite differed from the Tamil practice in that it was offered by a male relative, not by the widow, and in an extremely complicated ritual. The similarities, however, are striking: the Aryan rite also involved spreading grass (*darbha* grass)[4] on a place previously cleaned with cow dung[5] and offering piṇḍas, which at least sometimes were composed of boiled rice.[6] The practice of first smearing dung on the place where the piṇḍa is to be offered may be Dravidian, for it is first mentioned in Indo-Aryan in the *Matsyapurāṇa* and is lacking in earlier texts. The fact that the widow offers the piṇṭam in the Tamil version, while she does not do so in the Aryan ritual (unless there is no one else to do so), indicates that the Aryan rite was not borrowed directly by the Tamils. It will be seen below that the Tamil version of this rite appears in Sanskrit very late, in an interpolated passage in the *Skandapurāṇa*. Grass was used by both the Aryans and Dravidians as a sort of insulating agent. The Tamils used it, as has been seen, as a base when the piṇṭam was offered to the corpse and when a widow offered piṇṭam to her dead husband. Dead bodies were laid out on grass before being cut with swords to ensure that they would go to paradise (Puṟ. 93). Similarly, the Aryans would strew darbha grass around at the cremation ceremony (when offering piṇḍa) and at other ceremonies.

There were among the Aryans virtually thousands of variations in the cremation procedures and subsequent rites;[7] certain elements, however, notably the use of the piṇḍa and of darbha grass, are common to almost all. It is significant that these same two elements are found among the early Tamils, but in contexts that show they were not borrowed through the Brahmins: the cutting of bodies and the offering of liquor with the piṇṭam, for example.

[4] Pandurang Vaman Kane, *The History of Dharmaśāstra* (Poona, 1930–62), IV:262.

[5] Ibid.; *Matsyapurāṇa* 16.45–65.

[6] Kane, *History of Dharmaśāstra*, IV:478.

[7] Ibid., p. 210.

There is no archaeological evidence for cremation in the megalithic age in South India; therefore, it seems likely that cremation came from the North. However, the use of a low caste person to perform the cremation, something not found in the *śāstras* cited by Kane, suggests that the ceremony was not borrowed from the Aryans.

Throughout the descriptions of the funeral rites and post-funeral rites discussed above, there is a unifying element: that there is danger associated with death, and that it is necessary somehow to insulate oneself from this danger. Thus corpses are laid out on grass, an insulating agent; a man of the lowest caste, whose job was to control dangerous forces, offered to the corpse the sacrifice of the piṇṭam; the widow had to place the piṇṭam to be offered to her dead husband on grass on a surface cleaned with cowdung, a purifying agent. It has been seen that memorial stones would be erected to eminent men who died in battle, and that they would be propitiated with wine and lambs. It is significant that, after worshiping a memorial, a man was supposed to bathe and burn incense (Puṟ. 329), and that one of those who worshiped the memorial stone was the player of the tuṭi drum (Ak. 35), a man of low caste whose primary function was to control sacred power. The danger that death carried with it can also be seen in the war sacrifice, a rite in which the victorious king seeks to offset the danger he has incurred by killing enemy kings and soldiers (see chapter 3 above). The position of the widow also demonstrates vividly the danger that was thought to accompany death: she is infected by the power unleashed upon the death of her husband, and therefore she must either take her own life or devote the rest of her days to practicing severe mortification. In all of these cases, there is an attempt to control the sacred power that goes out of control at death. It has been stated above that the two primary loci of the sacred in ancient Tamilnad were woman and the king. It is now necessary to investigate the role of each; their behavior when associated with death throws light on the nature of the sacred.

The King

The status of the king and the various sacred objects with which he surrounds himself have been discussed in chapter 2.

It has been seen that in ancient Tamilnad the king was the center of sacred forces, and that if those forces were kept under control the kingdom would flourish, while if they went out of control the kingdom would suffer drought or be taken by enemies. An excellent example is Patiṟ. 13:

In those lands,
fields were full of cattle,
eels flashed,
farmers sowed without plowing fields rooted up by boars,
lilies bloomed with sugarcane,
large-eyed buffaloes stayed in fenced fields,
plump-headed cows ate lilies with luscious coconut,
paddy fields were full of the chattering of birds,
canals led from blossom-covered ponds,
and rich cities were filled with singing.
Now you have become enraged
and smashed them fearfully,
and their beauty is ruined.
Their cities are changed
like sick bodies relentlessly assaulted by Death.
Fields of flowering sugarcane are barren
and demon women with curly hair
ride donkeys amongst *viṭattēr* trees with twisted fruits
and amongst dark *uṭai.*
There, battlefields covered with thorns are strewn with ashes
and, spread over by dust, have lost their loveliness.
The bleakness there makes the hearts of the mighty perish
and destroys the strength of those who think on them, so that they tremble.
But, great lord, the land you guard blossoms,
devoid of hunger and disease.
Ascetics live in its forests,
warriors inhabit its meadows with shining-bangled girls,
and its roads are easy to pass over.
In your land,
those who watch over the folk
are watched over in turn.
There, Venus never joins with Mars,

and showers pour down
whenever the land needs rain.

The conjunction of Venus and Mars was thought to accompany drought. The point of this poem is that the sacred power of the king being praised is so great that it easily overcomes the sacred power of his enemies. That is why the lands of the enemy kings are described as the haunt of demons, filled with plants of the wasteland and with fields that are veritable burning grounds, the most inauspicious of places because they are places of death. But the land of the king who is addressed is full of signs of sacred power under control: ascetics live in its forests, its meadows are inhabited by warriors and their wives (not by widows), and there is no drought. Indeed, the one word that describes the kingdom of sacred power under control is *order*; that is why in it "those who watch over the folk are watched over in turn." On the other hand, there is anarchy in the land of the enemy kings.

The rite of the war sacrifice has already been discussed in detail in chapter 3. Here, it is necessary to repeat some of the conclusions drawn above. At the end of a battle, a war sacrifice would be celebrated at which the flesh of slain enemies would be ritually cooked. The purpose of this ritual was to establish a close bond between the victorious king and the kings who were slain in battle, and thereby to protect the victorious king from the power unleashed on the death of his rivals, to which he was particularly vulnerable because he too was a king and a locus of sacred power and because he was responsible for their death. This rite is homologized to the marriage ceremony in one description, marriage also being a rite in which a bond is created between two people. Moreover, in marriage, the woman protects her husband with her power, just as in the war sacrifice the dead king is supposed to lend his power to the victor.

A rite that lends further insight into the connection of the sacred and the king is ritual suicide. A king who felt that he had incurred an unbearable loss of honor could fast himself to death in a rite named *vaṭakkiruttal* ("sitting [facing the] North"). One king who resorted to this expedient was Cēramāṉ Peruñcēralātaṉ, who was wounded in battle by a spear that entered his back. Ashamed at his back wound, he starved himself to death (Puṟ. 65; Ak. 55). Another was Kōpperuñcōḻaṉ, whose sons rose up against him in battle to take his kingdom from him. In Pur̲. 213, the poet Pullār̲r̲ūr Eyir̲r̲iyan̲ār addresses the king, telling him, "If these young ones, their judgment uninformed by reason, who have risen against you with unshakable resolve, should be defeated, to whom would you leave your great wealth, lord of raging battle? And if you should lose to them, you would leave behind contempt so that they who scorn you [would] rejoice. Renounce therefore your valor. . . . You must do what is right . . . so that they who abide in the world of the gods hard to attain [will] welcome you with quick eagerness as a guest." Persuaded, the king decides to fast to death. In Pur̲. 214, he addresses his comrades, evidently attempting to persuade them to join him. His words indicate that he was influenced by Jainism: "O you with unclear views, who do not give up in your hearts your stained outlooks . . . , a man hunting an elephant may get his elephant while a hunter of little birds may return empty handed. If noble men with lofty aims receive reward for a portion of their good acts, they may experience delight in the eternal world. If they do not experience delight in that world, they may not have to be born again. And if they are not born again, it is crucial that they die with bodies devoid of evil, establishing their fame like a Himalayan peak."

He goes to starve himself "in the dappled shade of a river island" (Pur̲. 219), a sacred place,[8] surrounded by those good men who saw fit to join him (Pur̲. 218, 219). His friend, Picirāntaiyār, who lived in Pandya country and whom Kōpperuñcōl̲an̲ had never seen, their friendship being based on mutual respect of one another's renown, arrived to join him, much to the amazement of those who surrounded him, who say (in Pur̲. 217),

If you ponder it, this resolute act
undertaken while still in the prime of greatness
is amazing.
And it is even more amazing
that a man from another land,
renowned and successful,
should come here at such a time, out of love for his friend,
with fame his companion and friendship his staff.

[8] Even today Śrīrañgam, one of the most sacred Vaishnava temples, is on an island in the Kāvēri river.

The assurance of the king who said, "He will come,"
is amazing,
and the wisdom of him who came
is amazing.
Indeed, it crosses the limit of wonder,
and so what will become of this world,
which has lost a man whose long-lasting fame is so great
that another, from a country his scepter did not rule,
gave him his heart?
That land is pitiful indeed.

One bard, Karvūrp Peruñcatukkattup Pūtanātanār, hears by chance of the king's resolve and addresses him in Puṟ. 219:

Warrior who wastes all your flesh away
in the spotted shade of a river islet,
do you hate me?
Many are here at your behest.

Another bard, Pottiyār, wishes to join him, but the king tells him to come back later, after his pregnant wife has given birth to a son. He does so, but on returning he finds that all that is left of the king and his followers are the memorial stones erected to them. He addresses a poignant poem to the stones:

You said,
"After she who loves you,
who no more leaves you than your shadow,
whose body shines with ornaments as radiant as fire,
has given birth to a renowned son, come."
O loveless one who banished me from here,
surely you will not remain silent,
unmindful of me.
Which place is mine,
O you who yearn for fame? (Puṟ. 222.)

In describing the rite of vaṭakkiruttal, Singaravelu writes, "When someone chose to die by means of 'fasting unto death,' groups of men and women sat on the ground at certain times during the period of mourning for the chieftain who had decided to forsake his earthly existence."[9] He then gives as examples of such invitees Picirāntaiyār and Pottiyār, saying that the latter

[9] S. Singaravelu, *Social Life of the Tamils: The Classical Period* (Kuala Lumpur, 1966), p. 127.

was obliged to bring his wife (which is why he states that women were invited as well as men). He has entirely missed the point. Those who joined the king died with him, a fact made clear in Ak. 55, which mentions "those who underwent the great change of death to go to the world hard to attain with Cēralātan̲ when they heard the news both harsh and sweet that that hero, ashamed at the wound he had received, had faced north." That Pottiyār did not bring his wife with him is quite clear from the grammar of Pur̲. 222, where the king tells him, "[After a son has been born], come," using the singular imperative (*vā*). The reason why he had to wait for a son to be born was to ensure that there would be someone to carry on his line, not, as Singaravelu states, "Since Pottiyār's wife was then pregnant, social sentiment probably rendered it incumbent upon the ruler to persuade the poet and his wife to return home first and then come back to the place of the ceremony after his wife had given birth to the child."[10]

Both of the kings who performed this rite did so to go to the "world hard to attain," and Kōpperuñcōl̲an̲ uses arguments that seem influenced by Jainism when he tries to persuade his comrades to join him. In spite of these elements that appear northern, however, it seems to me that vaṭakkiruttal is essentially an indigenous institution. The kings who performed it were motivated more by shame than by the religious desires of Jaina ascetics. They sat with their swords next to them, and, after they died, stones were erected to them as memorials. Suicide customs in Aryan India are described by Kane,[11] but nothing mentioned is shared with the Tamil rite of vaṭakkiruttal except that the means employed is sometimes starvation.

The megalithic graves, which precede the period under study by several centuries, often contain the bones of several individuals, a fact that according to Banerjee, shows that "obviously there was a time-lag between the erection of the tomb and the actual interment so that as many as could be accommodated at a single ceremony were interred at a time and the burial sealed once for all."[12] One wonders whether such tombs could have been used

[10] Ibid., p. 128.

[11] Kane, *History of Dharmaśāstra*, II:925ff and IV:605ff.

[12] N. R. Banerjee, *The Iron Age of India* (Delhi, 1965), p. 213.

for interring the king and those who chose to die with him. It is true that only in the rite of vaṭakkiruttal is the practice of dying with the king mentioned; however, there is some evidence that the custom was more widespread.

Thus, in Puṟ. 236, the widow of a king addresses his ministers: "The pyre of black wood heaped on the burning ground may be abhorrent to you, but to me, since my great-armed husband is dead, that fire and a large pond of lotuses . . . are the same." It seems quite likely to me that she is scorning the ministers because they are too cowardly to join her in committing suicide. A thousand years after the anthologies, Marco Polo wrote about Maabar (the Pandyan country), "The king retains about his person many knights, who are called 'the devoted servants of his majesty, in this world and the next.' These attend upon his person at court, ride by his side in processions, and accompany him on all occasions. They exercise considerable authority in every part of the realm. Upon the death of the king, and when the ceremony of burning his body takes place, all these devoted servants throw themselves into the same fire, and are consumed with the royal corpse; intending by this act to bear him company in another life."[13]

When the king died, sacred power went out of control all over his kingdom. Especially affected were those who were close to him, just as a wife was especially affected upon the death of her husband. In fact, so strongly did sacred power out of control affect such people that it was thought best for them to take their own lives. It is notable that in the poems those who die with the king do so willingly, inspired by their friendship and love for the dead man; nevertheless, I believe that originally the reason for the custom must have been the same as for suttee: those close to the king were infected by sacred power out of control upon the death of the king to whom they were so close, and there was little that they could do but take their own lives. There is perhaps another element as well. By agreeing to join the king in death, they could increase his fame and thereby improve his position in the next world, and, since they would be followers of his there also, improve their own positions after death. Thus memorial

[13] Marco Polo, *The Travels of Marco Polo* (New York, 1930), p. 287

stones were erected not only to Kōpperuñcōḻaṉ when he starved himself to death, but also to all of those who accompanied him. One supposes that the place where the stones were erected was considered a sacred place, and that rites were undertaken to propitiate the spirits of the men that dwelt in the stones. It is likely that many temples in South India were originally places where memorial stones were worshiped, and that their idols were originally memorial stones.[14]

Woman

Women in ancient Tamilnad were strongly tabooed when they were menstruous or when they had just given birth. Puṟ. 299 describes how an enemy's horses "stand terrified like women who cannot touch dishes [that is, are menstruous] [when they are] in the temple of Murukaṉ." In Ak. 7, the foster mother describes what she told the heroine when she came of age: "I told her, 'Your breasts are budding, your sharp teeth glisten, your hair is coiled, and you wear a *taḻai* [a dress of leaves strung together, worn by girls after puberty]. Do not go anywhere with your friends who love to wander about. Our ancient town Mutupati has places where aṇaṅku assaults [*tākkaṇaṅku*]. You are under [our] protection [now that you have reached puberty], and you should not go outside. You are no longer a little girl, wise, lovely child. At the time of puberty [?—*petumpai paruvattu*] you had to be outside [while you were menstruous?].' " Though the meaning of the last line translated above is not certain, I have given this quotation because of the importance of the rest of the poem. It shows that a profound change was thought to come over a girl when she reaches puberty and first begins to menstruate, and that suddenly she becomes vulnerable to the dangerous forces that inhabit her town. Therefore she must be protected, she must put her hair up (as loose hair is dangerous), and she must wear a special dress of leaves, probably because of the ability of the leaves to protect her from aṇaṅku. Even today, puberty is extremely important for women in South India. Great efforts are

[14] In *The Cult of Viṭhobā* (Poona, 1960), pp. 193–208, G. A. Deleury argues persuasively that the temple to Viṭhobā at Paṇḍharpūr arose around the memorial stone originally erected to a hero named Biṭṭaga.

made to determine the exact time of its onset, as the position of the stars at that time is thought to be crucial to the woman's relationship with her future husband (or with her husband if she were already married, as she probably would have been if she lived in a village a hundred years ago).

The time of impurity after giving birth was called *puṉiṟu*, and it lasted for ten days, after which the woman bathed at night in a tank (such, at least, was the custom a few hundred years after the anthologies).[15] Puṟ. 68 compares the Kāviri river to a breast trickling with milk after puṉiṟu, showing that the milk was thought to be impure before that time, while Ak. 139 describes "white clouds that are impure [*vālā*] in the days after they have given birth." It is possible that animals as well as human beings were thought to be impure in the period after they gave birth, for Ak. 56 says that to get out of the way of a cow in its puṉiṟu period, the hero's bard dropped his lute and unwittingly ran into the heroine's house.

Though it is nowhere stated, it is probable that until puṉiṟu was over, the father was not allowed to see the child, a custom that is common among archaic peoples. Thus Crawley writes, "Separation between husband and wife at birth is often prolonged until the child is weaned, the idea being that milk, a female secretion, is a specially dangerous vehicle for transmission of her effeminate properties. Hence the infant, from contact with the mother, is also 'unclean,' that is, 'dangerous' in the taboo sense no less than it is in danger. . . . Among the northern [American] Indians, the mother is unclean for five weeks after birth and remains in a separate hut—no male may approach her, even the husband."[16] He also describes the ceremony in which the father first sees the infant. Among the Basutos, the father is separated from the mother and child for four days, and then the medicine man performs a ceremony at which they are introduced.[17]

A ceremony at which the father first sees his son is described in Puṟ. 100. In it, according to the colophon, "Auvaiyār sings Atiyamāṉ [Neṭumāṉ Añci] as he sees his newborn son." Duraicami Pillai, a modern commentator, clarifies, "When a first son

[15] *Maṇimēkalai* 7.75–76.

[16] Ernest Crawley, *The Mystic Rose* (New York, 1927), II:198.

[17] Ibid., p. 199.

was born to a family, a few days after his birth, the father put on war dress and, surrounded by good men, go to se son. Such was the custom among the ancient Tamils. The p pose of this was to imprint on the heart of the child a warli mentality and spirit when he first saw his father." The poem says:

In his hand is a spear
and on his feet are battle anklets.
Sweat glistens on his body
and on his neck is a fresh wound.
Adorning his curly black hair
he wears a *vēṅkai* blossom
together with a large *veṭci* flower
and with needly white leaves
from the top
of the fast-growing young palmyra,
which causes foes to flee [presumably, the tutelary tree].
His rage,
like that of an elephant
that dares to fight a tiger,
is still unspent;
none escaped
who angered him.
His eyes, which glared at foes,
are still red
though they see his son.

The poem places great emphasis on the sacred accouterments of war that characterize the hero: his spear, his anklets, and the flowers and leaves he wears, especially the palmyra leaves taken from the tutelary tree (the reason why the tree is said to make foes flee). The sweat and wound of the warrior indicate his emotional state, the sacred frenzy of battle. All of these elements help him to offset the effeminate qualities of the nursing mother, whose state is equally sacred, though of a different nature. The danger inherent in the situation of a father's first sight of his child is also suggested by a ceremony practiced in modern Andhra, at which the father must first see the child as a reflection in a bowl of oil as the child and its mother sit behind a curtain.[18]

[18] I am indebted to Velcheru Narayanarao for information concerning the ceremony of first seeing a child in Andhra.

Several poems describe the husband avoiding his wife's embrace while she is nursing their child. In Ak. 26, the wife complains, "There were times when at night he would say in ecstasy, 'Pressing my chest hard, do not stop embracing me with your black nipples,' as they resembled iron rings on the tusks of an elephant who attacks great doors. . . . Now those breasts are pendulous with milk for our son, and when I longed to embrace closely his ornamented chest . . . , he feared some sweet milk might fall on him." Finally he embraces her carefully from behind. Similarly in Aiñ. 65, the heroine says to her husband, "Do not embrace my body, which has given birth to our son—your chest might be spoiled." (See also Aiñ. 404.) It is notable that the women who are the subjects of these poems have obviously passed their periods of impurity; yet even after that period, their milk is dangerous to their husbands.

One of the five akam categories, *marutam*, concerns the hero's abandoning his wife and visiting courtesans, generally after their first son has been born (Ak. 16, 26, 66, 176). One of the reasons for the hero's disaffection for his wife would appear to be the danger to his manhood that her milk represents, as well as the pendulous state of her breasts, which rendered her unattractive (the importance assigned to women's breasts will be discussed below). Thus in Ak. 16, the heroine speaks of the courtesan's "young breasts ornamented with gold," even though the courtesan is older than she is.

The fact that women were tabooed when they were menstruous and when they had given birth suggests that they were thought to possess sacred power that at certain times became dangerous and had to be carefully controlled by subjecting the woman to some sort of mortification. This inference is confirmed by the fact that the sacred power of woman is actually mentioned, usually in conjuction with her chastity (*kaṟpu*), a virtue as important in ancient South India as it is today. Puṟ. 198 speaks of a woman's chastity as "joined with a god [*kaṭavuḷ cāṉṟa kaṟpu*]," while Kuṟ. 252 and Ak. 184 mention "chastity [which has] a god [*kaṭavuṭ kaṟpu*]." In Ak. 73, the friend describes the heroine as having "chastity full of aṇaṅku [*aṇaṅku uṟu kaṟpu*]" as she suffers while her husband is away, and, in Ak. 198, the hero exclaims, "She was no excellent woman with perfect chastity, but a goddess [*cūrmakaḷ*—literally "fear-inflicting woman"] who lives in the spring full of soft flowers." The sacred power of a woman is thought to dwell especially in her breasts, and many poems state this fact; for example, Ak. 177 speaks of "breasts with aṇañku."

It appears from the above references that a woman's chastity is very closely related to the sacred power she possesses. The nature of chastity is made clear in several references. It consisted in a sort of asceticism, the restraining of all impulses that were in any way immodest. Thus Puṟ. 196 describes the bard's wife as being "a delicate woman with a shining face and chastity that [knows] only modesty [*nāṉ alatu illāk kaṟpu*]," Puṟ. 249 speaks of "chastity that is restrained [*aṭañkiya*]," and Puṟ. 361 says that the king's wives are "women of chastity increased by patience, with sharp teeth, which their tongues fear if they speak loudly." Puṟ. 166 describes the wife of an orthodox Brahmin as one who has "chastity hard to obtain, which banishes all harshness [*maṟam*], with a small forehead, large wide loins, few words, and ample hair, a woman who fits exactly her husband's state." In Ak. 86, women who have given birth bless the bride saying, "May you be filled with desire so that you love him whom you get [as husband], so that you are a help in many things and do not slip from chastity." In Kuṟ. 252, the heroine's friend scolds her, saying, "[When he returned from his courtesan], you, without changing your sweet expression, served him, you with your divine chastity [*kaṭavuṭ kaṟpu*]," to which the heroine replies, "Good men are ashamed when praised to their face; how could they bear abuse?" Chastity is often attributed to a woman who is extremely attractive, with large loins and breasts (Puṟ. 166, 361): clearly the more sexually attractive a woman is, the more power her chastity endows her with. Chastity is also attributed to woman as a mother (Puṟ. 198; Ak. 16, 184); in Ak. 184, the son of a chaste woman is called the light of his clan (*kuṭi*). Chastity was conceived of as an almost tangible quality in the woman who possessed it, producing domestic peace and light, as in Kuṟ. 336, where a woman's chastity is said to shine in her house.

The importance of chastity to a prospective husband may be inferred from the fact that when Kapilar took the daughters of his dead friend Pāri around to kings in order to marry them off, he had to insist that he was a Brahmin and a Pulavaṉ (poet) lest they think he had spoiled them (Pur̲. 201). It was thought degrading to a man to make love to an unchaste woman who did not love him, for in Pur̲. 73 the king exclaims:

If he would come gently,
prostrate himself before my good feet,
and beg, saying, "Give!"
then it would be a trifle
to give him my kingdom
and the right to it
conferred by the drum.
And even if it were my sweet life he desired,
I would give it here and now
while still in this world.
But that fool who mocks my purpose,
not heeding the strength of the mighty,
is like a blind man
stumbling on a tiger
asleep
in the plain sight of all.
If I do not go,
fight him,
and make him suffer just where he is
like a long pole
of strong thick bamboo
caught in the feet of a grazing elephant,
then may my garland wither
in the unresponsive embraces
of women with thick black hair
who have no love
in faultless hearts.

Several times, a woman's chastity is compared to the star Arundhatī (Pur̲. 122; Ak. 16; Aiṅ. 422).

Any woman who had come of age and was sexually attractive was thought to be filled with aṇañku. This sacred power was thought to reside in her breasts and, to a lesser extent, in her loins. Thus, in Kur̲. 337, the hero exclaims, "The buds of her breasts have blossomed, and soft thick hair falls from her head. Her compact rows of white teeth are full, [having completely replaced] her baby teeth, and [on her body] spots have appeared [a sign of puberty]. . . . I know her, so she afflicts [aṇañku, here used as a verb] me." In Ak. 161, the friend describes how the heroine weeps "so that cold drops wet her finely rising young breasts, vexing because aṇañku is there," and Ak. 177 speaks of "breasts with aṇañku." In Ak. 220, the breasts of the heroine are said to be "as hard to get to see as the well-guarded post . . . of the sacrifice completed by the one with an axe . . . at Cellūr." In Aiñ. 363, the hero laments, "You think there are spots on your breasts, but my afflicted [*aṇañkuṟu*] heart thinks that there is aṇañku." In Naṟ. 9, the presence of aṇañku in the breasts of a woman and the role of plants worn as ornaments in controlling it are stated as the hero says to his beloved, "Put bright shoots of lovely *puṉku* with its dotted flowers on your spotted breasts so that aṇañku stays there, and come with no regrets, O you whose teeth are bright." If a woman's breasts can best be described to invoke her beauty, since they are the seat of her aṇañku, they can also be used to invoke her wretchedness. Thus, when the poet wishes to show how poor he is, he often makes a point of describing the pitiable condition of his wife, mentioning that her breasts are ugly and empty even though she has nursing children (Puṟ. 159, 160, 164, 211, 276). In Puṟ. 295, when a mother sees the valor of her dead son, her breasts give milk again: her joy is so profound that the seat of her aṇañku, long since impotent, is suddenly charged with power again.

The sacred power that a woman possesses can work two ways: if she is married and in an auspicious condition, it protects her husband; if she is not, it can bring destruction. The first of these roles is illustrated by the convention in which the hero, wandering through the wilderness in search of gold, is given the strength to continue by thinking of his beloved, as in Kuṟ. 274:

In the desert
a cruel man,
his readied arrow fitted to his bow,
looks for wayfarers
as he climbs a hill
to shake down
thick, sapphire-dark fruits
of an *ukāy* tree,
its trunk as soft

as a dove's back,
and he chews bark
to assuage his thirst.
Yet even this fearful desert is sweet
if I go
thinking of my woman,
her loins decorated with jewels and gold,
her breasts lovely.

(See also Aḳ. 83; Aiñ. 203, 303, 322, 327, 328, 360.)

The dangerous aspect of a woman's power can be seen in the conventional poems on the destruction of the city by suitors whose request has been denied by the girl's relatives. In these poems, the girl has just passed puberty; the bewitching nature of her breasts is often stressed. An example is Pur̲. 350:

The moats are filled with dirt,
the bastions ruined,
and the walls broken
in our scarred, ancient city.
It cannot prevail in battle;
what will become of it?
Kings with swift horses
and drums
that roar like thunder during the rains
came in the morning
and roamed about the lofty gate.
Her brothers,
strong in the hatred of murderous battle,
will not be content without a fight.
For spots have spread
on the breasts
of the young girl
whose red, blackened eyes
are like the sharp blades of brandished spears
and whose bangled arms sway.

In Pur̲. 336 the poet describes the preparations for war and then exclaims, "Surely the mother is without principles and evil who created this enmity and happily nurtured until they were beautiful those still unmatured young breasts, as lovely as buds of flowering *koñku.*" In Pur̲. 337, Kapilar asks, "Even though they are so courageous, who will squeeze her fine young tusklike breasts, spread over with many spots and marked with ornaments?" (See also Puṟ. 336–355).

An inauspicious state of a woman's powers is brought about by her fall from chastity. The ancient Tamil poems nowhere describe this eventuality, as they are idealized; however, it is well treated by a modern Malayalam novel, *Chemmeen*, by Thakazhi Sivasankara Pillai, about the life of the fishermen of the Malabar coast, which has changed little in the last two thousand years.[19]

The heroine of the story is Karuthamma, a young girl. One day, she is talking and laughing with a Muslim trader named Pareekutti when suddenly she feels embarrassed: "Karuthamma had felt as if she stood naked in front of him. She had wished she could vanish from his sight. She had never experienced such a feeling until then.

"Her breasts were a symbol of the exuberance of youth, throbbing with life. When he looked at her and fixed his eyes on her breasts, Pareekutti had felt as if his nerves were on end and shivering. Was that why the laughter ended?"[20]

Karuthamma's mother hears of the incident and gives her daughter a lecture:

> "This wide-open sea contains everything, my child. Everything. Why do you think all the men who go out there come back safely? It is because of the women at home who live clean lives. Otherwise the currents in the sea will swallow them up. The lives of the men at sea are in the hands of the women on shore. . . .
>
> "Do you know why the sea goes dark sometimes? That is when the anger of the goddess of the sea is roused. Then she would destroy everything. At other times she would give her children everything. There is gold in the sea, child, gold," Chakki [Karuthamma's mother] said.
>
> "Purity is the great thing, child. Purity. The strength and the wealth of the fisherman lie in the purity of his wife. . . .
>
> "You are no longer a girl, but in the full bloom of your youth [that is, you have passed puberty]. Kochumuthalalis [Muslim

[19] Thakazhi Sivasankara Pillai, *Chemmeen*, trans. Narayana Menon (London, 1962).

[20] Ibid., p. 5.

> traders] and young reckless fishermen with neither morals nor character will stare at your bare breasts and eye you with lecherous eyes. . . .
>
> "My child, you must not be the cause of the ruin of the seafront."[21]

Subsequently, Karuthamma is married to the fisherman Palani. But all the time she feels a vague longing for Pareekutti. Finally, one night when Palani is out fishing, she meets Pareekutti and embraces him. Palani's boat is caught in a storm and sinks; she and Pareekutti are found dead the next day.

From the above references, it may be inferred that a woman was thought to be filled with sacred power, or aṇaṅku, as soon as she passed puberty. The more attractive she was, the stronger was her power; for it manifested itself in making men desire her. Even before marriage, it had to be controlled by the woman's self-restraint and chastity; that is why Karuthamma is warned by her mother not to talk to the Muslim trader, and why a man would not marry a woman who was not chaste (as he still will not).[22] After marriage, also, it had to be restrained, through the chastity and modesty of the woman; otherwise, it would lead to her husband's destruction. But, if a woman was chaste, her power was under control and she was a source of strength to her husband.

The nature of a woman's power is clarified by the conduct expected of her when as a widow she was in close association with death. Widows did not wear ornaments (Puṟ. 224, 253, 261), they caked their shaven heads with mud (Puṟ. 280), and they slept on beds of stone (Puṟ. 246). It has already been seen that a widow was supposed to offer piṇṭams for her dead husband to eat (Puṟ. 234, 249). It is not surprising, perhaps, that with such empty lives to look forward to many widows committed suicide upon their husbands' deaths. In Puṟ. 246, the chief wife of Pūtapāṇṭiyaṉ addresses those who were dependent on her husband and who urge her not to commit suttee so that she may become queen and continue to support them. It seems likely to me that her words are intended as a reprimand to the "good men"

[21] Ibid., p. 9.

[22] Today if a man finds that his bride is not a virgin, he often sends her back to her family and has nothing further to do with her.

who, even though they were close to the king, have refused to take their own lives upon his death:

Listen, all of you good men
with your wicked schemes,
who would hinder me with words of restraint
and not urge me to go.
Listen, you good men!
I am no woman to suffer austerities,
eating for food
vēḷai leaves
boiled with tamarind
with white sesame paste
and a squeezed ball of rice
untouched by fragrant ghee
whose light color
resembles the seeds of a curved cucumber
with chipmunk lines
split with a sword,
and to sleep on a bed
covered with stones
without even a mat.
Go ahead, spurn the pyre of black wood
heaped on the burning ground.
To me,
since my great-armed husband is dead,
that fire
and a large pond of lotuses
that have loosed from buds rich petals
are the same.

Yet it was not merely dread at the thought of the austerities to which she would have to submit or grief at the loss of her husband that motivated a widow to commit suttee. She was thought to be filled with aṇaṅku that might not be kept under control even by austerities, if she were young and chaste. Puṟ. 247 describes vividly the power of a young widow:

In a place
full of ominous power [aṇaṅku]
a herd of simple deer
slumbers in the light of a fire

kindled by forest men
from dry wood
brought by elephants
and is roused from sleep
by monkeys rooting about.
There
a woman wanders toward the burning ground,
her hair
streaming with water
spread down her back.
Though she is alone for only a moment
in the vast guarded palace of her husband
where the eye of the drum [the concert drum] never sleeps
her sweet life trembles
fleeing headlong from her youth. . . . .

Here the woman is going to burn herself after her husband has died. The image at the beginning of the poem shows clearly that there is danger—the simple deer sleeping in the light of the hunter's fire. Elsewhere also trembling is a sign of possession by a sacred power and thus of being dangerous to oneself and to others (Kuṟ. 105; Puṟ. 259, 299). Both this poem and Puṟ. 246, given above, suggest that the widow is filled by a power that she cannot control and that can be quenched only by fire. Moreover, it would appear that the power is the same that appears in young girls after puberty and makes men desire them; thus her life flees headlong from her youth—she must undertake measures to control her passion by eating unpleasant food and sleeping on stones; she must render herself unattractive to men by cutting off her hair and divesting herself of her ornaments. When her husband is alive, it is not a difficult matter to remain chaste; but, when he is dead, remaining faithful to him is not an easy matter, and the widow who does not take her own life must undertake extreme measures to keep her chastity.

The nature of a widow's power is further illumined by the *Cilappatikāram*, written in perhaps the sixth century by Iḷaṅkōvaṭikaḷ. Its principal characters are a merchant, Kōvalaṉ, and his wife, Kaṇṇaki. After he is married, Kōvalaṉ grows tired of his wife and lives with a courtesan, Mātavi, on whom he spends all of his money. He then returns to his forgiving wife and travels with her from the city of Pūmpukār to Maturai, where he intends to sell a pair of golden anklets she possesses and to establish himself as a merchant with the proceeds. He leaves his wife on the outskirts of the city and proceeds with one of the anklets in hand into Maturai. On his way he sees the king's goldsmith, who has stolen one of the queens anklets. The stolen anklet is identical to Kōvalaṉ's anklet in all respects, except that it is filled with pearls rather than with precious jewels. Kōvalaṉ shows his anklet to the goldsmith for appraisal. The goldsmith immediately goes to the king, tells him that the thief has been found, anklet in hand, and is dispatched with guards by the king to kill the thief and and bring back the anklet, which he does.

Kaṇṇaki hears of what has happened and goes into the city. She confronts the king, tells him of the injustice that has been committed, and, to prove it, tells him to open the anklet. When the anklet is opened and it is seen to contain precious stones, the king, his scepter and parasol bent, falls down dead, while his queen falls on top of him, dying. Kaṇṇaki says,

"It is no idle thing that the wise say,
that justice is death
for those who wreak evil.
See, queen of that mighty monarch
who has worked such evil,
what I,
doer of wickedness,
will do now."
[An onlooker speaks]:
"Her lily eyes streamed with water;
in her hand, a single anklet [the mate to the one given to the king];
her form untenanted by life.
What evil have I done that I saw her,
her black hair spread like a forest?
The king of Maturai beheld her
and terrified he died."[23]

Kaṇṇaki goes outside the city and says,

"Men and woman of Maturai, city of four temples!
Gods of the skies and men of austerities,

[23] Cil. 20 *veṇpā* 2.

hear me.
I am enraged at this city
whose king wrought injustice upon him I love,
and I am without fault."
With her hand she twisted off her left breast,
encircled Maturai three times keeping it to the right,
uttered a curse,
and shining with her ornaments
she threw her lovely breast on the pollen-covered street.
His color black,
his long, matted, twisted hair crimson,
his teeth white as milk,
the god of fire
who consumes in concentric order
appeared at her curse in a Brahmin's form.
"Woman of great chastity,
long ago I was commanded to leap forth and consume this city
on the day you would be so cruelly wronged.
Who shall escape here?"
he said.
"Brahmins, just men, cattle,
chaste women, the old, and children.
Spare them and go to those who are evil."
At the behest of the raging woman with golden bracelets,
smoking fire grew thick in Maturai,
the city of the good-charioted king.[24]

As a chaste, young woman, Kaṇṇaki is filled with aṇaṅku even while her husband is alive; but her power is in control. When he is killed, it goes out of control and is able to cause the city to be consumed because the city has been deprived of the protection of the king and of his power, which left at the moment he realized he had committed an injustice. It is notable that her power is concentrated in her breast. It is strengthened by her wildly flying hair and ornaments: it is because these things rendered a widow dangerous that she was supposed to shave her head and break her ornaments. Several elements in this telling are of northern

[24] Cil. 21.40–57.

provenance: the notion of karma, by which the burning of the city was ordained long ago, and the idea of saving Brahmins, cows, and others.

It was not only by self-immolation that the widow took her life. In Puṟ. 256, a widow asks the potter to make her husband's urn large so that it will hold her too:

Potter who makes vessels,
listen:
have compassion on me also,
for I have crossed
many barren places with him
like a little white lizard
on the spoke of a shafted wagon.
Make wide
the urn for the burial ground
on this earth
with all its great spaces.

It is interesting to note that urns containing the bones of two or three people have actually been found in Mouttrapaleon near Pondicherry. The bones were placed in the urns at one time, and J. M. Casal and G. Casal, who found them, suggest that they may represent cases of suttee.[25] Such multiple burials were not uncommon: out of thirty-four urns examined, two contained the bones of more than one person. Their date is about the first century B.C.

Before going on to contrast the Tamil view of woman with its northern counterparts, I wish to investigate other aspects and implications of a woman's power and to draw conclusions concerning them. It was not only her husband that a woman protected with her power, but also her brothers, her father, and, to an even greater extent, her son.

The relation between a woman and her father and brothers is suggested in poems in which those relatives try to keep the heroine from having anything to do with her lover. In Kuṟ. 123, for example, a woman about to meet her lover is anxious because the boats of her brothers, who hunt many fish, approach. In Puṟ. 350, the brothers play an important role in denying to her

[25] Casal and Casal, *Site Urbain*, p. 291.

suitors their sister who has just attained puberty (see also Pur̲. 352, 353, 355).[26] In Ak. 158, the father stands between the heroine and her lover. The heroine's friend insists to the mother that the heroine could not possibly be meeting her lover at night, "[For] father, as strong and wrathful as Murugan, is at home and has let his dogs, like a pack of tigers, run loose." The reason for the hostility of the father and brothers is suggested by a modern folk story, in which a woman's brothers try to keep her from being married so that they may continued to be protected by her power.[27]

The role of the mother's power in protecting her son is far more clear. It is suggested by the poetic convention in which a woman rejoices to learn that her son had died in battle, as in Pur̲. 277:

When she learned her son had died killing an elephant,
the joy of the old woman,
her hair pure grey like the feathers of a fish-eating heron,
was greater than the day she bore him;
her tears were more
than the drops that quiver on strong bamboo
on Mount Vetiram
after a rain.

The reason the mother rejoices when she learns that her son has died a hero is that she is ultimately responsible for his heroism, in that she has passed on to him her own power. For her entire life, she has had to undertake ascetic practices and had to hold herself in tight control in order to increase her power and keep it under control. The aim of that is to make her the center of a happy and successful family. By seeing that her son has died a hero, the mother realizes that she has succeeded in her aim, and that she has been able to impart enough of her power to her son to enable him to find what was for the Tamils (at least in theory)

[26] Thus Brenda Beck, to whom I am indebted for many ideas expressed here, includes a woman's brothers (as well as her father, husband, and son) in what she calls the nuclear family. I have investigated the role of the nuclear family in my paper "Some Aspects of Kinship in Ancient Tamil Literature," in *Michigan Papers on South and Southeast Asia* (Ann Arbor, Mich., forthcoming).

[27] See Brenda Beck's article in *Michigan Papers on South and Southeast Asia* (Ann Arbor, Mich., forthcoming).

the greatest fulfillment a man could find, a heroic death in battle. The mother's happiness at such an outcome is even more vividly described in Puṟ. 295, where her breasts flow with milk again when she sees the heroic death of her son: she is so moved that her breasts, the seat of her aṇaṅku, are again charged with power. In one poem, Puṟ. 373, soldiers' wives do not go to the courtyard (to burn themselves), but are thrilled at the wounds of their dead husbands; like the mother, the wife is a source of a man's power.

In the Tamil folk tradition, there is great competition between the wife and the mother after marriage, and the two are always fighting. It seems to me that this can be seen as inspired, at least in part, by the competition between them to lend their power to the man. After a son is born, there is competition of a different sort: both the husband and the son must compete for the mother's power. That is one reason for the conventions of the marutam division of the akam poems, where the hero abandons his wife after the birth of a son and goes to live with his courtesans. It is also the reason, it seems to me, why the wife generally goes to her mother's house to give birth for the first time: that is an occasion of great danger to the new son, and there must be no other man to compete for the mother's power. It has been seen that the father would first see his son while wearing war dress, and that, in modern Andhra, a father must first see his child as a reflection on the surface of oil as the child and its mother sit behind a curtain. These customs can be understood in terms of the disorder and danger that exist upon the birth of a son until harmony is reestablished. From the moment when a son is born, the mother's powers are shared between the son and the husband. Great care must be taken to control this power until the adjustment is made.

The relationship by which a woman protects her husband and other male relatives is not merely one-sided. By channeling her power to those men, and especially to her husband, the woman is able to keep her power under control and to exist in an auspicious state. That is why when a woman is widowed, and no longer has a husband to pass her power to, she must undertake extreme measures to keep her power under control.

The mutual nature of the relationship between husband and wife is of great importance. It appears from the poems that the object most filled with sacred power is also the object most threatened by sacred power present elsewhere. Thus, in Ak. 7, a girl who has reached puberty is subject to "aṇan̄ku that assaults" in her town, and menstruous women, in Pur̲. 299, stand terrified in the temple of Murukan̲. Similarly, in Ain̄. 250, the heroine's breasts, the seat of her aṇan̄ku, are themselves afflicted by that power, for, the poet says, "the one who afflicted [*aṇan̄kiyōn̲*] her young breasts, which bear ornaments, is the lord of the forest . . . not the victorious, manly Murukan̲."

In marriage, likewise, the husband and wife are dangerous to one another; therefore, the contacts between them must be carefully regulated. Thus, husband and wife did not eat together (Pur̲. 120; Kur̲. 167), and the husband was not allowed to see his wife or child in the impure period after she had given birth. It is likely also that, as in later times, the wife did not call her husband by name.

The nature of a woman's power is further illumined by the fact that in the poems, man is often homologized to nature, while woman is homologized to culture.[28] This notion is well expressed in Pur̲. 86:

Holding the pillar of my small house,
you ask, "Where is your son?"
Wherever my son is, I do not know.
This womb that has given birth to him
is like a rock cave
that a tiger has inhabited and left.
Somewhere on the battlefield you will find him.

Here the woman is likened to the house, which has a pillar to hold it up; she is like something artificial, which needs support to stand up. But the son is like a tiger who lives in a rock cave, a natural dwelling that needs no support. The woman continues to need her son, for he gives her emotional fulfillment and enables her to control her power, but the son no longer needs his mother. The same contrast is expressed in Pur̲. 251, which describes a man who has become an ascetic:

We saw then
a warrior
who made loose the ornaments

[28] Again, I am indebted to Brenda Beck, who noticed this distinction in folk literature.

of women with small bangles,
like dolls
in their houses,
which seemed paintings.
Now he bathes in a waterfall
from a high bamboo-filled summit,
goes to a red fire
hot and raging on logs
brought by forest elephants
and dries his curly matted hair,
which hangs low on his back.

The woman is like a doll; her house is like a painting. But the man lives in the midst of nature, in his natural state, after he has renounced women and family life.

The reason for this contrast between man and woman is partly a facile one. As in the poem adduced above, woman is associated with the home and with domestic life; indeed, her most common name in Tamil is *maṉaivi*, she who is associated with the house. On the other hand, the man is commonly associated with the harvest and with battle, both occupations that center on the real, uncultured world.

But another and more significant reason can be found for the identification of the man with the natural and of the woman with the cultured. Woman is dangerous unless she is carefully controlled; left in her natural state, she is a threat. Thus women are supposed to do many things to remove themselves from their natural state. They are supposed to put up their hair, to wear flowers in their hair, to wear a mark on their foreheads, and to wear many ornaments. Indeed, so strongly was the use of ornaments associated with women that a word meaning lovely ornament, *cēyiḻai*, is used by metonymy to mean woman in ancient Tamil. It was not only by physical means that a woman was supposed to remove herself from the natural state; I have argued that cross-cousin marriage is a means for binding a woman in a tight, interlocking family relationship.[29] Aiṅ. 405, which describes woman in her most auspicious state, makes her cultured, domestic nature clear:

[29] See Hart, "Some Aspects of Kinship."

She has become
the light of her house,
like the red flame
in the bowl
of a shining lamp,
for she gave birth
to his son
whose land
is ornamented with meadows
made lovely with flowers
in the pattering rain.

Here the woman is compared to the light in a man-made lamp; she is ultimately like a natural thing, fire. But just as fire is destructive in its natural state, but is a source of light when constrained by the wick of the lamp, so the woman, potentially dangerous if her power is not constrained, is a source of happiness and fulfillment if her power is controlled in artificial ways. The poem suggests that just as a house has no use if there is no lamp to enlighten it, so the distaff things and structures around which the Tamil woman's life is centered are meaningless unless there is a woman to animate them. Moreover, just as the flame can burn down the house if it goes out of control, so the power of woman can destroy those people closest to her if it is not restrained.

In descriptions of women who are not in an auspicious state, several passages in Tamil literature use natural comparisons. Thus, in the passage from the *Cilappatikāram* quoted above, the onlooker describes the widow Kaṇṇaki:

What evil have I done
that I saw her,
her black hair
spread
like a forest?[30]

Similarly, in Pur̲. 247, quoted above, a widow going to burn herself is associated with a natural scene.

I will now compare the ancient Tamil view of women with its ancient northern counterparts for two reasons. First, if in fact that view is as important in ancient Tamil society as I have indi-

[30] Cil. 20 *veṇpā* 2.

cated, then it is crucial to show that it was indigenous; and, secondly, if the South Indian view of woman, as exemplified by Tamil, spread to North India, this is an important example of the movement of cultural elements from the South to the North.

That the chastity of a woman was considered far less important in North India in Vedic times than it was later is proved by the ceremony of Varuṇapraghāsa, which is described in the *Śatapathabrāhmaṇa.*[31] Keith condenses as follows:

> On the first day of the offering, barley is roasted on the Dakṣiṇa fire, the one used for all ritual acts of an uncanny description: then a number of dishes of a porridge made from the barley are prepared, one for each member of the family with one over, apparently for the members yet unborn. The wife of the sacrificer is then asked by the priest what lovers she has; she must name them, or at least indicate the number by holding up as many stalks of grass as she has lovers, and by this action she purifies herself from her sins in this regard: otherwise, if she does not tell the truth, it will go badly for her connexions. She is then taken to the southern fire, in which she offers the plates with the words, 'Whatever sin we have committed in the village, in the forest, among men and in ourselves, that by sacrifice we remove here,' and further on an offering is made to Varuṇa, who is asked to spare the lives of his suppliants and not to be wroth.[32]

In another passage from the *Śatapathabrāhmaṇa*, Sukanyā says, when she is married to the old and decrepit sage Cyavana, "I shall not forsake my husband while he is alive, to whom my father gave me,"[33] showing that chastity did not demand of her the extreme of faithfulness found in Tamil and later Sanskrit, where the wife was expected to remain chaste even as a widow.

A view of chastity much more like the Tamil is found in the *Mahābhārata.* In the Vanaparva, when Damayantī curses a young hunter with evil designs on her by invoking her faithful-

[31] *Śatapathabrāhmaṇa* 11.5.2.20. For a fuller description of the development of attitudes regarding chastity in North India, see George L. Hart III, "Woman and the Sacred in Ancient Tamilnad," *Journal of Asian Studies* 32, no. 2 (1973): 233–250.

[32] Arthur Berriedale Keith, *The Religion and Philosophy of the Vedas and Upanishads* (Cambridge, Mass.), p. 265.

[33] *Śatapathabrāhmaṇa* iv.5.9.

ness to her husband, the hunter falls down dead.[34] Similarly, in the *Śalyaparva*, the power of a chaste woman (*pativratā*) is described: she can, if she chooses, burn the world or stop the motions of the sun and the moon.[35] Many similar descriptions appear elsewhere in the *Mahābhārata* and the Purāṇas.[36] In the *Mahābhārata*, however, there are also passages that show an attitude toward chastity more like the one that obtained in Vedic times than that of the Tamil poems. In the *Vanaparva*, for example, when Damayantī does not hear from Nala for a long time, she prepares to hold another *svayaṃvara*.[37]

There existed without question among the Aryans of Vedic times the practice of allowing a childless woman to conceive by her husband's brother and even, if she became a widow, to marry him.[38] This practice was called *niyoga*. The *Apastambadharmasūtra*, assigned by Kane to the period 600–300 B.C.,[39] states: "One shall not make over [his wife] to strangers [for a son by niyoga], but only to one who is *sagotra*."[40] Similar rules for niyoga are mentioned in the *Mānavadharmaśāstra*, and the practice is also mentioned in the *Mahābhārata*.[41] In both the *Apastambadharmasūtra* and the *Mānavadharmaśāstra*, the practice of niyoga is described and then condemned.[42] Later writers on *dharmaśāstra* invariably forbade niyoga and had recourse to rather desperate ways of explaining away what their predecessors had said.[43] It is clear that, in the time of the Vedas, the practice of niyoga and probably also of widow remarriage were common and accepted by all. By the time of the early writers on dharmaśāstra and of the *Mahābhārata*, the old customs had stiffer and stiffer competition from the newer standard of perfect chastity

[34] Mbh. 3.61.37–38.

[35] Mbh. 9.62.

[36] Kane, *History of Dharmaśāstra*, II:563ff.

[37] Mbh. 3.68.

[38] *Atharvaveda* 2.615; *Ṛgveda* X.40.2.

[39] Kane, *History of Dharmaśāstra*, I.135.

[40] *Āpastambadharmasūtra* 11.10.27.2–4.

[41] *Manusmṛti* IX.59–61; Mbh. 1.111–114.

[42] *Āpastambadharmasūtra* 11.10.27.5–7; *Manusmṛti* IX.64–68.

[43] Kane, *History of Dharmaśāstra*, II:604.

among widows. Thus there are found "bewildering and often conflicting rules about niyoga in the *smṛtis*."[44] Finally, a little after the time of Christ, the new customs won out entirely and the practice of niyoga was considered wrong. It is in this period that the passages were written that are so common in the two epics and the Purāṇas, describing the sacred power of a chaste woman.

A similar evolution is found in the development of other practices among widows. Unfortunately, there is no direct evidence from Vedic times, but the practices of niyoga and of widow remarriage indicate that the widow was not subject to the excessive ritual restrictions of later times. Manu speaks of the ascetic practices that may be performed by a widow: "A woman, when her husband is dead, may, if she chooses, emaciate her body by subsisting on flowers, roots, and fruits, but she should not even take the name of a stranger male. Till her death, she should be forbearing, observe vows, and be celibate."[45] By the time of the *Skandapurāṇa*, the author could write, "The widow is more inauspicious than all inauspicious things."[46] In another passage, which Kane shows is probably an interpolation, that same Purāṇa declares, "The tying up into a braid of the hair by the widow leads to the bondage of the husband; therefore, a widow should always shave her head. She should always take one meal a day and never a second. . . . A widow . . . should every day perform *tarpaṇa* with sesame, water, and *kuśa* grass for her husband, his father, and grandfather, after repeating their names and *gotra*."[47] This passage is extraordinary; it gives virtually every vow expected in the Tam̲il poems of at least six centuries earlier: tonsure, eating small amounts, not sleeping on a cot, and offering piṇṭam to the dead husband.[48] The vows of tonsure and of offering tarpaṇa do not appear earlier among the exhaustive references collected by Kane. It is this passage on which the medieval writers relied to prescribe the continual tonsure of widows.[49] Kane demonstrates

44 Ibid.

45 *Manusmṛti* V.157–160.

46 *Skandapurāṇa* III, *Brahmāraṇya* sect., ch. 7, vs. 50–51.

47 Ibid., *Kāśīkhāṇḍa*, ch. 4.

48 See Pur̲. 246, quoted above.

49 Kane, *History of Dharmaśāstra*, II:586.

conclusively that the practice of continuous tonsure by widows in Aryan India was late, arising only some time shortly before the fourteenth century.[50]

Another practice whose origin in Aryan India may be traced is the taboo on a wife's uttering her husband's name. Such practice was permitted when the *Rāmāyaṇa* was written, for over and over Sītā utters the name of Rāma. In one chapter she utters it six times as she talks to Hanumān,[51] and when she is abducted by Rāvaṇa she calls her husband by name again and again.[52] By the time of Kālidāsa, the taboo was observed in North India, for Śakuntalā and her friends refer to Duḥśyanta as *rājarṣi*, never uttering his name, and when Śakuntalā wishes to address him directly she says, "*paurava*."[53] Unfortunately, because the akam poems are anonymous, it is not possible to determine whether this taboo was present in early Tamil. Certainly it is very much present in Tamilnad today, and, in light of other related elements found in ancient Tamil, it seems quite likely that this taboo was observed by the Tamils eighteen centuries ago.

The final Aryan practice to be considered is that of widow burning, or suttee. Kane states, "It appears probable that the practice arose in Brahmanical India a few centuries before Christ."[54] It is first mentioned by Strabo, who says that the Greeks under Alexander found suttee practiced among the Cathaeoi in the Punjab.[55] It is mentioned several times in the *Mahābhārata*: Mādrī, the favorite wife of Pāṇḍu, burns herself with her husband,[56] Saurandhrī is ordered to be burned with Kīcaka,[57] and some wives of Vasudeva and Kṛṣṇa are said to have burned themselves when they were widowed.[58] On the other

[50] Ibid., pp. 587ff.

[51] *Vālmīkirāmāyaṇa* 5.31.12,13,15,16,17,21.

[52] Ibid., 3.47.

[53] *Abhijñānaśākuntala*, act 3.

[54] Kane, *History of Dharmaśāstra*, II:625.

[55] *The Geography of Strabo*, trans. Horace L. Jones (London, 1917–32), XV.1.30 and 62.

[56] Mbh. 1.90.75, 1.116.29.

[57] Mbh. 4.22.8.

[58] Mbh. 16.8.18.

hand, in the *Strīparva*, no mention is made of widows burning themselves, while the cremations of the Kauravas are described in detail. Winternitz considers the portions of the *Mahābhārata* that describe suttee to be insertions of later date than the main body of that epic. He points out that suttee is nowhere mentioned in the *Rāmāyaṇa*.[59] Several texts are cited by Aparārka that apparently forbid self-immolation to Brahmin widows.[60]

From the foregoing evidence, it appears virtually certain that the practice of attributing sacred power to woman as it is found in early Tamil and in Sanskrit, beginning with the epics, was one that originated with the indigenous peoples of India, and probably with the megalithic Deccan Dravidian civilization, which flourished in the first millennium B.C. It is in Dravidian India that it is still strongest, and it is only in Tamil literature that it is consistently and without exception observed. It is, moreover, only in early Tamil literature that the real reason for suttee and widow asceticism is stated: that the widow is full of sacred forces that would endanger her and others unless they were suppressed. Beginning about the third century B.C., practices associated with the sacred power attributed to woman began to make their way into Aryan India: the Greeks under Alexander found suttee practiced by at least one group in North India. However, it was not until about the time of Christ that the notions regarding woman in North India began really to resemble those found in Tamil: it is in the *Mahābhārata* that a woman's chastity is first considered a source of sacred power, which can destroy anything that threatens it. The influx of Dravidian elements into Aryan culture at about this time is clearly indicated by the great numbers of Dravidian words, probably from now-dead central Dravidian languages, which began to find their way into Sanskrit and Indo-Aryan during the period of the epics.[61] It will be seen below that in the first three or four centuries after Christ there was a considerable influx of poetic elements from the Deccan Dravidian tradition into Sanskrit. It is significant that this influx occurred

59 M. Winternitz, *A History of Indian Literature*, trans. S. Ketkar (Calcutta, 1962–63), I:444.

60 See Kane, *History of Dharmaśāstra*, II:627; Aparārka, *Yājñavalkyasmṛti* (Poona, 1903–04), p. 112.

61 T. Burrow, *The Sanskrit Language* (London, 1955), pp. 380–388.

at approximately the same time as the influx of Dravidian ideas regarding woman, for it is in the centuries after Christ that those ideas became predominant in North India.

As time went on, even more Dravidian elements entered Aryan India. The practice of widow tonsure, for example, did not penetrate into the North until at least six hundred years after it is noted in Tamil, and other elements of widow asceticism accompanied it. It is interesting that it is chiefly the Brahmins who practice the tonsure of widows today in Tamilnad, even though they are more of Aryan origin than the other Tamils. This shows how the indigenous customs spread into Indo-Aryan culture: before a group was assimilated, Brahmins would come into it and adopt those values most admired by that group in order to gain respect. Thus the custom would have gained a foothold in the Brahminic religion and would be perpetuated when descendents of the Brahmins wrote lawbooks or copied texts with the appropriate insertions. Today, an ideal of chastity not too different from the early Tamil one pervades virtually all of India, being perceptibly stronger than it was in medieval India, where Tantrism was practiced.[62] This trait of Hinduism, virtually uni-

[62] It is true that the indigenous South Indian view of woman bears a superficial resemblence to the Tantric view. However, I believe that the two views are unrelated and come from quite separate sources. For one thing, it was and is unthinkable to a South Indian that a woman's chastity be compromised for a religious cause. For another, while *śakti*, or power, is attributed to woman in Hindu Tantrism, among the Buddhists the woman is passive while the man symbolizes the active element. This could not be so if woman was identified with power in the earliest Tantra systems. Finally, Tantra is a system of personal salvation that is not consonant with any major South Indian religion, as may be inferred from the poem about ascetics given in chapter 4 in the section on Jainism, Buddhism, and Hinduism. Thus South India's major contribution to Indian religion was bhakti —devotional worship of an emotional nature. The South Indian antipathy to Tantrism is demonstrated by a story told by the Vīra-Śaivas about one of their saints, Allama Prabhu. When that devotee met Gorakhnath, a practitioner of Tantra and a great yogi, Gorakhnath gave him a sword and told him to cut him in half. When Allama Prabhu complied, he found that the sword would not penetrate the "diamond body" of the yogi. Thereupon Allama Prabhu told Gorakhnath to take the sword and thrust at him. The sword passed clean through the body of Allama Prabhu as if nothing were there, and the saint was unharmed. In other words, the yogi had made himself invulnerable by amassing power, while the devotee had eradicated self and so could not be harmed. It should be pointed out that when Tantrism penetrated to South India, it was influenced by the indigenous beliefs there regarding woman.

versal today, spread from indigenous groups, chiefly from the Deccan culture of the Dravidians, and was embraced more and more by Aryan society.

CASTE

The notion of caste in Tamilnad was and is based to a large extent on ideas of the sacred. Indeed, the ancient poems have much to say about caste before that institution was overlaid with a stratum of Aryan ideas. Therefore what they reveal regarding caste is of great importance both for an understanding of the sacred in ancient Tamilnad and for an understanding of the historical development of caste in Tamilnad and, it seems likely, in the rest of India as well.

The ancient Tamil poems refer to low-born people several times. In Puṟ. 82, a low man (*iḻiciṉaṉ*) "stitches a cot for a woman in labor," hurrying because a festival (in which he presumably must participate) is at hand. Nilakantasastri suggests that this man is called low because his occupation involves working with leather.[63] In Puṟ. 170, the man who plays the tuṭi drum in a village is called "the one of low birth" (*iḻi piṟappāḷaṉ*); in Puṟ. 287, the poet addresses the "*pulaiyaṉ* beating the tuṭi, low man [iḻiciṉaṉ] with striking drumstocks," where pulaiyaṉ comes from *pulai*, the ancient Dravidian word for pollution.[64] Similarly, in Naṟ. 77, the man playing the tuṭi as soldiers go into battle is called a pulaiyaṉ. In Puṟ. 289, the man who plays the taṇṇumai drum to summon men to battle is called a low man and a pulaiyaṉ. In Kali. 68.19, the harlot speaks scornfully of the pulaiyaṉ (the Pāṇaṉ, or bard, sent as a messenger by her husband) who entered her house saying, "May it flourish!" In Kali. 95.10, the heroine speaks of the pulaiyaṉ who sings and plays his lute. The low status of drummers and bards is confirmed in Puṟ. 335, where to describe a desolate land the poet says, "Its only clans [*kuṭi*, a word for caste in later literature] are Tuṭiyaṉs [who play the tuṭi drum], Pāṇaṉs, Paṟaiyaṉs [who play the *kiṇai* drum—see below in this chapter], and the Kaṭampaṉs." The meaning of Kaṭampaṉ

[63] K. A. Nilakantasastri, *The Cōḷas*, 2d ed. (Madras, 1955), p. 88.

[64] D.E.D. 3714.

is not certain. In the only two other occurrences of the word in early Tamil, it means Murukan̲, (Cil. 24.11.3; Maṇi. 4149), a name given to that god because he wears a garland of *kaṭampu* flowers. It is likely that, in this poem, Kaṭampan means a priest of Murukan̲, since like that god such a priest wore a garland of kaṭampu. In any case, he was probably a low man, for in later Tamil *kaṭampan̲* means an unruly person, *kaṭampi*, a lewd woman, and *kaṭampu*, evil, mishap, or misfortune. The low status of bards may also be inferred from the fact that several centuries after the anthologies, Tiruppāṇāḻvār, who was a Pāṇan̲ by caste, was considered to be so low that he was not allowed into the temple.

In his book *Tamil Heroic Poetry*, Kailasapathy is unaware of these references to bards as low and so he comes to unwarranted conclusions regarding their position in society: "The Pāṇar were minstrels who sang their songs to the accompaniment of the *yāḻ*, 'lute.' In medieval times the word came to denote a lower caste. But in the early poems not only do we note the absence of the caste system, but also find that the Pāṇars were held in high esteem as a vocational group. In a poem enumerating the names of excellent flowers, foods, gods, and other things, a bard speaks of the Pāṇar as one of the four noble clans. In passing, it is interesting to note that another ancient clan—the Par̲aiyar, 'drummers'—enumerated under the category [sic] in the same poem—was also degraded in the caste hierarchy of later times."[65] The poem he means is evidently Pur̲. 335, though he gives no reference, since that is the only poem in the anthologies that mentions Par̲aiyan̲s. That poem has occasioned an extraordinary number of misconceptions. Pillay writes, "It is noteworthy that a poem in the *Pur̲anān̲ūr̲u* says that there is no caste or tribe except the Tuṭiyar, Pāṇar, Par̲aiyar, and Kaṭampar. This is attempted to be explained as a reference only to the martial communities of the land. But it does not seem too much to consider them as the only four indigenous communities, then uninfluenced by the later caste system."[66] Nilakantasastri writes, "One poem in the *Pur̲anān̲ūr̲u* affirms that there are only four castes (*kuḍi*),

[65] K. Kailasapathy, *Tamil Heroic Poetry* (London, 1968), p. 95.

[66] K. K. Pillay, "Landmarks in the History of Tamilnad," *Proceedings of the Second International Conference Seminar of Tamil Studies* (Madras, 1971), I:18.

viz., Tuṭiyan̲, Pāṇan̲, Par̲aiyan̲, and Kaṭampan̲, and only one god worthy of being worshiped with paddy strewn before him, namely the hero-stone recalling the fall of a brave warrior in battle. These castes and this worship were of very great antiquity, perhaps survivals from pre-Aryan times."[67] It seems best to translate the poem here in order to lay to rest the many misconceptions it has occasioned:

> If strength hard to subdue . . .
> . . . .
> Except for *kuravu*, *taḷavu*, *kuruntu*, and *mullai*,
> there are no flowers.
> Except for black-stemmed *varaku* [a kind of millet],
> large-eared *tin̲ai* [a kind of millet],
> the little creeper *koḷ*, and *avarai* [beans] with round pods,
> there is no food.
> Except for the Tuṭiyan̲, the Pāṇan̲,
> the Par̲aiyan̲, and the Kaṭampan̲,
> there are no clans.
> Except for stones worshiped
> because [men] stood before hostile enemies
> and blocked them
> and killed elephants with high gleaming tusks,
> and died,
> there are no gods worshiped
> with offering of paddy.

All of the flowers and foods enumerated here are peculiar to the less productive mountainous and forested land that is called *van̲pulam* in Tamil and is differentiated from land on the more prosperous plains, called *men̲pulam*, where paddy is cultivated. They all grow in the mullai, or forest, tract. Context demands that the four castes here mentioned be as lowly with respect to the prestigious groups of society as the varaku, tin̲ai, koḷ, and avarai are to the rice and other food of favored provinces. Thus Duraicami Pillai must be correct when he suggests, in his commentary on the poem, that the purpose of the poet here is to paint a desolate picture of mullai, or forested, land, a fact no doubt made clear in the lines that have been lost. This example

[67] K. A. Nilakantasastri, *A History of South India from Prehistoric Times to the Fall of Vijayanagar*, 3d ed. (London, 1966), p. 131.

indicates how unreliable many of the secondary sources for ancient Tamil literature are.

To return to a consideration of low castes in ancient Tamilnad, Pur̲. 360 and 363 describe how, at the cremation ceremony, a man called a pulaiyan̲ (Pur̲. 360) or "one of low birth" (*il̲i pir̲appin̲ōn̲*, in Pur̲. 363) places a few grains of boiled rice in the dead man's mouth before he is burned, without looking around at the corpse. *Pulaittis* (the feminine of pulaiyan̲) appear several times, most commonly as washerwomen (Ak. 34, 387; Pur̲. 311). In Pur̲. 259, the poet describes how a bull "jumps and frolics like a pulaitti whose body has been taken over by Murukan̲," and Subrahmanian, neglecting to cite a source, states that the pulaitti would prophesy while under the influence of Murukan̲.[68]

There is one mention of the *varṇa* system: in Pur̲. 183, the poet, expounding the virtues of learning, says, "in the four divisions . . . if one in the lowest should study [and become a learned man], someone in the highest will come to him [to learn]." The notion of varṇa here is borrowed entirely from the North; there is no evidence that it described Tamil society in any manner.

Among those called low in the examples just given, there is one factor that virtually all share: they are rendered dangerous by the sacred power with which they come into contact in their occupations. The leather worker is infected by the soul of the cow with whose skin he works; the man at the funeral, by the spirit of the dead man; the washerwoman, by the dirt (and especially menstrual discharge) on the clothes she cleans; and the pulaitti by the dangerous gods who possess her. The drummers and the bards were rendered dangerous by the gods (aṇaṅku) who were thought to reside in their drums and lutes, and by their occupation, which involved controlling dangerous forces by playing during battle, when the naṭukal was worshiped, at executions, in the presence of the king, and in the presence of the gravely wounded.

Concerning these low-caste men, Kailasapathy writes, "In the early period, the word [*il̲icin̲ar*, the low men] and what is but a synonym of it, *pulaiyar*, denoted the perfect antithesis of *cān̲r̲ōr*, 'the great and noble ones.' *Pulaiyan̲* from *pul*, 'meanness, base-

[68] N. Subrahmanian, *Pre-Pallavan Tamil Index* (Madras, 1966), p. 582.

ness,' came to mean the pariahs in later times. But as will be shown below, in the poems themselves it denotes people engaged in what were considered 'mean, low, servile' jobs." His proof is as follows: "We may now cite a few examples of the lower people. The instances are not many, but sufficient to illustrate the point.

(1) a person tying (stitching) beds (*iḻiciṉaṉ*)
(2) a person who beats large drums (*iḻiciṉaṉ*)
(3) a person who beats large drums (*pulaiyaṉ*)
(4) a washerwoman (*pulaitti*).

The last example shows most clearly the very basis of the odium attached to these people. Such work is considered as 'labor' which 'falls beneath the dignity of able-bodied men.'"[69] He has entirely missed the point. If one used his criterion, many of the drummers and Pāṇaṉs were low only by their having to go from one king to another to beg for a living. The Pulavaṉs also had to do that, but rather than being looked down upon, they were praised and admired. Thus, in Puṟ. 201, Kapilar proudly says, "I am a Brahmin and a Pulavaṉ." It is striking, moreover, that all of the so-called low or base people have occupations that bring them into contact with dangerous sacred power, while many others, such as the foster mother and the servants, have demeaning occupations but are nowhere called low. Even today, something of the ancient power to control the sacred clings to the Paṟaiyaṉ. Thurston points out that Brahmins consider Paṟaiyaṉs to possess special magic power, so that a forsaken *paṟaiccēri* (Paṟaiyaṉ quarter) is considered a good site for a Brahmin *agrahāra*, and Brahmins are not allowed to enter the Paṟaiyaṉ quarter just as Paṟaiyaṉs are excluded from the agrahāra.[70] He also cites instances of Brahmin women worshiping at Paṟaiyaṉ shrines for children and of Brahmins consulting Paṟaiyaṉ mediums.[71]

If the ancient Tamils considered many persons low because their occupations brought them into contact with dangerous sacred power, it is natural to wonder whether the Vēlaṉ, the priest

[69] Kailasapathy, *Tamil Heroic Poetry*, pp. 258-262.

[70] Edgar T. Thurston, *Castes and Tribes of Southern India* (Madras, 1909), VI:88ff.

[71] Ibid., p. 84.

of Murukaṉ, who is in more intimate contact with such power than anyone else, was also considered to be low. It is true that the Vēlaṉ is never called low or base in the poems, but in modern Kerala members of one of the subcastes of Paṟaiyaṉs are called Vēlaṉs. One of their jobs is to tell the future, like the Vēlaṉs of ancient Tamil literature, from whom they are no doubt descended. Furthermore, it has been seen that in Puṟ. 259 a pulaitti, or base woman, is possessed by Murukaṉ and shakes, much like the Vēlaṉ, and that, in Puṟ. 335, the Kaṭampaṉ, who was probably a priest of Murukaṉ, is classed among the low castes. In light of this evidence, it is likely that the Vēlaṉ was in fact considered a low person.

It is difficult to determine exactly what restrictions were applied to these low-born people. In Puṟ. 363, quoted above, the poet stresses the dreadful nature of death by describing how the corpse is fed by a pulaiyaṉ. From this it would appear that in ancient times, as now, a man of higher caste would refuse food from the hands of a low-caste man and would consider such food polluted. Kuṟ. 169 seems also to imply that people of low caste—in this case, bards—were considered to be polluting:

> With these pure white teeth I used to laugh with you.
> Now I wish only that they would break off cleanly
> like the tusks of an elephant that butts against rocks
> as he goes in the wilderness.
> My life is polluted [*pul*]
> like the dishes from which bards eat fresh fish.
> I cannot have you,
> and so I wish I were dead.

Ak. 110 also suggests that certain foods were considered polluting by the higher castes. In it, a man comes up to girls who are the daughters of fishermen as they play in the sand. He asks,

> "Foolish girls
> with wide, soft, bamboolike arms!
> The light of the sun has faded
> and I am very tired.
> Would there be anything wrong
> if I ate a guest's meal
> on a soft, open leaf
> and then stayed

in your noisy little village?"

The girls lower their faces in modesty and reply politely,

"This food is not fit for you—
succulent fish,
which only low people eat."

In the *Paṭṭiṉappālai*, one of the *Pattuppāṭṭu*, line 77, the outer streets of a town (*puṟaccēri*) are said to be inhabited by fishermen. It is quite likely that then, as now, the fishermen lived in the outer parts of the city because they were considered of low caste, probably because they were infected by the spirits of the fish they killed. Thus in the poem given above, the guest who is of high caste would be polluted by eating fish, which are fit only for the lower castes.

Curiously, some poems suggest that the commensal taboo between high and low castes was not as universally observed as it is today, especially between the bards and the king. Thus, in Puṟ. 361, the king gives liquor to bards (Pāṇaṉs) and their families, sometimes joining in the drinking himself, and, in Puṟ. 235, the poetess Auvaiyār, putting her poem in the mouth of a low-caste bard (for as a Pulavaṉ she certainly would not say that her head stank of flesh), says of the dead king Atiyamāṉ:

If he had a little toddy, he would give it to us.
If he had much, after offering it to us,
he would drink it happily as we sang.
If there were a little rice,
he would put it on many plates.
He would give to us whole pieces of meat with bones.
He would stand where spears and arrows came.
With his hand fragrant with orange blossoms
he would stroke my head, which stank of flesh.
Before it fell,
the spear that penetrated his breast
made holes in the wide dishes of the foremost of bards;
it went through the hands of suppliants;
and it pierced the tongues of poets
of subtle skill in eloquent words,
making dim the pupils in the empty eyes of those who depend on them.

Where is my lord who loved me?

Now there are no singers,
and there are none who give to singers.
Like the dark *pakaṉṟai* flowers,
flowing with honey in a cool bay,
that fade unworn,
there are many many lives that pass
without giving one thing to others.

It is possible that in these poems, the poets wish to emphasize the greatness of the king by stating that he considers generosity more important than the pollution he may incur by eating with low-caste bards, just as, in Puṟ. 50, which is quoted above in chapter 2, the poet glorifies the king because he serves the poet who desecrated the royal drum rather than executing him. Another indication that pollution taboos were not as strong in ancient times is the custom among rich people of keeping Pāṇaṉs at home to serenade them, for today men of very low castes are not allowed even to enter the homes of those of high caste.

That the ancient Tamils had, like their modern counterparts, a sense of pollution is suggested by several customs not related to caste. It has already been seen how menstruous women were not allowed to touch dishes and how women who had just given birth were thought to be unclean. Ceremonial bathing is mentioned in several contexts: warriors bathed before going to war (Puṟ. 79, 341, 354); men would bathe and kindle incense after worshiping the memorial stone (Puṟ. 329); women would bathe after the puerperal period of impurity; and the king's ceremonial drum would be taken out and bathed at certain times (Puṟ. 50).

The society of the ancient Tamils appears to have consisted of many groups, each of which performed a different occupation, much as it does today. It has been seen that, in Puṟ. 335, the only clans (kuṭis) in a desolate land are said to be Tuṭiyaṉs, Pāṇaṉs, Paṟaiyaṉs, and Kaṭampaṉs, where at least the first three are named for their occupation. Other such groups include Kuṟavaṉs (hill people, a low caste today); Eyiṉaṉs (hunters); Taccaṉs (carpenters); Vēḷirs (a ruling class, probably the ancestors of the modern Vēḷāḷaṉs); Iṭaiyaṉs (cowherds); Paratavaṉs (fishermen); Umaṇaṉs (salt merchants); Kollaṉs (blacksmiths); potters; mahouts; and chariot drivers.

That membership in these groups was hereditary is suggested by many poems that describe the sons or daughters of a group following the same occupation as their fathers. Thus, in Ak. 1, the hero swears to his beloved, "We will never part, just as the resin never leaves the stone once put there by the whetstone-maker's son [literally "little whetstone-maker"]." Similar passages show the sons of carpenters (Puṟ. 206), potters (Puṟ. 32), cowherds (Kuṟ. 241), and "foulmouthed hunters" (Puṟ. 324) helping their fathers with their work. In Ak. 140, the hero says, "The beloved little girl of the salt merchants, who goes [crossing] hills cracked by the heat and telling the price of white rock salt got without plowing in the field of the black pan of the fishermen . . . goes swinging so her bangles with little decorations ring and cries out the barter price in the street, 'White rock salt for paddy!' A house dog, knowing her voice [as different] barks. Her eyes . . . are for me hot pain, so I grieve like the ox in the hand of her father, pulling so that the wagon stuck in the muddy field is freed." Other poems describe the women of the Pāṇaṉ clan helping their men in entertaining kings and others (Puṟ. 64, 89, 103), the women of the hunter clan (Aiṅ. 364, 365; Puṟ. 181), and the wife of a fisherman who, when her husband goes to fish, goes to the salt pan to get salt to exchange for paddy (Kuṟ. 269). At least some of the clans lived in different places in the city, for Puṟ. 348 speaks of a city "where men . . . cut paddy and where there are streets [*cēri*] of bards [Pāṇaṉs] who exchange little fish," while, in *Paṭṭiṉappālai* 77, the outer streets (puṟaccēri) of a town are said to be inhabited by fishermen.

There is little question that in ancient Tamilnad, as in modern South India, cross-cousin marriage was the norm. Certainly, arranged marriages were standard. Thus, in Kuṟ. 40, the hero indicates that it was common to marry a relative when he says,

My mother and yours,
what were they to one another?
My father and yours,
what kin?
I and you,
how did we come to know each other?
And yet
like rain falling on red fields

our loving hearts
have mixed together.

In Kur̲. 229, the heroine's friend says,

He would take her hair
and pull;
and she would grab his hair,
not yet thick,
twist it,
pull it,
and run.
And though their loving foster mothers
stopped them,
they paid no heed
but right in front of them
had their little fights.
Certainly fate is a wonderful thing,
for now it has made them rejoice in marriage
like a garland
woven of two strands of flowers.

It is true that many of the Tamil poems concern love between strangers; yet such love was not common, as can be seen by the extreme measures taken by the parents to keep the girl at home once she is suspected. Thus, in Ak. 20, the girl's friend says, "Mother has begun to guard you, friend, because she says that there is a lone chariot that whirls the moonlight sand . . . oblivious to day or night by the great bay." (See also Kur̲. 246, 292, 294; Ak. 90.)

There is much evidence in addition to the two poems given above that cross-cousin marriage was in fact practiced in ancient South India. The *Baudhāyanadharmasūtra* (1.1.19–26) states that the practice of such marriage was peculiar to the South, and Trautmann has adduced many cases of cross-cousin marriage being introduced into Sanskrit or Pali stories by the Ceylonese Buddhists and the South Indians.[72] Indeed, Trautmann's arguments are so persuasive that they admit of no reasonable doubt

[72] See Thomas Trautmann's paper "Cross-Cousin Marriage in Ancient North India?" in *Michigan Papers on South and Southeast Asia* (Ann Arbor, Mich., forthcoming).

that cross-cousin marriage was in fact practiced in ancient South India.

The picture that emerges is of a social system in ancient Tamilnad not too different from that of later times. There were many endogamous groups, ranging from the ruling classes on one end to the low castes on the other. Then, as now, a person of high caste would not take food from the hands of someone of low caste; however, the restriction on contacts between different groups was not as extreme as it later became, for the poems indicate that people of high status kept Pāṇaṉs, who were very low, in their houses to play and sing for them.

It is extremely significant that the most differentiation is found among the low groups. Thus the clan of the Tuṭiyaṉs, who play the tuṭi drum, is distinguished from that of the Paṟaiyaṉs, who play the *paṟai* drum, and from that of the Pāṇaṉs, who play the yāḻ (lute). *Paripāṭal* 7.31–32 says that dancers and singers had their own (and presumably different) streets. The reason this differentiation among the low groups is important is that it is just these groups who were charged with the control of sacred power. On the other hand, among groups at the top of society, or in the middle, there appears to be no such extreme differentiation, though no doubt each occupation did form roughly a different caste.

The extreme differentiation within the lowest stratum of society could only be motivated by the belief that each low group had a fitness to deal with one aspect of the sacred, but not with any others. Thus, only one group could play the tuṭi drum, and it could not play the kiṇai drum. It has been suggested above that fishermen were of low caste in ancient times as they are today. In *Chemmeen*, the importance of having just the right caste for the various tasks involved in fishing is suggested: "Fisherman Andi . . . turned the conversation in another direction. 'Are there any instances of any fishermen of the wrong caste getting a boat and net?' 'Yes. But the boat and the net did not last long,' Ramanmuppan said."[73]

[73] T. S. Pillai, *Chemmeen*, p. 31. An interesting passage on page 132 of the same book shows how the sacred power that a fisherman possesses because he kills fish must be controlled by the vow of not saving: "Palani described a belief current among the fishermen. 'A fisherman cannot save. This is because he makes his

It is difficult to know how large a role the notion of fitness played among the higher castes. It would appear that it was important for them also. Thus, in Pur̲. 87, the poet appears to be invoking the special ability of a man of the carpenter caste when he compares the king to "a wheel made in a month by a carpenter who can complete eight chariots in one day." The idea of special fitness because of birth is also invoked by the poets when they praise the king's ancestors and describe their exploits. A similar point of view is adopted toward things: the skin of the royal drum must be made from the hide of a bull that vanquished another bull; pictures of gods and designs must be drawn in houses to make them fit for habitation; men must put certain flowers in their hair to go to battle; a Pāṇan̲ must sing in a house to make it habitable and put it in an auspicious condition.

Of course, these notions are found in virtually every other culture, but in ancient Tamil society the notion of fitness seems to have been stronger and more pervasive than in most. This is indicated by the fact that the sacred elements that determined fitness were not transcendent deities who had to be invoked, like the Vedic or Homeric gods, but rather were concentrations of power immanent in certain objects. The omnipresence of these forces is suggested by a poem by the medieval Kannada poet Basavaṇṇa, well translated by Ramanujan as follows:

The pot is a god. The winnowing
fan is a god. The stone in the
street is a god. The comb is a
god. The bowstring is also a
god. The bushel is a god and the
sprouted cup is a god.

Gods, gods, there are so many
there's no place left
for a foot.

money at the cost of millions of lives. He makes his money by cheating and catching innocent beings moving freely in the sea. To look upon those millions dying with their eyes open was nothing to those who saw that sight every day. But you cannot save money made at the cost of innocent lives. It was not possible. Otherwise, why should fishermen starve?' he said. This was not only Palani's belief. This was a belief shared by fishermen all along the long, long coast over hundreds and hundreds of years."

There is only
one god. He is our Lord
of the Meeting Rivers.[74]

It is because of the omnipresence and impersonal nature of the indigenous gods that the Tamils had virtually no mythology (except for one or two stories about Murukaṉ and Koṟṟavai) before the incursion of Aryan elements. Thus for the Tamils there were discrete sacred forces that inhered in many everyday things, made them fit for certain uses, and dictated the manner in which they were to be used. It is not surprising that the fitness determined by the presence of sacred forces included specification of the class of men who could use the object. Thus one kind of drum could be played by only one clan, and another by another. Only one kind of man could fish, or hunt, or, apparently, make chariots.

And yet, after all this is said, it must be acknowledged that ancient Tamil society was not segmented to the extent that it later was. There is no question that the ancient Tamils had a conception of pollution, and that it worked in a manner similar to the way it worked later. But the fact remains that the poems do not describe as rigid a society as existed in medieval times, and the ritual distance they describe between the highest members of the society (if one excludes Brahmins) and the lowest is not as great as it later became. This fact is indicated by the *Tolkāppiyam* itself, which divides society into two categories, the high ones and the low ones.[75]

It seems to me that two factors can be isolated as responsible for the extremely segmented society that developed in medieval times. For one thing, as urbanization increased, more and more specialization developed, and the caste system grew more complex. But even more important, the Brahmins consolidated their position in Tamilnad and by their example made purity a virtue to be cultivated by all but the lowest. Even in ancient times, the more orthodox Brahmins set themselves apart from the population and observed strong pollution taboos. Kuṟ. 277 describes a street (*teru*, evidently then, as now, a more respectable term than

[74] A. K. Ramanujan, *Speaking of Siva* (Baltimore, 1973), p. 84.

[75] See Kailasapathy, *Tamil Heroic Poetry*, pp. 258ff.

cēri) "where there are no dogs in the wide doorways." Similarly, the *Perumpāṇā<u>r</u><u>r</u>uppaṭai* (at lines 297 ff.) mentions a village of Brahmins where dogs and chickens are banned. Brahmins went to extremes to keep their rites from being polluted by non-Brahmins, for, in Ak. 220, the heroine's friend says to the hero, "You grieve, standing a long time outside our house, your heart quivering every time you think of her lovely breasts, as hard to get to see as the well-guarded post . . . of the sacrifice completed by him with an axe [Paraśurāma] . . . at Cellūr." It has been seen in chapter 4 that at least some Brahmins evidently did not eat meat, a custom probably not followed by all North Indian Brahmins of the time and motivated, perhaps, by the fear of being polluted by the spirits of the dead animals consumed. There is no mention at all of a Brahmin's presence in a temple of Muruka<u>n</u>, or of a Vela<u>n</u>'s or similar ecstatic's performance in a Śiva temple, and it seems certain that the two kinds of priests never took part in the rituals of each other's temples, just as today some village temples are run by non-Brahmin Pūjāris while those of the Hindu pantheon are in the hands of the Brahmins. As late as the time of Rāmānuja, there were many Brahmins who felt that service in a temple was not fitting for a Brahmin, the only duty of the highest varṇa being the six *kriyās*. In the Vaishnava tradition, these orthodox Brahmins refused to accept the *Pañcarātra Āgamas*, which described the duties of a temple Brahmin, and denied the Brahminhood of all who served in temples. It is possible, I believe, to see in this disassociation from the temples by the twice-born a continuation of the ancient taboo on the sacred power of indigenous elements to the Aryan. It look all of the genius of Rāmānuja to dispel this taboo on temple worship, and he was able to do so only after many generations of Ā<u>l</u>vārs had worked to make an acceptable synthesis of the two traditions.

It must be remembered that, to the ancient Tamils, sacred forces were dangerous accretions of power that could be controlled only by those of low status. When the Brahmins arrived in Tamilnad, it was natural for them to disassociate themselves from these indigenous forces and to characterize themselves as "pure," that is, isolated to the greatest possible extent from polluting sacred forces; indeed, if they were to gain the people's respect, they had very little choice. It was also natural for the

Brahmins to characterize the gods they introduced as pure and unsullied by pollution; thus men of low caste were not allowed into Brahminic temples, and, in Rāmānuja's system, one of the most important attributes of God is *nirmalatvam*, freedom from taint. It follows that the Brahmins had to adopt from the high-caste non-Brahmins many of the customs whose purpose was to isolate a person from dangerous sacred power. Thus Brahmin widows became even more ascetic than their non-Brahmin counterparts; Brahmin wives became as careful of their chastity as other high-born women. At the same time, because of the example of the Brahmins, the other high-caste people increased their awareness of purity and pollution, and they gradually adopted stronger and stronger measures to insulate themselves from dangerous sacred forces. Thus, after a time, no high-class non-Brahmin would let an untouchable, as the lowest classes became, into his house. This process has been called Sanskritization erroneously, I believe, by Srinivasan and others. It is not an imitation of the Brahmins and an adopting of their values by other members of the society, but rather an attempt on the part of any group that seeks to better its position in society to isolate itself from pollution-causing elements. This tendency was present in Tamilnad even before the arrival of the Brahmins, for those castes who manipulated the sacred were of low status; however, the Brahmins catalyzed this process and made it more universal. It is no accident that in Kerala, where Brahmins had more power than anywhere else in South India, caste differences became more pronounced and intercaste behavior more strongly regulated than anywhere else in India.

The Nature of the Sacred in Ancient Tamilnad

The early Tamils did not believe in karma, the theory of northern origin that all of one's suffering or happiness comes as a result of what was done in previous lives. Their explanation for the seemingly undeserved suffering with which the world abounds was that a wild and capricious power was working its unpredictable will. This power they called aṇaṅku, a word that also means "fear" and "malevolent deity." The most distinguishing quality of aṇaṅku is that it is capricious; in other words, it is characterized by disorder.

It is natural that it should have been associated with events connected with disorder, with the increase of entropy. Most notable of such events from a human viewpoint are death and, to a lesser extent, disease or any other condition different from a normal state. Especially in the case of death, the most extreme case of human disorder, aṇaṅku was felt not only to be involved as a cause, but also to be produced. A locus of irremediable (but, in certain situations, controllable) disorder was thought to touch all around death, like a whirlpool.

It is from this starting point that the negative characteristics of sacred power for the Tamils can be derived. The disorder resulting from death must be controlled by certain people, the low castes, who are also affected by the disorder they help control. Any dead substance which comes from the body, such as menstrual discharge, blood, or hair, carries with it a potential for disorder and chaos and must be carefully controlled.

For woman, the time of greatest departure from her normal state was when she gave birth; moreover, birth was a time of great danger for both mother and child and was, as the opposite of death, naturally a time at which the forces of the sacred were present in a dangerous manner. When a woman gave birth and the forces of disorder hovered about her, ready to take her life or the life of the child, extreme measures had to be taken to isolate her from danger and to isolate others from the danger she represented. A woman gave birth in her parents' house, and her husband was not allowed to see her or the child for some time. Similarly, when a woman was menstruous, a time when she was discharging a dead substance from her body and when she was to an extent in the same condition as when she had just given birth, she was dangerous, she had to be isolated from those around her, and she had to eat from special dishes.

Of all objects in the world, the most dangerous was the widow, a woman identical to a man who had died, and therefore a person in whom all of the forces of chaos lurked. Therefore, she was supposed to undergo rigorous self-mortification, or, even better, take her own life on her husband's pyre, for it was only by her own death that she could really bring under control the power in her if she were young and chaste.

For man, the time of greatest danger and disorder was battle. There had to be present in battle men—the low-caste drummers —who could help keep the chaotic forces under control, and many rituals had to be observed before and during battle: the participants had to bathe beforehand; they had to wear certain flowers; they had to smell burning mustard; and so on.

The key word characterizing the expedients adopted to control aṇañku is order, the creation of an artificial but effective structure around dangerous objects or persons to neutralize the threat that they represent. That is why rites and festivals of ancient and modern South India are so complex: the more complicated and intricate an event is, the more order is present in it. That is also why those low castes whose primary function was to control sacred power were musicians (the Pāṇan̲s), drummers (the Tuṭiyan̲s and Par̲aiyan̲s), or dancers (the Vēlan̲s), for music and dance are highly ordered and can help keep under control the forces of disorder. This fact is shown vividly by those poems about wounded heroes: the first thing that had to be done when a man was wounded was for a bard or drummer to stand next to him and to play. Similarly, a bard was supposed to play the lute and sing in the houses of the high-class people in order to create an auspicious atmosphere, that is to say, an aura of order, there. It seems to me that the complexity of the music of the ancient South Indians can be attributed to the necessity that it be ordered so as to offset the forces of disorder. Thus the music had *paṇs*, the same as modern *rāgas*, each of which fit a certain situation and a certain time of day.

Like all ancient peoples, the ancient Tamils found it important to have regulated contact with the sacred, for through such contact the future could be predicted and exorcisms of the possessed performed. Such contact took place when a priest or other susceptible person went into a trance and danced (and it still does today). It is important that such behavior did and does not take place at random, but rather in carefully controlled situations. Thus the Vēlan̲, when he danced to exorcise the spirit from a woman who was thought to be possessed, did so in a special temple decorated with special flowers and prepared very carefully. Similarly, when there is frenzied dancing, in Kuṟ. 366, it is at a festival. In other words, when contact with the sacred was made, it was under circumstances in which the sacred was carefully controlled, either through rites or simply because the time was auspicious, and there was less danger that it might get out of hand. Today those who practice firewalking or other similar rites of mortification must undergo many weeks of painstaking preparation in which they practice many kinds of asceticism: if they are to be filled with the sacred without its going out of control, they must make themselves into fit receptacles.

The motives of controlling the sacred were not merely to be able to tell the future, or exorcise, or prevent catastrophe. When the sacred was under control, an auspicious state was achieved in which things occurred in an ordered way. Thus if a woman was in an auspicious state—married and chaste—she could protect her husband and keep evil from befalling him. If a king was in an auspicious state, then his kingdom would flourish, and there would be no drought or incursions of enemies. In other words, two conditions were possible for things charged with the sacred: dangerous and auspicious. Some things, such as the low castes, were always dangerous. Others, such as women and the king, might be in either condition. The king had to remain in an auspicious condition if his rule was to be prosperous; he had to maintain that condition through the help of the Pāṇaṉs and others (which is why they, and not he, were low: they controlled his power, while he merely possessed it), through his just rule, and through his heroism. If the king fell from an auspicious state through failing to be just, as in the *Cilappatikāram*, or through being defeated in battle, then his kingdom would suffer, and he personally would be destroyed. It is in this light that the custom of vaṭakkiruttal, or facing north to starve to death, must be viewed. Both of the kings who resorted to this expedient had fallen from their auspicious condition, Peruñcēralātaṉ because he had received a back wound, and Kōpperuñcōḻaṉ because his own sons were raising an army against him. Like the widow who is young and chaste, the best expedient remaining to them was to take their own lives.

An important consequence of the Tamils' conception of the sacred is that the sacred was thought of as a force immanent in certain objects at certain times, not as the property of transcendent gods who could be invoked at special ceremonies and about whom stories could be told. Thus, in Naṟ. 8, the hero tells his beloved, "Put bright shoots of lovely *puṉku* with its dotted flowers on your spotted breasts so that aṇaṅku stays there." The idols worshiped in South Indian temples are considered not mere symbols of a transcendent reality, but actual bodies inhabited by the gods. They are awakened in the morning with music and poetry; their teeth are brushed; they are bathed; and they are treated as if they were actually persons.

Consideration of the immanence of the sacred for the Tamils leads to one final notion of considerable importance: that the sacred had to be held in some object where it could be propitiated and controlled if an auspicious condition were to exist. When a hero died or a woman committed suttee, a stone was erected to house the dead spirit, for in this way it could be contained and kept under restraint. On the other hand, in Ak. 167, a deserted village has a house whose veranda is "not smeared with dung, where sacrifices formerly constant have been forgotten, empty because the lovely god drawn there has departed," while, in Puṟ. 54, in a desolate land, "gods who were worshiped with much noise have forsaken their columns so that there can be no sacrifices there." There appears to be a notion that the presence of sacred forces in an auspicious condition is able to keep away forces that are in a state of disorder. That is why at critical times, drums, which have aṇaṅku in them, and other instruments must be played.

6

THE BARDS AND POETS OF ANCIENT TAMILNAD

The assortment of poets, bards, drummers, dancers, and other performers that existed in ancient Tamilnad is bewildering, to say the least, at first glance. Yet the fact is that a proper understanding of the types of performers and their interrelations is of crucial importance if the ancient Tamil poems are to be understood. Indeed, faulty analysis of this subject has led the authors of two recent and important books to the incorrect conclusion that the ancient Tamil poems were oral.[1] In order to set the record straight, and to elucidate the nature of the poetry itself, the various types of performers are described in some detail below.

The bard called Pāṇaṉ took his name from the word *paṇ*, a generic name for modes of music much like the modern *rāga*. The principal instrument of the Pāṇaṉ was the *yāḻ*, a kind of lute. Unlike the many drums that were played in Tamilnad, it was suitable for establishing a paṇ. Thus, in Puṟ. 152, when the concert leader tells various performers to take up their instru-

[1] K. Kailasapathy in *Tamil Heroic Poetry* (London, 1968), and Kamil Zvelebil, who repeats what Kailasapathy has said, in *The Smile of Murugan: On Tamil Literature of South India* (Leiden, 1973).

ments, he asks one person "to play the paṇ on the yāl̲," while, in Ak. 186, the word yāl̲ is used as a synonym for paṇ.

The music-making activities of the Pāṇan̲s are various. Most commonly Pāṇan̲s are described as they travel from the court of one king to another to make music and receive a gift from the monarch to sustain the wretched existence they and their families led. They would be accompanied by their wives, called Vir̲alis (from *vir̲al*, "victory"), who would dance as they performed.

Pāṇan̲s would be kept in the houses of the rich to impart to the family life of a man and his wife an aura of auspiciousness, and to entertain them by singing songs appropriate to the various times of the day and the various activities of the house. Thus, in Aiñ. 407 and 410, a Pāṇan̲ plays his yāl̲ as the hero and his wife play with their son, while, in Aiñ. 408, many bards are present singing mullai songs (which evoke the fertility of the rainy season) as the couple stays at home. In Ak. 214, the absent hero wonders with trepidation how his beloved will feel as "alone on a rainy evening she hears the clear music, threatening [aṇañku] her life, as grieving yāl̲s play *cevval̲i* [the paṇ of grief], mixing with the music of flutes of cowherds bringing back their cattle." The Pāṇan̲ kept at home is said in many poems to have been sent as a messenger by the hero to his wife when he is away or after he has been with his courtesan (in which case his task is to mollify her anger).

Like the other bards and drummers, the Pāṇan̲s had certain ritual duties. During battle, the Pāṇan̲ would play the taṇṇumai drum (Ak. 106; Nar̲. 310). That drum was also beaten before the battle to assemble the soldiers and tell them to take flowers for the battle (Pur̲. 289), and after the battle when heroes were honored by being presented with flowers (Ak. 106); it seems reasonable to suppose that the Pāṇan̲ played it in those instances also. In Kur̲. 328, Pāṇan̲s are said to be trapped between the two sides of opposing armies. When a king or hero lay wounded, a Pāṇan̲ would stand over him and hold his sword and shield (Pur̲. 285) or perform (Pur̲. 281, 291) in order to keep away dangerous forces. In Pur̲. 332, the spears of warriors are taken around the city in procession before a battle "while the voices of girls mix with the [sound of] yāl̲s."

The yāḻ was thought to be filled with the sacred. In Ak. 115, lutes that used to be worshiped are said to lie broken on the battlefield, while, in Ak. 14, as he plays, a bard worships a god (*kaṭavuḷ vāḻtti*), presumably the god in his lute. In Puṟ. 260, when a bard tries to play his yāḻ after the king has died, the strings leave their usual state and play *viḷari*, a melody of grief and mourning, against his will, showing that sacred forces were thought to reside in his instrument. The connection of the sacred with a stringed instrument has continued until today: while playing the *vīṇā*, the performer must be careful not to let his foot touch the instrument.

Several other tasks that may have been the lot of the Pāṇaṉs deserve mention. Since the taṇṇumai drum was played by Pāṇaṉs in battle, it seems likely that that drum was played by men of the Pāṇaṉ caste in its other uses as well: it was beaten as men cut paddy (Puṟ. 348; Ak. 40; Patiṟ. 90.41); it was struck as a caravan came through the forest surrounding a fort, to inform all of its approach (Kuṟ. 390); in Ak. 63, it is beaten as Kaḷvaṉs (a thieving tribe) bring stolen cows home; and, in Ak. 87, the wilderness is said to resound with the sound of the taṇṇumai rising in the strong fortresses of Maṟavaṉs, who rob wayfarers. It seems a justified inference from the uses of the taṇṇumai that that drum was the largest and loudest of all the drums used by the ancient Tamils. In Puṟ. 15, a Pāṭiṉi (woman singer; according to the old commentary, a Viṟali) sings as the king sits atop his elephant planning an invasion. Pāṇaṉs who could not make their living by performing would catch fish, residing in their own part of the city and exchanging some of the fish for paddy (Puṟ. 348; Ak. 196; Aiṅ. 47, 48, 49, 111). This confirms their low status: bards were allowed the low task of catching fish, but were not allowed to raise paddy.

There existed in ancient Tamilnad entourages of performers called Vayiriyaṉs and Kōṭiyaṉs. Though these performers played the yāḻ in addition to their other instruments (see the beginning of *Porunarāṟṟuppaṭai*; Puṟ. 164), and though their women were called Viṟalis (Ak. 82, 352), they were different from the Pāṇaṉs, for *Maturaikkāñci*, line 750, says, "Let Pāṇaṉs come; let women singers [*pāṭṭiyar*—women Pāṇaṉs, according to Nacciṉārkkiṉiyar] come; let prosperous Pulavaṉs come; let Vayiriyaṉs come."

It seems likely that the Kōṭiyaṉs and Vayiriyaṉs were subcastes of the Pāṇaṉs, for they are the only other groups mentioned who played the yāl and whose women were called Viralis.

The Kōṭiyaṉs received their name from *kōṭu*, a horned instrument, and *iyaṉ* ("player"). Their special instrument was the *tūmpu*, a long horn that resembled the trunk of an elephant (Ak. 111), also called an *uyir* according to Naccinārkkiniyar's commentary on *Malaippaṭukaṭām*, line 6, and the old commentary on Pur. 152. The etymology of Vayiriyaṉ is *vayir*, a kind of large horn, and *iyaṉ*. It is not possible to discern any difference between the Kōṭiyaṉs and Vayiriyaṉs; indeed, the two names are never used in juxtaposition, and it seems possible that vayir is a multiform of uyir, and thus that the two groups are the same.

These performers would dance at festivals (*Maturaikkāñci* 628) and give concerts, going from place to place. A typical concert is described in Pur. 152, where the leader of the group says, "I'll sing a song, Virali. You there beat the *mulavu* drum; you play the paṇ on the yāl; and you play the *uyir*, like a hollow elephant's trunk open at one end. You play the *ellari* and the *ākuḷi*, and beat the *patalai* drum softly on one of its eyes. And give in my hand the black staff." Another concert is described in Ak. 82, where the heroine remembers how she first met her lover:

Many saw him
as he stood with a flowering garland on his breast
to one side of the entrance of the ripe millet field
and asked which way the elephant he was fighting had gone,
carefully choosing an arrow
and holding in his hand his strong well-shaped bow,
he from a land
where the summer westwind makes flute music
in the shining holes bored in swaying bamboo by bees,
where the music of the cool water of sweet-songed falls
is the thick voice of gathered concert drums [mulavu],
where the harsh calling voices of a herd of deer
are the brass tūmpu,
where the bees on the flowering mountainside are the lute
[yāl],
and where,
as a court of monkeys looks on entranced,

loud in their appreciation as they hear the melodic music,
a peacock swaying in dance on that slope thick with bamboo
looks like a Viṟali entering the stage.
Friend,
of all those who saw, why am I the only one who,
staying on my bed in the night with its difficult darkness,
my eyes streaming water,
feels my arms grow thin?

Another class of performers the poems mention are dancing men and women. In Kuṟ. 31, the heroine, who calls herself a dancing woman [*āṭukaḷamakaḷ*], searches in the *tuṇañkai* dance at the festival for her lover, a dancing man. In Puṟ. 393, the poet says that he became as exhausted praising the king "as the loins of a dancing girl." In Naṟ. 95, there is a description of a dancing girl walking on a rope of twisted fiber as the flute is played with other instruments. It seems likely that such dancing women were courtesans, for, in Ak. 76, the *parattai* (courtesan whom the hero visits) says that her lover "has come to our street as we dance ecstatically to the resounding drum [muḻavu]." Similarly, in Ak. 186 the heroine says that her lover is with the courtesan, "taking her cool arms fragrant with sandal as shining-bangled girls sing their old yāḻ [meaning paṇ] and beat the clear muḻavu drum," and, in Ak. 66, the muḻavu is said to resound in the house of the courtesan. In Kuṟ. 363, it appears that the woman who danced the tuṇañkai dance was a courtesan, for the heroine, called "the courtesan kept at home" (*iṟparattai*) by the colophon, says of the hero's other courtesan, "they say [she] . . . talked behind my back. To show that she is wrong [and that he does love me], the [festival] time for the tuṇañkai dance has come [and he will choose me rather than her in that]." The parattai often speaks of "our street" (for example, in Ak. 76), and that street is always different from the street on which the higher class heroine lives. In light of *Paripāṭal* 7.31–32, which speaks of "the dancers' street" (*āṭavar cēri*), it seems likely that the parattai lived with the other dancers in a separate part of the city. It has been seen that music and dancing had religious significance in ancient Tamilnad. It seems natural therefore that dancing girls, who continued to be courtesans, should later come to be associated with temples.

The Pāṇaṉs, the concert-givers, and the dancers all resembled one another in that they sang and performed in the various paṇs, or modes. The concert-givers and dancers (and perhaps the Pāṇaṉs as well) played the muḻavu, a concert drum that was the ancestor of the modern mṛdaṅgam; thus that drum is said to be played by the Vayiriyaṉs (Puṟ. 164; Kuṟ. 78; Ak. 155), by concert-givers (Puṟ. 152; Ak. 82), by players of the yāḻ (Puṟ. 164), by Viṟalis (Puṟ. 103), and by dancers (Ak. 76, 189). There are two references to rich houses "where the muḻavu never sleeps" (Puṟ. 247; Ak. 145), showing that if a man were rich enough, he would keep a man to play the drum as well as a Pāṇaṉ at home.

To a very different category than the Pāṇaṉ, the concert-giver, and the dancer, belonged the man who played the *kiṇai* drum. It is likely that one of the names of the kiṇai drummer was Paṟaiyaṉ, and that the modern Paṟaiyaṉ is his descendent. Thus Puṟ. 388 says that a kiṇai player plays the *paṟai* (a generic term for drum), while, in Puṟ. 371, a suppliant packs up his paṟai, goes to the king, and plays the *taṭāri* (another name for the kiṇai). In Puṟ. 335, the Paṟaiyaṉ clan is distinguished from the Pāṇaṉ and Tuṭiyaṉ clan, while, in the *Puṟapporuḷveṇpāmālai*, a later work, a verse mentions the Kiṇaiyaṉ, Tuṭiyaṉ, and Pāṇaṉ as three different clans; thus it seems natural to identify the Kiṇaiyaṉ and the Paṟaiyaṉ.

Like the Pāṇaṉ, the Kiṇaiyaṉ was supposed to drum during battle (Puṟ. 79), a task whose importance is suggested by Patiṟ. 75.9, where "those whose job it is to beat the difficult paṟai" are said to be the cause of the enemy's defeat. In Puṟ. 78, the kiṇai is beaten as enemy kings are executed, a reference suggesting that perhaps, like the Paṟaiyaṉs of today, the kiṇai players were supposed to play at funerals to keep dangerous forces under control.

The most commonly mentioned office of the kiṇai player is to come to the king's door as a suppliant in the morning and to receive gifts (Puṟ. 369–400). Puṟ. 399 is a noteworthy example of this theme; in it, the drummer speaks: "My food [was] tamarind curry cooked by the drummer woman [Kiṇaimakaḷ] after selling fish caught on a hook with a long bamboo pole and eaten at the wrong time; I was shrinking to one side [from shame]. [People] said, 'What is this? He who is just to the just . . . has love [for you].

Eat the nectar [food] you crave!' I considered what I should do next; then I went, cleaned my strong black stick [poet's stick or drumstick?], tied up [with new strings] my clear-eyed black kiṇai, which was lying with its strings useless, played its new tightly fitting cover so that its measured garland [?—*alakin̲ mālai*] resounded sharply, and, thinking, 'Food, hard to get, is at hand,' I did not worship the god [kaṭavuḷ; the god in the drum is meant] who keeps food away. Before I had asked for one thing . . . he gave many herds [of cattle] whose shapes resembled stars flowering in the sky." The explanation of the drummer's failure to worship the god in the drum is that he considers the king more efficacious than the divinity who has for so long allowed him to go hungry.

In Pur̲. 225, the par̲ai drum is said to be beaten in the morning as conchs sound at the doorways of kings. From this it appears that it was the ritual duty of the kiṇai player to go to the palace and wake the king with his drumming. That may be why, in Pur̲. 379, the Kiṇaiyan̲'s livelihood is said to be "to come in the morning." Elsewhere, the drum played for the king in the morning is the muracu (Pur̲. 61, 397; Aiñ. 448). While there is nowhere any indication of who played the muracu, it is not unlikely that a subcaste of the Par̲aiyan̲s had that office, especially as one of the modern subdivisions of that caste is called Muracu.[2] The task of awakening the king was one fraught with sacred importance, for it involved bringing the most important representative of the sacred back from symbolic death into this world. Even today, the gods in temples have to be awakened by the proper songs, sung in the proper manner, while most people in South India try to look at something auspicious when they first awake in the morning.

In Ak. 249, the kiṇai drum is said to be played by a group called Akavunan̲s. There is no way of determining just what the relationship of the Akavunan̲ was to the kiṇai player described above, but the fact that both play the same drum indicates that they were closely related indeed. The root *akavu* means to call; it is generally applied to birds, and, as has been seen, these were considered ominous. In what is evidently an extension of the

[2] Edgar T. Thurston, *Castes and Tribes of Southern India* (Madras, 1909), VI:80.

meaning of the root akavu, *akaval* means a prophetic utterance, Akavunan̠ a man of the Akavunan̠ clan who tells the future, and Akavan̠makaḷ a woman of that clan. It is extremely significant that the name of the meter used for all of the early anthologies is akaval, for that shows that the meter was first used for oracular purposes, probably by the Akavunan̠s.

When they prophesied or sang, Akavunan̠s would hold in their hands a small staff of bamboo, called in the old commentaries on Pur̠. 152 and Patir̠. 43.27 the *pir̠appuṇarttuñkōl*, or the staff that gives knowledge of the future.[3] The care with which such staffs were selected is described in Ak. 97, where the poet tells of a king "whose love protects Akavunan̠s with their women whose limbs are curved, who hold small sticks with tiny joints carefully taken and cut in a little forest of bamboo." Like the Akavunan̠, the Akavan̠makaḷ would also hold a small staff (Kur̠. 298). One of the duties of the Akavunan̠ was to hold his stick in hand and praise the field of fighting after a battle was over, perhaps to bring it back to a normal condition, just as the kiṇai player brings the king back to his normal waking condition in the morning (Patir̠. 43.28).

In Kur̠. 23, the heroine's friend addresses the Akavan̠makaḷ who has been hired by the mother to determine what is the matter with the lovesick heroine. In form, this verse appears to imitate the utterance of the Akavan̠makaḷ:

> Singer of rhymes [*Akavan̠makaḷē*],
> singer of rhymes,
> your long hair as white as strings of shells,
> sing a song,
> just sing a song—
> sing of his tall hill.

[3] *Pir̠appu* means literally "birth"; here it takes the secondary meaning "future" or, perhaps, "character of things." Kailasapathy is almost certainly wrong when, on p. 111 of *Tamil Heroic Poetry*, he translates *pir̠appuṇarttuñkōl* as "the rod [that] makes known the circumstances of birth [that is, caste]." In Pur̠. 152, the leader of a group of concert players says, "Give in my hand the black staff." In spite of U. V. Swaminathaier's identification of this man as an Akavunan̠, in his commentary on the poem, I do not believe that he belonged to that caste. It is true that in some manuscripts the old commentary identifies the staff here with the fortune-telling rod of the Akavunan̠; however in other manuscripts, that passage, which Swaminathaier relies upon for his identification, is missing. It is therefore almost certainly an interpolation.

Here the friend asks the Akavaṉmakaḷ to sing of the true cause of the heroine's distress, that is, of the man she has fallen in love with, and not of the god who everyone thinks has possessed her. It may be remarked parenthetically that even today there is a low caste called Kuṟavaṉs one of whose duties is to tell the future with a staff in hand.

The final important group of low-caste people whose office included some kind of music-making was the Tuṭiyaṉs. These men would beat their drum, called a tuṭi, before and during battle (Puṟ. 260, 287); indeed, so important was this function that, in Puṟ. 260, the tuṭi is said to be the raft in which a chieftain crosses the flood of arrows in battle to get back his stolen cattle. The Tuṭiyaṉ was low-born (Puṟ. 287); in Puṟ. 170, enemies are warned to be careful when they approach Pittaṉ, lord of a village "where people who use their bows for plows [that is, to make a living], unlearned in outlook, wander the whole day, and a tuṭi beaten by a low-born one, his strong hand growing red, resounds with the owl." Like other music-makers, the Tuṭiyaṉ was often a suppliant (Puṟ. 269, 280). In most places where the tuṭi is mentioned, it is associated with rude and dangerous men who live in the wilderness. In Ak. 159, men steal cattle and dance to the time of the tuṭi; in Ak. 79, hunters (Eyiṉaṉs) go in the wilderness to plunder "with curved bows and loud tuṭis whose lovely mouths resound with every dance" (see also Ak. 261); and, in Ak. 89, Maṟavaṉs attack a caravan as the tuṭi is played. Elsewhere, the tuṭi is associated with cattle raiding (Puṟ. 260, 269). Perhaps this association of the drum with thieves and cattle robbers in wild places accounts for the ominous connotations the drum has. In Ak. 19, owls hoot in the wilderness "so that one can tell their meaning, like tuṭi drums (on which sticks are rolled)." The Tuṭiyaṉ stands as guard over heroes wounded in battle, in Puṟ. 285 and Puṟ. 291, and, in Ak. 35, he is said to play his drum when the memorial stone is worshiped.

This concludes the enumeration of low-caste performers. It is possible, I believe, to discern three general groups: the Pāṇaṉs, which includes the Kōṭiyaṉs and Vayiriyaṉs as well as the dancing men and women; the kiṇai players, which includes the Akavunaṉs; and the Tuṭiyaṉs. The first two of these groups are well differentiated by function. The Pāṇaṉ group consisted of individuals who played the yā<u>l</u> or other concert instruments, such as the mu<u>l</u>avu drum, and whose performances were characterized by music in one of the modes called paṇs. The second group, the kiṇai players, are never said to play any instrument except drums, which they would accompany by singing. Their music appears to have been less sophisticated than that of the Pāṇa<u>n</u> group, and they are never said to entertain the rich with their performances (although they would go to kings, sing their exploits, and receive recompense). The tuṭi players resemble the second group: they also never play any instrument except their own drum, the tuṭi (for they are never said to play any of the drums that the kiṇai player would beat). They appear to be even less sophisticated than the kiṇai drummers, for their drum is mentioned for the most part in wild surroundings among dangerous and unlearned men.

We now turn to a very different group of performers, the Pulava<u>n</u>s, or poets, who wrote the poems in the anthologies. Probably during the reign of the Mauryas in the second or third century B.C., the Brāhmī syllabary was introduced into Tamilnad. In all likelihood, this was the first alphabet the Tamils used, though it is conceivable that they wrote previously in the Indus-Valley script.[4] In any case, it seems certain that, just as the Phoenician-derived Greek script was easier to use than Linear B, the Brāhmī writing system was far more efficient than what existed before it. The result was similar to what happened in Greece: a few centuries after a practical writing system was introduced, there sprang up a lyric poetry, which, perhaps because of its freshness, because of the fact that its authors felt that they were the first to write down poems in a permanent form, is quite excellent. The men who

[4] B. B. Lal has shown in an article entitled "From the Megalithic to the Harappan: Tracing Back the Graffiti in the Pottery," *Ancient India* no. 6. 1960 (New Delhi, 1962), pp. 1–24, that 90 percent of the graffiti on the red-and-black ware of the megalithic people in South India are identical to various signs used in the Harappan writing. Two groups have recently found that the Harappan writings is proto-Dravidian, and, while their conjectured meanings for many of the signs are dubious, their findings concerning the structure of the language, which fits only Dravidian, are compelling. See Asko Parpola, Seppo Koskenniemi, Simo Parpola, and Pentti Aalto, *Decipherment of the Proto-Dravidian Inscriptions of the Indus Civilization* (Copenhagen, 1969). For a fuller explanation of the structure of the language, see Y. Knorozov, *Predvaritel'nye Soobshcheniya ob Issledovanii Protoindiǐskikh Tekstov* (Moscow, 1965).

wrote this poetry were called Pulavaṉs; it is their poems that were collected to form the anthologies that are the principal subject of this book.

Like all writers, the authors of this poetry modeled their compositions on forms with which they were familiar. The only models they had were the oral poems being composed by low-caste performers all around them. As a result, they took most of their poetic themes from the Pāṇaṉs and others, and even copied their life-style to an extent—though it must be kept in mind that the Pulavaṉs were of high caste, while the oral bards were low. Specifically, one of the most important functions of the oral poets was to enhance the sacred aura of the kings by their songs of praise. If such a result could be accomplished by illiterate men of low caste, then it could also be accomplished by literate poets of higher status, especially as the new poems were written down, thus preserving the fame of the king for all time. Even though the Pulavaṉs did not belong to the low castes, and did not have the ritual status to play the instruments of those castes, they did compose songs modeled on those of the oral bards. Thus there are found in the anthologies many poems whose purpose is to enhance the king's fame and prestige.

Two points need to be made here. First, the poets took their conventions and subject matter almost entirely from the oral bards; and, secondly, they copied the bards' life-style, at least to the extent of going from one court to another until they found a king who would support them in return for their poems. The first point is well exemplified by Puṟam 60, by Uṟaiyūr Maruttuvaṉ Tāmōtaraṉār, who was a physician (*maruttuvaṉ*) and a devotee of Vishnu (Tāmōtaraṉār, from Sanskrit Dāmodara), both of which facts indicate that he belonged to a high caste. The poem is placed in the mouth of a Pāṇaṉ, as is shown by the reference to a Viṟali, or female Pāṇaṉ, here the speaker's wife:

In the vault of the sky where the red planet twinkled
like a lamp on a ship amidst the sea,
we saw the full moon standing at the zenith.
Then I and my Viṟali, her bangles few,
standing like a forest peacock in that wilderness
worshiped it at once, again and again,
as we considered how it resembled the umbrella

white, fearful, and garlanded
as it shields from the heat of the sun,
which belongs to Vaḷavaṉ whose sword does not err
and whose royal drum [muracu] roars in victory,
our king who is like a mighty ox
pulling out of holes an axled wagon full of salt
from pans by the sea
and taking it to mountainous lands.

There are many other poems placed by Pulavaṉs in the mouths of bards or drummers. In Puṟ. 390 and 392, for example, the poetess Auvaiyār has a drummer narrate how he came to the king's palace in the morning, played his kiṇai, was invited inside by the king, and was given many gifts; similarly, in Puṟ. 373, 382, and 400, Kōvūrkiḻār, whose name indicates that he was a Vēḷāḷaṉ (because of the ending -kiḻār), puts the poem in the mouth of a kiṇai drummer.[5] The high status of Pulavaṉs, which is in marked contrast to the status of the Pāṇaṉs and other performers, is indicated by the fact that, from their names, at least one-tenth of them appear to have been Brahmins (a figure that is probably low, since not all Brahmins could have had telltale names).[6]

One of the most common conventions that was obviously borrowed from the oral poetry of the bards and others concerns one bard, decked out with new clothes, ornaments, elephants, chariots, or other good things, who meets an indigent bard on the road and tells him to go to the king if he also would be rich (Puṟ. 48, 68, 69, 70, 103, 105, 133, 141, 155, 180, 181, 353, 379). A good example is Puṟ. 141:

O suppliant who suffers from cruel hunger,
whose family is blackened by the sun,

[5] Zvelebil is certainly wrong when he calls Auvaiyār a Viṟali, on p. 14 of *The Smile of Murugan*. Thus, in *Puṟanāṉūṟu*, comm. U. V. Swaminathaier (Madras, 1963), p. xxxii, Swaminathaier writes: "Many poems appear in this book and other books which she [Auvaiyār] sings not through her own mouth but through the mouth of someone else, such as a Viṟali. [Some] scholars have hastily concluded that she is a Viṟali or some other such person, but this is incorrect. Her singing in that way [as if she were a Viṟali] is poetic license. This license is observed in the songs of other Pulavaṉs as well." See Kōvintaṉ, *Cañkat Tamiḻp Pulavar Varicai* (Madras, 1961), II:9ff.

[6] K. K. Pillay, "Aryan Influences in Tamilaham during the Sangam Epoch," *Tamil Culture* 12, nos. 2 and 3 (1966): 159–170.

you do not stop asking,
"Who are you who stop in the wasteland as if it were your home town,
unhitching from your high chariot the swift horses
as your Virali shines with her garland and fine ornaments
and a lotus of fresh gold put on her by her Pāṇaṉ?"
We were worse off than you
before we saw the lord with a white spear.

It is obvious that these poems were copied from the oral poets.

Like the bards, the Pulavaṉs went from court to court, hoping to find a king who would support them for a time. A few found permanent patrons. Puṟ. 47 describes well the life-style of the Pulavaṉs. It is supposed to have been addressed by the poet Kōvūrkiḻār to the king Kāriyāṟṟut Tuñciya Neṭuṅkiḷḷi, who was about to execute the poet Iḷantattaṉ as a spy. It shows that poetry writing in Tamilnad had become a sophisticated art, replete with contests in writing verse:

The life of suppliants such as us
consists of discovering benefactors,
going like birds across many wastelands
thinking nothing of the long distances,
singing as well as we can with tongues that form words imperfectly,
rejoicing at what we receive,
feeding our families,
eating without saving anything,
giving without holding back,
and suffering for the king's good favor.
Never do our lives bring harm to others,
unless you count rejoicing,
walking with heads held high,
when [poet] enemies are put to shame in each category.
Indeed, our suppliants' life
is as fine as the existence you lead
with your wealth from ruling the earth and your lofty fame.

Pulavaṉs, being of high caste, and being in close contact with kings, naturally became the advisers of kings. Indeed, they came to be considered sages and became the moral custodians of society. There are many poems in which Pulavaṉs take it upon themselves to criticize the actions of kings, seemingly with impunity. An example is Pur̲am 47, just given, or Pur̲. 96, in which Auvaiyār describes the son of her patron, Atiyamān̲ Neṭumān̲ Añci:

Two foes have arisen for the son of my lord
who has thick long arms
and a handsome breast garlanded with flowering *tumpai.*
One is his passion for girls who look at him,
their blackened flower-like eyes pale,
their arms thin.
The other is that cities he visits do not wish him to stay,
thinking, "Even though there is no festival
he will not be moderate in eating
with his retinue, which feasts on mutton;
and his elephants will drink and spoil
the water in our reservoirs."

In some instances, kings themselves became Pulavan̲s and perpetuated their own fame. A good example is Pur̲. 71, in which Ollaiyūrtanta Pūtappāṇṭiyan̲ says,

Kings angry like lions,
their hearts unrelenting
their armies unrestrained
have made alliance
and say they will fight with me.
If I do not see their backs as they flee with their chariots,
attacking them so they cry out in the hard-to-bear tumult,
then may I be separated from her
whose blackened eyes are large and lovely set on her face.
And in my court where love established with justice is never forsaken,
may I give authority to someone unfit
and make my scepter bent by straying from the right.
And may I lose the happy laughter that comes from being with my friends
who are as close to me as my eyes:
Māvan̲, chief of Maiyal,
a place surrounded by the famed Vaiyai
and known even in flourishing towns for its unfailing prosperity;
Āntai of ancient Eyil;

renowned Antuvañcāttaṉ;
Ātaṉaḻici;
and violent Iyakkaṉ.
And, no longer king of the southern land,
distinguished for its ancient dynasty, which has protected humanity,
may I be born again
to watch over the dry lands of others.

It is possible, of course, that many such poems were composed by nonroyal Pulavaṉs and attributed to kings.

In his recent book, *Heroic Tamil Poetry*, Kailasapathy attempts to establish that the puṟam poems in the Tamil anthologies are oral poetry and that they conform to the requirements laid down by Parry and Lord for such poetry. He shows correctly that the poems possess both themes and formulas; that is, that they have thematic matter that occurs again and again with similar treatment, and that they have certain phrases or word groups that appear again and again, like Homer's "swift-footed Achilles." The purpose of such repeated themes and formulas is to enable an oral poet to extemporize in meter: clearly, if he has a stock of phrases at hand that fit neatly into the meter in which he is composing, and a stock of themes that he can use over and over in different compositions, he can extemporize more readily than if he must build up each composition word by word and incident by incident. Kailasapathy has shown that, without question, ancient Tamil poetry is full of both themes and formulas. He concludes, "The application to early Tamil literature of the details of oral techniques postulated for Homer and many other oral bards by the Chadwicks, Parry, Thomson, Bowra, Lord, and others justifies the method [of analysis of the poems undertaken earlier in the book] and warrants the conclusion that it, too, belongs to the same category of literature. All indications examined in this study bear out the conclusion beyond reasonable doubt."[7] Zvelebil in his recent book *The Smile of Murugan* repeats Kailasapathy's conclusions without questioning them.

Unfortunately, Kailasapathy has neglected two criteria that literature must meet to come under Parry's and Lord's category

[7] Kailasapathy, *Tamil Heroic Poetry*, p. 288.

of oral poetry. First, the poetry Lord and Parry have described is epic poetry. It narrates a story, usually with many subplots, at length. Such poetry in fact exists in South India today and, no doubt, existed two thousand years ago, but it is not the type of poetry represented by the anthologies.[8] Rather, the anthologies consist of short poems, never more than a few hundred lines in length, and usually shorter than twenty lines. The *Kuṟuntokai* has poems shorter than nine lines, while the *Aiṅkuṟunūṟu* consists of poems of five or fewer lines. Such poetry cannot be classified as epic literature by any stretch of the imagination; it could not have been composed under the same conditions as the compositions Lord describes, which were extemporized by poets who continued narrating one story for many hours (or, in some cases, for days at a time).

The second criterion Kailasapathy has neglected is the complexity of the poems. Lord shows that in an oral text, the great majority of sentences either conclude at the end of the line or are written in such a way that the thought is complete at the end of the line but can be added to within the same sentence. An example of this adding style, which Lord terms *nonperiodic enjambement*, would be "And then Achilles came / And Patroclus and Agamemnon." Lord writes, "nonperiodic enjambement, the 'adding' style, is characteristic of oral composition; whereas periodic enjambement is characteristic of 'literary' style. Obviously, then, the oral text will yield a predominance of nonperiodic enjambement, and a 'literary' text a predominance of periodic."[9] This is so because the illiterate singer must improvise quickly line by line before an audience and cannot handle a complicated sentence that continues over many lines, unless that sentence is constructed by the "adding" style described above. While some written material may contain little periodic enjambement, as Lord points out,[10] it is quite impossible for material that can be termed oral epic poetry to contain a predominance of periodic enjambement.

[8] Many Tamil works that are true oral epics have been published by the R. G. Pathi Company, Madras; for example, *Kāttavarāya Cuvāmi Katai* (1972).

[9] Albert B. Lord, *The Singer of Tales* (Cambridge, Mass., 1964), p. 131.

[10] Ibid.

The fact is that the majority of the Tamil poems is full of periodic enjambement of the most complex sort. It is not unusual for one sentence to run on for twenty or thirty lines in the longer poems and to be so complicated that it takes a detailed commentary for even a reader skilled in the language to determine the exact sense and the precise grammatical function of each clause without painstaking analysis, as a glance at almost any poem in the *Patiṟṟuppattu* will disclose. Furthermore, it is not only the sentence structure that is complex in the Tamil poems; their symbolism and use of suggestion are often extraordinarily complex, as will be seen below when several poems are analysed in the beginning of chapter 7. It is simply not possible for illiterate bards to extemporize poetry as dense as the Tamil poems.

This is not to say that the poems were not uttered before being committed to writing. It is quite possible that at the poetry contests mentioned in Puṟ. 47 above, the poets spent some time mentally composing their poems and then recited them for the audience, and that they were committed to writing only afterward. Indeed, in view of their brevity, it is likely that many of the poems were composed in this way. But this does not make the poetry oral in the sense in which Lord uses the term. It is known that Shakespeare himself composed large parts of his plays in his head before he wrote them down; yet no one would call Shakespeare's creations oral literature. Similarly, Milton dictated much of his poetry after he had gone blind, yet his works are as "literary" as any in the English language.

At this point, the dichotomy of "oral" and "literary" becomes misleading, for Lord has used the word "oral" in a very special manner to describe only the compositions of illiterate bards who extemporize long epic stories in meter. He does not use it to describe other oral literature, such as the *Ṛg Veda*, for which Ṛṣis took a long time to compose each verse. In order to avoid confusion, it is best here to introduce new terminology: let us call the literature that Lord has described, which is characterized by fast extemporization and by many formulas and themes, *simple*. Such literature is almost always composed by illiterate people, but there are some exceptions. For example, there are even today perfectly literate pundits in India who can extemporize material that is virtually impossible to distinguish from simple material by illiterate bards such as the parts of the *Mahābhārata* that tell the story of the Kauravas and Pāṇḍavas.[11] Thus it is necessary to distinguish between unlettered simple material, which Lord has described, and lettered simple material, which is virtually indistinguishable from the material of illiterate epic bards but is composed by literate men.

Let us call *complex* any work that the author has an opportunity to polish and rewrite (either in his mind or on paper) over and over. Most of these works can be characterized as lettered—that is, as the products of literate men. Some, however, such as the *Ṛg-Vedic* hymns, are unlettered; that is, they are by illiterate authors. Most literature falls into the category of either "unlettered and simple," which Lord has described as "oral" literature, or "lettered and complex," which Lord calls "literary." However there exists without question "lettered and simple" literature (such as many of the later Sanskrit Purāṇas) and "unlettered and complex" literature (such as the *Ṛg Veda*).

In the early stages of most literatures, and occasionally even in the later stages, much lettered material is copied from unlettered material. Most commonly, the unlettered models that are used are "simple"; and because such models are replete with formulas and themes, the lettered compositions modeled on them also have formulas and themes, though to a lesser extent. But, because the lettered poet has much more time at his disposal to mold each line, his composition is complex; that is, its language is more difficult and it contains much periodic enjambement. A comparison of Vergil, who spent as much as a day on each line, and Homer, who was a true oral bard (that is, whose compositions are unlettered and simple) makes this clear: Vergil uses both formulas and themes, like his model, Homer; but his sentences are invariably longer and more complex. The same is true of the great Sanskrit poet Kālidāsa, who imitated the simple style of the Sanskrit epics. His works are full of epic formulas and epic themes, but the diction of his works is far more complex and difficult than that of the epics.

It has been seen that the ancient Tamil poems are characterized by formulas and themes. Why not explain this fact by saying

[11] Thus every Sanskrit epic has many interpolations that must have been inserted by literate persons but are uniform in style with the older portions of the text.

that they are lettered imitations of unlettered simple verse, like most of Kālidāsa's poems? Unfortunately, this solution is ruled out by one of the important considerations given above: the subject matter of the Tamil poems is not epic story, but short, dense poems. They could not be imitations of unlettered epic stories, for their subject matter has nothing in common with such stories.

Rather than being copied from the compositions of epic singers, the Tamil poems must have been modeled on the songs of the Pāṇaṉs, at least for the most part. This is suggested by the fact that each of the five akam categories is associated with a paṇ, or musical mode, from which word the Pāṇaṉs take their name, and which characterized their songs (but, it would appear, not the songs of the drummers). Judging from the akam anthologies, the compositions of the Pāṇaṉs must have been short pieces that were created in a laborious manner and memorized; in other words, they were unlettered but complex. Such compositions would be suitable for being sung to the complicated musical patterns called paṇs; one surmises that the Pāṇaṉ did not utter his composition as a recitative (in which case a four-line composition would last a short time indeed), but rather that he repeated each line many times.

The question remains why the poems should be characterized by themes and formulas if in fact they are copied from the compositions of the Pāṇaṉs, which were unlettered but complex. Unfortunately, such works have not been much studied. One important example of such literature is the *Ṛg Veda*; if the reader works through several hymns of that work in the original, he will discover that it contains many themes and formulas. Similarly, it seems likely that the songs of the Pāṇaṉs contained both of these elements. The reason that such literature contains themes is simply that it is highly conventional, as a glance at the akam poems or the *Ṛg Veda* will disclose. As far as formulas are concerned, it is natural that poets composing in meter in a society where true epic poetry is flourishing (as it must have been in Vedic India and ancient Tamilnad) should use many formulas. I believe that a study of the *Ṛg Veda* would indicate that it contains far fewer formulas than true simple works, like the dramatic parts of the *Mahābhārata*. Certainly, Kailasapathy's analysis of the puṟam poems shows that, while they do contain many formulas, they have far fewer than a true simple work in a Dravidian language has, such as the first portion of the Telugu *Palnāṭivīracaritramu*, of which virtually every line and every phrase is repeated many times.[12]

While the poetry of the Pāṇaṉs could not accurately be described as simple, it seems likely to me that the compositions of the kiṇai players and the tuṭi players were of the same nature as the unlettered and simple literature described by Lord. The songs of those players were recited to the drum beat, which makes it unlikely that they were sung with many repetitions. It is noteworthy that, in *Paripāṭal* 8.27-28, the tuṭi sounds to tell people that water covers the young paddy and harvested sheaves in the field, for this suggests that in ancient times the drummers had the same function as in later times—of spreading news through the countryside.[13] It does not take much imagination to see that such news must have been extemporized by the drummer in meter, that is, that it fits the requirements of unlettered simple literature. It is significant that those poems at the end of the *Puṟanāṉūṟu* that are put into the mouths of kiṇai players are quite long, and that the structure of almost every poem in the series Puṟ. 369–400 is virtually identical (in other words, that these poems are more thematic than most of the poems), for these facts suggest that, in these poems, the Pulavaṉs were trying to copy the long, extemporized poetry of the drummers. Of course, the Pulavaṉs were restricted regarding length and could not make their poems nearly as long as the songs of the drummers must have been.

To sum up, then, the poems of the Tamil anthologies were composed by poets called Pulavaṉs, who were men and women of high status. The poems were modeled on the compositions of illiterate and low-class performers, of whom there were many sorts in ancient Tamilnad; but chiefly they were modeled on the compositions of the Pāṇaṉs, who would sing in modes called paṇs to the accompaniment of the yāḻ and sometimes other instru-

[12] For this information I am indebted to Gene Roghair, a student of Velcheru Narayanarao's and mine, whose thesis will concern this fascinating work.

[13] In the *Kamparāmāyaṇam* (in 1.30), the paṟai is beaten to warn of an impending flood.

ments. Some of their poems, but not many, were modeled on the songs of the drummers, the kiṇai players and the tuṭi players, who would recite as they played the drum. The Pulavaṉs were of recent origin, arising only after the introduction of the Brāhmī syllabary in Tamilnad about the second century B.C.; however the bards whose works they copied must have been far more ancient. Thus all over South India, even today music-making is associated with the low castes. The Paṟaiyaṉ is found in Tamilnad, Kerala, and the Kota-speaking areas,[14] while the Pāṇaṉ is found in modern Kerala and Orissa, and in parts of ancient North India, where Pāṇa meant a low-class bard.[15] Because the institution of the Pāṇaṉ is so ancient, and because he is of low class, it seems almost impossible that the musical system of ancient South India, which was based on modes called paṇs (from which the Pāṇaṉ took his name), could have been borrowed from the North. Rather, it seems likely that later Indian music, with its rāgas (which are only more elaborate paṇs), has its origin in the music of ancient South India. It will be seen in the next section of this book that much of the impetus that produced Sanskrit classical poetry came the literature of the Deccan megalithic culture, which was the product of Pāṇaṉs and other illiterate bards and which spread into Maharashtrian Prakrit in about the first century A.D. It seems to me that the musical system must have spread into North India at about this same time, or perhaps a bit earlier, though of course nothing can be said with certainty without extensive research of the sort that has never been undertaken. If so, then an extensive portion of India's music and poetry has its origin in the art of the bards, who were one of the lowest of the South Indian castes, a curious and rather gratifying fact.

[14] D.E.D. 3319.

[15] D.E.D. 3351.

Part II

ANCIENT TAMIL POETRY AND INDO-ARYAN PARALLELS

7

THE TECHNIQUE OF SUGGESTION IN TAMIL AND INDO-ARYAN

SUGGESTION IN ANCIENT TAMIL

The old Tamil poems use a complex technique of suggestion to achieve their effect, and, while much in the poems is accessible to a newcomer to them, each poem inevitably contains some suggestion that can be apprehended only by someone who has studied the poems at some length. I have therefore analyzed several of the poems here so that the reader can form an accurate idea of the technique of suggestion they use.

> Holding the pillar of my small house,
> you ask, "Where is your son?"
> Wherever my son is, I do not know.
> This womb, which has given birth to him,
> is like a rock cave
> that a tiger has inhabited and left.
> Somewhere on the battlefield you will find him. (Puṟ. 86.)

The contrast that animates the poem is between the house, whose artificial nature is emphasized by mention of the pillar that supports it, and the natural cave of rock. The poet seems to be contrasting the appearance, which is that the son comes from a domestic environment where everything is constructed for human convenience, with the reality, which is that the son is not at all effeminate or domesticated, that he is actually like the tiger that lives in a natural cave. Another idea suggested by the contrast is that the house, with its support, can be easily destroyed by nature, unlike the rock cave. Ultimately the contrast is between the two modalities of the sacred: woman and domestic life, and the king and battle. The poet also means the son to be likened to the pillar of the house. The mother and the rest of the family are dependent on him in spite of his nature, which, like that of the tiger, is to be unattached.

When she learned her son had died killing an elephant,
the joy of the old woman,
her hair pure grey like the feathers of a fish-eating heron,
was greater than the day she bore him.
Her tears were more
than the drops that quiver on strong bamboo
on mount Vetiram
after a rain. (Pur̲. 277.)

The comparison of the old woman's hair to the feathers of a heron emphasizes her toughness, for the heron is a predatory, merciless creature. It also indicates that in spite of her age she still retains sexual vigor, as the heron searching for and eating fish is often used in the poems as a symbol of sexual activity. In other words, her power as a woman has not yet been sapped by old age. For the Tamils, the greatest fulfillment for a woman was to have a son; her greatest time of fulfillment was when she gave birth to a son. But in this poem, the discovery of the mother that her son has died heroically in battle is a source of greater fulfillment than giving birth to him, because she discovers that the life she brought into the world has attained the most excellent kind of fulfillment. Much of the poem's power is derived from the woman's unnatural joy at what she considers to be her son's good fortune. This idea is developed by the final image, in which her tears are compared to drops that have fallen from the sky and quiver on bamboo in the wind before dropping to earth. This image suggests the state of the mother. Her life is spent in anticipation of her son's fulfillment, just as the drops on the tree quiver in anticipation of their fall to earth, where they will attain the fulfillment of supporting the life that grows there. When her son dies, she has reached her fulfillment. As I see it, the image can be taken even further. The descent of rain to the earth is homologized to sexual union in almost all cultures. Here, the falling of the rain is like the union that led to the son's conception. The period when the drops are suspended is like his life, which passes in anticipation of his final fulfillment. Finally, the falling of the drops is like his dying on the battlefield, an act that is necessary for the future prosperity of his people, just as the mixing of the drops with the earth is necessary for the flourishing of the plants that grow on the mountain. Mountains were the abode of ineffable and mysterious sacred forces for the Tamils. The poet seems to suggest that the son's death on the battlefield, a locus of the sacred, is not simply an ordinary death, but one in which sacred forces are involved. The wind, which causes the drops to fall, may perhaps be likened to the mysterious power whose unleashing occasioned the death of the son. The reader should note that in this poem, and in most of the other poems, suggestion is not tied down; there is no one correct solution. Rather, each image raises many suggestions. There is more in each poem than my analysis suggests.

O man of fields,
is your woman so lovely
that you can desert this girl,
leaving to languish her beauty,
which resembles Tēṉūr city,
its fields beautiful with lilies,
its many-rayed sacrificial fires
like the sun making the day? (Aiṅ. 57.)

Here the friend addresses the heroine's husband, who has deserted his wife for a courtesan. She suggests the excellence of the woman whom he has abandoned. In general, the comparison of a woman to a field is made to suggest that the woman is a sexual object; the act of union is compared to the sowing of the field with seed. Here, the friend suggests that the heroine is sexually attractive, just as the field is attractive with its lilies. She is, moreover, the proper place for him to put his seed, which will flourish and produce offspring just as the seed in the fields of Tēṉūr will produce excellent crops. But Tēṉūr is also a sacred place, filled with the fires of Brahmins. This suggests that the wife is a source of sacred experience and of prosperity and happiness, like the fires of the Brahmins, which help to keep the world in an auspicious and prosperous state. Indeed, the fires, and by implication the wife, are as indispensable for the proper order of the world as is the sun itself. Without them, life becomes disordered, with no day or night and no ordered activity. Thus the friend suggests the dissipation of the hero.

O man in whose bay girls dry their hair
streaming with water
and resemble a flock of herons,
they said,
"A chariot comes often to this bay
spraying the dark waterlilies
by the seething backwater."
And mother said,
"Do not go out." (Aiñ. 186.)

Before girls can dry their hair, they must bathe in the bay. Naturally, when a girl is bathing it is an ideal time for her to meet her lover. Here the friend, who means to invite the hero to meet the heroine as she bathes, makes her meaning quite clear by comparing the girls drying the hair to a flock of herons, birds whose searching for fish is conventionally likened to sexual union. In the second half of the poem, the invitation is made even more obvious, and the feelings of the heroine are suggested. A man has been coming along the shore spraying the waterlilies with the water splashed by the wheels of his chariot, a sexual image. The hero should come in his chariot to make love to the heroine, for she is so much in love that her mother has noticed and denied her permission to go out. The first image of the poem may also be interpreted as a warning: girls habitually bathe in the bay, and they are as vicious and uncaring as herons. Thus it is necessary to be extremely carefully in meeting the heroine lest some of the women notice and begin to gossip.

Embracing the green *taḷavu* creeper,
jasmine, yearning for the rains
and nurturing its straight buds like moonlight,
will find fulfillment.
My black loveliness abides
yearning for his chariot. (Aiñ. 454.)

The hero has promised to return by the time of the monsoon rains. The poem suggests the state of mind of the heroine as she awaits the start of the rainy season. When she sees two creepers together, she is reminded of lovemaking. She imagines that the jasmine is preparing for the rains, ready to open its buds when the monsoon begins, just as she is prepared to give herself to her lover then. The buds are like the light of the waxing moon, just as her readiness for her lover becomes more and more heightened until he returns and can make love to her under the light of the moon. The fulfillment of jasmine comes when it flowers, to be fertilized and go to seed; the fulfillment of the wife comes when she is impregnated and conceives. The poem contains a threat: if the rains do not come, the jasmine will wither and die without ever flowering, just as the heroine will wither if her lover does not return. The use of color in the poem is interesting: the whiteness of the jasmine is likened to the dark color of the heroine. Ultimately, the effect of the poem lies in the comparison of the slow, deliberate growth of the buds of jasmine with the mental state of the heroine, and the promised fulfillment of the jasmine, opening its white buds and spreading its fragrance under the full moon with the fulfillment of the heroine in union with her lover.

> Larger than earth,
> higher than sky,
> harder to measure than the waters
> is my love for the man from a hillside
> where black stalks support *kuṟiñci* flowers
> from which rich honey is made. (Kuṟ. 3.)

Swaminathaier remarks, "They say that this [kuṟiñci] blooms once in twelve years, that the honey which bees make from its flowers is quite delicious, and that a tribe called the Totuvaṉs who live in the Nilgiris reckon their ages by counting the number of times this plant has bloomed from birth." The poem begins by focusing on cosmic phenomena—the earth, the sky, and the waters, all three of which must come together to produce fertility for crops. The focus narrows to a hillside, then to black stalks, then to flowers, and finally to the honey produced from the pollen of the flowers. It is as if the poet were saying that for the tiny amount of honey that bees are able to make from the pollen of the flowers, the participation of earth, sky, waters, hillside, stalks, and flowers all is required, and that in a sense the honey sums up in itself all of creation. It is conventional in Tamil to liken bees' taking pollen from flowers to sexual union. Here, the poet's intention is to suggest that, in the union of the couple, all of existence is made purposeful. In the Tamil version, "my love for the man" comes at the end of the poem and does not interrupt the sequence of objects described.

"Don't grieve," you say, "he will be back."
Don't grieve?
Friend who suffer for me,
now a black cuckoo with glistening wings,
preening himself with fragrant pollen on a mango branch,
looks like a touchstone gleaming with streaks of gold;
and I stroke my empty hair. (Kuṟ. 192.)

The hero has gone off to find wealth, promising to return by early summer (*iḷavēṉil*, the time that corresponds to spring, or *vasanta*, in Sanskrit). Here his wife sees the signs about her that early summer has arrived and grieves that her husband has not returned. Women in South India are supposed to keep their hair empty of ornament and flowers while their husbands are away, but must wear flowers after their return. The heroine sees the cuckoo on the mango branch, a sign of the fertility and loveliness of the season. As the cuckoo preens itself with pollen, the heroine first likens its wings to a touchstone gleaming with streaks of gold. Her man has left to bring back gold; by her comparison, she questions the worth of his endeavor, just as the touchstone evaluates the genuineness of the gold. The bird is also meant to be likened to her husband: it is concerned only with collecting the goldlike pollen of the mango, not with its family. Finally, the cuckoo is reveling in the fertility of the season, covering itself with fragrant pollen, while the heroine can only stroke her empty hair.

Like a broken bangle,
the crescent moon has appeared in the red sky
for men to worship.
Has he forgotten me?
He left me to weep
and goes on long, barren paths
where an elephant,

not bearing to see the suffering of his mate
staggering as she walks,
gores a high *yā* tree so it is ruined,
takes its white fibrous bark with his trunk,
tastes it,
and trumpets, his heart filled with pain. (Kuṟ. 307.)

When women are widowed in South India, their bangles are broken to help control the dangerous power that fills the new widow. In this poem, the crescent moon suggests a broken bangle to the woman whose lover has left to find wealth: an object that is normally so auspicious that men worship it suggests to her the most inauspicious of all states, widowhood. The time that she sees the moon is the evening, when all activity ceases and the anguish of night is anticipated, the time when the suffering of women separated from their lovers is most acute, at least conventionally in Tamil. Then the heroine describes the wilderness to which her lover has gone. An elephant tries to help his suffering mate by feeding her bark, only to find that it is inedible. This suggests that the attempt of the hero to make his beloved's life pleasant by bringing home wealth will miscarry; wealth cannot be enjoyed in the same way as union, to which eating is often compared. The poet also wishes to liken the heroine herself to the gored tree: the hero, he suggests, has tasted her sexually, ruining her in the process, found her unpalatable, and abandoned her.

Even if the earth should move from its place;
even if water should cease to wet
or fire cease to burn;
even if a limit should be found to the great sea,
I would not fear the gossip of evil-mouthed women
and harm the love I bear him from a slope
where a village, lovely with *kāntaḷ* flowers,
is filled with redolence
when an ape with black fingers, sharp teeth, and long hair
grubs in the dirt
and breaks jack fruits that are as fragrant as flowers.
(Kuṟ. 373.)

The poem begins with a conventional and hackneyed invocation of cosmic phenomena, which are likened to the love the heroine bears her man. Her motive in making this comparison is sarcastic; if she really meant to exalt her love, she would not use words that are so unoriginal. In the latter half of the poem, the fragrance of the fruits is meant to be likened to the gossip being spread about, and the hero, who has caused the gossip, is meant to be compared to the ape. In other words, in his managing of the affair with the heroine, the hero has been as clumsy and stupid as an ape grubbing in the dirt. Just as the ape breaks jack fruits out of lust and desire, and not out of any higher motive, the hero has enjoyed his woman for the basest reasons. The heroine hints that love must be delicate, especially for the first time—the jack fruit is as fragrant as delicate flowers. But the hero has not realized the delicate nature of woman and enjoys her with as little regard for her nature as the ape has for the jack fruits. One might paraphrase the poem, "Oh no, I will not fear gossip. Even if the earth should move or water cease to wet, I will not fear gossip—not about this fool who used me, making love to me like an animal, and then was so irresponsible that now everyone knows of our affair."

Light dwindles,
jasmine flowers open,
the rage of the sun is spent,
and activity comes to an end.
Though I swim the whole of evening, friend,
toward the dark,
it is no use.
The night is vaster than the flood of the sea. (Kuṟ. 387.)

The heroine has been left by her lover; her life is ruined, for no one will marry a woman once she has been spoiled by another man. Here, she expresses her anguish in the evening, when the activity of the day is at an end and the suffering that will come during the night is anticipated. The first half of the poem describes evèning; but its images, except for the opening of the jasmine flowers, apply also to the state of mind that immediately precedes death, the evening of life. In the last half of the poem, the night toward which she is going is likened to death itself: it cannot be crossed over, any more than the ocean can be crossed by swimming. Moreover, in looking back on her life, the heroine can see nothing of value: it is only like the raging of the sun, with no reason or purpose. The poem as a whole evokes an unearthly landscape: light grows less and less, jasmine buds open slowly and spread their fragrance about, and the heroine struggles to reach the boundary where night begins, only to realize that she cannot possibly pass through the night.

The Technique of Suggestion in Indo-Aryan

From these examples, the technique of the Tamil poets should be evident. Every image in the poem has an often complex symbolic function, and the interplay of symbols causes the poems to create a resonant effect in the reader's mind, with each symbol reinforcing the others to create an almost inexhaustible variety. That is why the deeper one goes into these poems, the more one can find in them. It is curious that this technique fits the *dhvani* theory of Sanskrit poetry, propounded best by Ānandavardhana in his *Dhvanyāloka,* far better than most of the Sanskrit poems that the *alaṅkārikas* sought to analyze by it. I know of no Sanskrit or Prakrit poem that produces *anuraṇanarūpadhvani,* suggestion that takes the form of resonance, so richly and wonderfully as the poems just analyzed. It is evident to anyone with a fair acquaintance with Sanskrit literature that the use of suggestion and symbolism as poetic techniques is scarcely found at all in the epics, but gradually becomes more common as the literature develops, until by the time of the last great poet, Jagannātha, it is the most important thing in a poem. One naturally wonders whether this technique could have been influenced in some way by the poetry of South India, in which it is found several centuries before it appeared in Sanskrit and Prakrit literature. In order to determine whether the Indo-Aryan development may in fact have been a result of southern stimuli, it is necessary to analyze some typical poems in Sanskrit and Prakrit to show how the poets achieved poetic effect in those languages. Since there is a historical evolution, the earliest will be examined first. Even in the rather brief treatment that follows, I believe the general development of the use of suggestion in Indo-Aryan will be clearly shown.

In the *Mahābhārata,* figures tend to be straightforward, stating in so many words the fact that there is a likeness and giving explicitly the points of resemblance. Thus, in 3.75.26, the poet says,

"Damayantī was exceedingly delighted when she had recovered her husband, like the earth with crops half-grown on obtaining a shower." This verse, which uses symbolism much more than most in the *Mahābhārata*, states the similarity and leaves only one fact for the reader to infer: that Damayantī was only half-fulfilled when Nala left her and that, if he had not returned, the fulfillment that she had obtained by being with him previously would have been wasted like the half-grown crop.

The different approach of the Tamil poets can be seen in a similar, very simple poem from the *Aiṅkuṟunūṟu*:

In her father's town
mud plowed by stately-gaited buffaloes
grows thick with *āmpal*
and with waterlilies colored like blue sapphires.
She is the sweet bed companion
for the man from a town of paddy fields. (Aiṅ. 96.)

This poem is spoken by the neighbors in surprise when they see the hero and heroine happy together again after he has been with his harlots. The heroine is meant to be compared to the fields of her father. The plowing of the fields by buffaloes is likened to the hero's making love to her, and the subsequent production of flowers is compared to her happiness after union. In the final line, the fields refer to his other harlots. In these two verses, while the same image is used, the technique is quite different. In the *Mahābhārata*, the similarity between the two things meant to be compared is explicitly mentioned, leaving the reader to infer one further likeness, which is really only a part of the original comparison. In the *Aiṅkuṟunūṟu* poem, on the other hand, there is no stated figure at all. All similarities must be discovered by the reader after a few minutes of pondering. Because no correspondences are stated, the poem is richer in implications than the *Mahābhārata* verse. Curiously, it is exactly this device found in the Tamil poem that is approved by the dhavni writers: the poet must not express the figure of speech that is the main point of the poem but must imply it instead.

Besides simile another figure found in the *Mahābhārata* is metaphor (*rūpaka*), of which a typical example is 3.84.11-12: "The rising Arjuna-cloud, excited by the Draupadī wind, with the divine missile as rain cloud, great, having white horses as cranes, bright with the bow Gāṇḍīva as its rainbow, will always extinguish the kindled Karṇa-fire with showers of arrows on the battlefield." This may be compared with the more profound use of similar imagery in Tamil, already described above. Other types of figures found in the *Mahābhārata* and given by Sharma in his book *Elements of Poetry in the Mahābhārata*, are irrelevant to the technique of suggestion. (One of them, *bhrāntimadalaṅkāra*, is described in chapter 10.)

Elsewhere in the *Mahābhārata*, similes, metaphors, and other figures are invariably as straightforward as the ones just given. Generally the poet has in mind one quality that he wishes to emphasize in a certain person or object, and he uses a figure in which that quality is prominent in the object used for the comparison. I have been able to discover no instance in which the two objects meant to be compared are mentioned without any word or immediate context that makes the reader compare them, as in the Tamil poems; nor are there any poems where the comparison extends far beyond one or two qualities in the two objects, as in Tamil. In the *Mahābhārata*, a reader would have to be slow-witted indeed to miss the entire point of any of the figures; in Tamil, on the other hand, the poems are so complex that the interplay and implications of the figures in the better poems are virtually inexhaustible and are occasionally even so difficult that the point of the figure cannot be determined today with certainty.

The situation in the *Rāmāyaṇa* is similar to that in the *Mahābhārata*. However, the figures become more elaborate and occasionally contain more suggestion. With the elaboration of the figures, they become artificial and often forced. Thus, in Su. 2.22, the city of Laṅkā is said to have fences of tanks for its hips, water for its garment, and missiles (*śataghnī* and *śūla*) for its hair. A typical use of suggestion occurs in Su. 7.32, where Hanumān sees Rāvaṇa's harem asleep, the women's ornaments quiet, like a lotus garden whose geese and bees are silent. The poet wishes to suggest that the talking of the women is like the cackling of geese and that the tinkling of their ornaments is like the humming of bees. In Su. 7.44, there is a figure that uses suggestive symbolism to a greater degree. In Rāvaṇa's harem, some women have torn or dirty garlands like blooming creepers dirtied by elephants in a forest. The suggestion is that the garlands have been spoiled in love play with Rāvaṇa (who is like an elephant). The image of elephants trampling plants is often used in Tamil to symbolize sexual enjoyment by a man of a woman (for example, Kuṟ. 348), as is the image of a garland withering in an embrace (Puṟ. 73). Such suggestive figures are unusual in the *Rāmāyaṇa*, and, where they appear, they often use images found also in Tamil poetry, as in the above example. It has been seen that many Dravidian elements were entering Aryan culture at the time of the epics. From the stronger emphasis on chastity in the *Rāmāyaṇa*, it is likely that Dravidian influence is stronger in that epic than in the *Mahābhārata*. This fits well with what is observed of the technique of symbolic suggestion, which was absent in the *Mahābhārata* and begins to appear in the *Rāmāyaṇa*, often using conventions that are found in Tamil poetry and that probably originated with the Dravidians. The conventions that the Sanskrit epics and Tamil poetry share will be discussed below.

In the *Buddhacarita*, figures are even more elaborate than in the *Rāmāyaṇa*, and the technique of suggestion appears occasionally, though it is still rare. In 5.51, Aśvaghoṣa, describing the sleeping harem, writes, "So others, decked with ornaments of fresh gold and wearing peerless yellow garments, fell down helpless with deep sleep, like *karṇikāra* boughs broken by an elephant," and the comments given above for Su. 7.44 apply. Like Vālmīki, Aśvaghoṣa's main concern was with descriptive rather than suggestive figures: "Another, lying with her bamboo pipe in her hands and her white robe slipping off her breasts, resembled a river with lotuses being enjoyed by a straight row of bees and with banks laughing with the foam of the water" (8.26). Here the woman is the river, her bamboo pipe the bees, her face or eyes the lotuses, her breasts (or hips) the shore and her white robe the foam. The enjoyment of the river by the bees has no sexual connotations as it would in Tamil or later Sanskrit poetry.

In the *Sattasaī* the suggestive technique becomes much more prominent, though a large number of the verses are still mainly descriptive. In 43, the heroine addresses her mother, "People bear separation by hope—but being separated by [only] one village is worse than death, mother." The hint is that her beloved does not love her, and so, though he is only one village away, he will not come to see her. In Sa. 92, the female messenger says to the hero, pretending to be addressing a bee, "O bee, before you never sported among other flowers; yet now that the *mālatī* jasmine is pregnant with fruit, you forsake it." She means to say that the hero never used to go to other women, but now that the heroine is pregnant, he leaves her. In these and other examples of the suggestive technique in the *Sattasaī*, certain one-to-one correspondences are suggested and the entire effect of the poem lies in the reader's making the proper connections, so that he can ascertain a situation or set of facts that he does not know. The poet usually relies upon only one facet of the object used as the image to do this. Thus, in the poem just examined, the relevant facts about the jasmine are straightforward and easily discernible: before it got fruit, the bee visited it; now, it does not. Other connotations of the image are secondary and of minor importance. In Tamil, on the other hand, the suggestion is usually more complex. The reader already knows the situation and the facts surrounding it. The imagery of the poem serves instead to bring out certain implications or connotations of the situation by use of properties of the object used for the image. Usually many connotations of the image are invoked, and they are of equal importance. For example, in Kuṟ. 25, the feeding heron is meant to be likened to the hero as a symbol of sexual self-gratification and to the world in general, whose only interest in the heroine's seduction is as a subject of gossip:

No one was there except that thief,
and if he lies what can I do?
There was a heron
looking for eels in running water,
its green legs like millet stalks,
when he took me.

It will be seen later that in the *Sattasaī* many conventions and figures found in Tamil first appear in Indo-Aryan. It should be remembered that the *Sattasaī* was written in Māhārāṣṭrī, the southernmost Prakrit, and that at least part of it was composed under the Sātavāhanas, who ruled both Maharashtra and the Telugu country. Considering that the poetry of the *Sattasaī* was popular and lacked the tendency toward conservatism of classical Sanskrit, it is not surprising that so many conventions and techniques that must have been used in the Dravidian Deccani culture found their way into it. The poetry we possess in the *Sattasaī* is, however, not of purely Dravidian inspiration. While many poems in it use suggestion, many others are purely descriptive, with little or no use made of the technique of suggestion under discussion. An example is Sa. 315: "The lightning flash of the clouds seems to point out [Sanskrit *darśayatīva*] the traveler's wife sunk down in despair and weeping in her house whose roof has been blown off by the strong wind." Such poems, which achieve effect purely by description, are hardly found at all in early Tamil. Another kind of poem found in the *Sattasaī* that is foreign to Tamil is the type that uses elaborate figures. An example is Sa. 106: "The redness of her lower lip, which is taken at night by her lover, is seen in the morning in the eyes of her rival wives." It should be pointed out that the society described by the *Sattasaī* put far less value on chastity than did ancient Tamil society, a fact that indicates it was of mixed Dravidian and Aryan origin.

In Kālidāsa, the technique of suggestion introduced into Indo-Aryan by the *Sattasaī* is elaborated and reaches its full development in the North. A few examples from the *Raghuvaṃśa*, book 6, devoted to the *svayaṃvara* of the princess Indumatī, are given below to show exactly how Kālidāsa uses suggestion:

> The prince [Aja] ascended the platform . . . by means of a well-constructed flight of steps, as a whelp of the lord of beasts climbs to the lofty peak of a mountain by means of projecting rocks. (3.)
>
> Seated on his throne, Aja resembled Guha riding a peacock. (4.)
>
> Śrī shone among the kings at the svayaṃvara like lightning that apportions itself out among many clouds. (5.)
>
> The rows of eyes of citizens left all [other] princes and fell on Aja just as black bees vacate flower trees and fall upon a wild elephant flowing with rut. (7.)
>
> [As a gesture of love] one king whirled a lotus whose pollen formed a circle within it, holding its stalk with both hands as its restless petals struck black bees. (13.)
>
> The very same maid . . . conducted the princess to a second king just as a wave raised by the wind carries a female goose on Mānasa lake from one lotus to another. (26.)
>
> [As the princess passed by each suitor at the svayaṃvara], like the flame of a moving lamp at night, that same king turned pale

[*vivarṇa*] just as a mansion on the highroad is shrouded in darkness [*vivarṇa*] when left behind [by a moving light]. (67.)

In verses 3, 4, and 5, the chief purpose of the images is to enhance the description of the subjects; no subtle interplay of connotations is intended. In all of these images there is some exchange of connotations between the two things compared: in verse 3, the kingliness and youth of Raghu are implied, while, in verse 4, his godlike stature is suggested; but these implications are straightforward and do not belong to the special technique of suggestion. In verse 7, the figure is more complex. First, there is a similarity in appearance between the eyes of the citizens and the bees. But the real point of the simile is that, while the other kings are handsome but innocuous like flower trees, Aja is heroic, fearful, and virile like a rutting elephant. The citizens are thrilled at his appearance, and, abandoning the rather commonplace pastime of looking at other kings, gaze at Aja just as bees when given a chance stop tasting the sweet but unexciting pollen of flowers and taste instead the fragrant rut of an elephant. A final suggestion is that, just as the flowers produce pollen perfunctorily as a matter of course while the elephant ruts only when maddened by lust, so the other kings' desire is commonplace while that of Aja is entirely out of the ordinary. In verse 13, the king's whirling lotus with its circle of pollen and its restless petals striking bees is a figure that suggests sexual intercourse. The king hints at the strength of his desire to make love to the princess.

In verse 26, the figure of the female goose going from one lotus to another on lake Mānasa would be an uninspired, purely descriptive image with few or no connotations were it not for the skillful introduction of the wind and the wave. The wind represents fate or the inexorable unfolding of events and is something external to the lake and not dependent on it. It produces a wave, likened to the maid, that moves the goose, or princess, from one lotus to another. Thus the princess is fated to marry Aja, as is shown by the fact that her right arm throbs when she sees him (6.68), and the outcome of the svayaṃvara is predetermined by the exterior force of fate. That in turn emphasizes the godlike character of the line of Raghu, for which all events happen as ordained by the gods. In verse 67, one of the most famous similes that Kālidāsa created, the princess moving from one suitor to another is likened to a lamp moving along a road at night. The houses on the road are dark and uninhabited; their existence is purposeless until they are used and filled with light. Just so, the lives of the suitors are not fulfilled until a fitting beloved inhabits their hearts and sheds her light there. The traveler is going to a predetermined place with his light, just as the eventual choice of Aja is preordained. As the traveler goes past each empty house, a little light falls on it making it lose something of its forlorn appearance and suggesting to a small extent what it might be like if inhabited. Just so, the joy that appears on the faces of the kings as the princess approaches them is only a small part of what their happiness would be if they were chosen. The subsequent darkness of the houses and the pallor of the kings shows how utterly wretched their state is, deprived now even of hope.

In these verses the technique of suggestion is similar in many respects to that of Tamil; yet there are important differences. In Tamil the comparison between the two things is often not implied by a word such as *like* or by an evident metaphor. Rather, the two objects are simply mentioned in different parts of the poem with no apparent connection, and it is left to the reader to relate them. In Indo-Aryan such a device is not as common as in Tamil, and even when it is employed the connection between the two objects is generally made clearer than in Tamil, as is evident from a comparison of Sa. 92, given above, with any of the Tamil poems analyzed. Kālidāsa generally (though not always) states the relation between the two things or sets of things he wishes to compare and then allows the interplay between the various properties of those two things or sets of things to be established through suggestion. Indeed, the main difference between the images used by Kālidāsa and the cruder images of the earlier Sanskrit tradition is that in the former, there are usually many relevant aspects of the things compared whereas in the latter there is usually one and other aspects are quite incompatible, so that the figure seems awkward and shallow, as in the examples given above from the *Mahābhārata*.

Kālidāsa also has instances of implied comparison of two things not specifically related by a figure, especially in his Prakrit verses.[1] In the fourth act of the *Vikramorvaśīyam*, for example,

[1] See also Megh. 106, analyzed below in this chapter.

the friends of Urvaśī speak of the suffering of that heroine, interspersing their conversation with verses whose situations are supposed to be compared with that of Urvaśī and her lover: "Two [female] geese grieve, their eyes filled with tears, full of love, on the shore of a lake, sharing the grief of their friend" (IV.2). The two female geese are Citralekhā and Sahajanyā, their friend is Urvaśī, and the point of the verse is that they grieve at her suffering in separation from her lover. This is exactly the type of verse common in the *Sattasaī*, as has been seen; indeed, this type of verse, which describes situations that have relevance to a situation to which they are supposed to be compared, is found chiefly in Prakrit. It is evident that such verses were current in that language.

It is important in terms of the history of Sanskrit poetry to determine how indebted Kālidāsa was to the Prakrit technique of suggestion for the somewhat different technique he used in most of his poems, as exemplified above. Of course, some use of suggestion is employed by virtually every poet, and it is likely that Kālidāsa's technique was to some extent developed by the poet himself. There are, however, reasons to believe that the greatest of Sanskrit poets was profoundly influenced by the use of suggestion in the popular poetry of Maharashtra, of which the *Sattasaī* is an example. First, he was fully aware of it: the Prakrit verses of his plays are in Māhārāṣṭrī, and several of those verses employ the same technique as the *Sattasaī* poems. Furthermore, the objects Kālidāsa uses for figures and the connotations of the objects he uses for suggestive purposes are often startlingly similar to the ones employed in the *Sattasaī* and ultimately in Tamil, while they are not found in the epics, as will be shown in the section on common elements used in figures of speech in ancient Tamil and Indo-Aryan. These elements of southern verse are uncommon (though present to some extent) in the Sanskrit epics; they increase in the *Buddhacarita*, and finally they become extremely prominent in the *Sattasaī*. The increase in the use of these southern elements is accompanied by a corresponding increase in the use of the technique of suggestion. In Kālidāsa, suggestion is even more prominent than in the *Sattasaī*, and southern elements abound. Thus Kālidāsa's technique may be seen as part of an evolution in which ever more southern elements were entering northern poetry.

There is, however, much more to Kālidāsa's poetry than the foregoing discussion would imply. He used many figures and instances of suggestion that are wholly foreign to the *Sattasaī* and the Tamil tradition; his poetry is modeled closely on the epics and even earlier Sanskrit sources and uses many elements of the Sanskrit tradition that do not appear in southern poetry. Especially conspicuous in Kālidāsa, and lacking almost entirely in early Tamil and largely in the *Sattasaī*, are the many descriptions and figures of speech in which Hindu mythology is used. Much of Kālidāsa's greatness may in fact be attributed to the synthesis that he represents between two quite separate traditions. He does not hesitate to apply the technique of suggestion to elements of the northern tradition, and in fact nowhere can one point to a verse that could be called purely northern or southern. He was creating his own type of poetry, using the two traditions; since he had no previous harmony to follow, his poetry is not the unimaginative rehearsal of images used many times before, which much of later Sanskrit poetry was. If the sudden influx of northern culture into the South was responsible for much of the freshness and imaginativeness of early Tamil literature, the converse is true for Kālidāsa.

The way in which Kālidāsa used the technique of the South with northern elements is well exemplified in *Meghadūta* 106, where the hero tells the cloud what to say to his beloved:

> "'When Vishnu [Śārṅgapāṇi] has risen from his serpent bed, my curse will end. Close your eyes and endure the four months that remain. Afterwards we will enjoy every wish we had apart in nights full of light from the ripened [that is, full] autumn moon.'"

Vishnu sleeps during the rainy season and during *pralaya*, while the world is absorbed. When he arises, he creates the world, full of new living things. Just so, as soon as the hero's and heroine's time of separation is over, new life will begin for them. He tells his beloved to pass the time of separation with her eyes closed: it will pass as quickly as a dream. The suffering of separation is as insubstantial as the experiences in a dream, but the happiness that comes after that will be true, like waking experience. When the darkness of *māyā* is dispelled, the light of truth shines forth. This light is symbolized in the poem by the full moon that illumines their lovemaking. Further, the moon has "matured" (*pariṇata*) so that it is now full through the dark clouded nights of the rainy season, just as the happiness of the saint is the result of suffering through long seasons of self-mortification and the ecstasy of the couple is occasioned by the long time they have suffered apart from one another. On the Gangetic plains, rice and millet are harvested in the fall.[2] Just as crops produce their harvest under the light of the autumn moon, the suffering of the couple produces its harvest then.

In this verse, nowhere does Kālidāsa express any simile or metaphor; as in Tamil, all comparison is implied, not stated. Moreover, Kālidāsa has in this one small verse incorporated and reconciled, unwittingly no doubt, the fundamental difference in the world views of the ancient North and South. In the North, the sacred authority lay with the Brahmin and with the Vedas, whose message was that final bliss in life was to be obtained through austerity and ultimate union with Brahma. In the South, the most sacred thing in life was the family, and the proper relationship between man and wife was the source of the happiness of the individual and the proper functioning of society. That Kālidāsa compares the bliss of the saint with the happiness of the reunited couple, thus equating the northern and southern views of the sacred, is no mere coincidence. At the time he wrote, the southern system of values regarding chastity and marriage was well established in Aryan India, and it was natural that he should have related these values to the orthodox Brahminical values regarding the ascetic. It is significant that the interplay between the two sets of values is the most prominent feature of his greatest *kāvya*, the *Kumārasaṃbhava*.

It is true that the comparison of divine union to the union of man and woman is commonplace in the mystical literature of the world. Nowhere else, however, is the erotic element emphasized so much as in Indian literature, whether in Sanskrit, starting with Kālidāsa, or in Tamil, beginning with the Nāyaṉmārs and the Āḻvārs. The reason for this is that, in India, the comparison was motivated by the notion that all aspects of love between man and woman are animated by the sacred, an attitude found first in the early Tamil poems and then in Kālidāsa, so that even the detailed descriptions of the loveplay between Śiva and Pārvatī

[2] O. H. K. Spate and A. T. A. Learmonth, *India and Pakistan: a General and Regional Geography*, 3d ed. (Bungay, England, 1967), p. 555.

in the eighth book of the *Kumārasaṃbhava* and the sensuous descriptions of Krishna by Āṇṭāḷ were not deemed unfitting.[3]

It has been seen that the real advent of suggestion into Indo-Aryan as an accepted and conscious technique of poetry is marked by the *Sattasaī* and that, while suggestion occurs occasionally in the epics and the *Buddhacarita*, it does not seem to be consciously cultivated in those works as it is in the *Sattasaī* and Kālidāsa. It is thus of great importance to define exactly the relation between the technique of the *Sattasaī* and that of early Tamil. In Tamil, suggestion is often far more complex than in Prakrit. One reason for this complexity is the circumstances under which the poems were written. The Tamil poetry was composed by sophisticated poets who had written poems for much of their lives and who used a group of conventions that had been refined and made more sophisticated for many years. They often wrote poems of thirty or forty lines in which many different figures were used and allowed to interact to produce suggestive effects whose permutations are virtually unlimited. The Prakrit poems, on the other hand, are all quite short and almost never contain more than one image. They appear to be much closer to folk poetry than most of the Tamil poems, and they are consequently simpler. A few Tamil poems seem closer to folk models than the others; their similarity to their Prakrit counterparts is striking. The *Aiṅkuṟunūṟu* opens, for example, with ten poems in which the heroine's friend says that the heroine in her innocence wishes for the good of the world while the friend wishes that the heroine would get her lover. Each of these begins with the heroine's words, "Long live [King] Ātaṉ, long live [King] Aviṉi," the repetition of which indicates their folk source. In Aiṅ. 5, the heroine's friend says:

"Long live Ātaṉ! Long live Aviṉi!
May hunger disappear
and sickness be banished far away,"
wished my friend. But I wished,

[3] An example of Āṇṭāḷ's verse is *Nāycciyār Tirumoḻi* 7.1:
Is camphor the most redolent, or is the lotus the most fragrant?
Or is it his red mouth like coral
that is the sweetest?
Longing for the fragrance and the taste
of Mādhava's mouth, who broke the tusks,
I ask—tell me, deep, white conch.

"May the chariot stand by our front door,
driven by the man from a cool bay
where a male crocodile eats fish whole."

Here there is only one image, and, as in the Prakrit poems, that image is to be related to the situation of the heroine. Like the crocodile that eats the fish with which he has long shared the bay, the hero cares nothing for the life of the heroine, with whom he has shared his life. Thus he has begun to visit harlots, a fact indicated by the akam category to which the poem belongs, marutam.

This may be compared with Sa. 92, where the female messenger says to the hero, pretending to be addressing a bee, "O bee, before you never sported among other flowers; yet now that the *mālatī* jasmine is pregnant with fruit, you forsake it," or with Sa. 594, "Struck by the sharp arrow drawn back to the ear [of the bowman], the doe, thinking 'I will never see my beloved again,' looked about for a long time," where the heroine is like the doe, struck with the shaft of desire and suffering, which will kill her before she can see her absent lover again. It should be noticed that in the Tamil poem the image is less well defined than in Prakrit, and therefore there are more connotations. While the similarities are obvious, the differences between the Tamil and Prakrit poems are too great to be explained simply by the fact that the Tamil poems are the product of more sophisticated authors than the Prakrit ones. Rather it may be said that while the Tamil and Māhārāṣṭrī poets both made use of a technique of suggestion that developed in South India, they exploited that technique in different ways. When Prakrit poets use suggestion, the elements involved usually have a one-to-one correspondence, which allows the poem to be "solved," that is, it permits the reader to determine exactly what element of the situation each part of the image is meant to correspond to. In Tamil, even in the simplest poems, which seem closest to folk models, such a solution is not possible; the correspondence between the two things compared is too inexact and the resulting suggestion too complex. The reasons for this different application of suggestion are investigated in the next sections.

Language as a Factor in the Use of Suggestion

In seeking to learn why suggestion is used differently in Tamil than in Sanskrit and Prakrit, even though the technique has the same origin in both traditions, the character of the Aryan languages as opposed to the Dravidian languages is one of the first and most important reasons that come to mind; for the Tamil language is especially well adapted to the development and use of suggestion, while the ancient Indo-Aryan languages are not.

In Tamil, it is difficult to make two or more long adjectival subordinate clauses modify the same noun. The reason for this is that in Tamil such clauses must be turned into phrases ending in adjectival participles. For example, "the chair in which I am sitting" would be *nāṉ uṭkārntirukkiṟa nāṟkāli* (literally "the I-am-sitting chair"). The adjectival participle must ordinarily modify the word that immediately follows it. Thus it is often impossible to translate literally into Tamil two adjectival subordinate clauses modifying the same word by using adjectival participles, which are the only Tamil forms that are reasonably close to the Indo-European adjectival subordinate clause. For example, it is impossible to translate literally, "The hero whom the king had sent and who had come to the city sat down." The result of such an attempt, *ūrukku vanta aracaṉ aṉuppiya vīraṉ uṭkārntāṉ* ("the city-come king-sent hero sat") would mean "the hero who had been sent by the king who came to the city sat down." Even when given its proper meaning, the sentence sounds unnatural.

To express such compound ideas, Tamil has developed a system of relating verbs either by continuatives (adverbial participles), which are used for previous or closely related action, or by infinitives, which are used for simultaneous or causally related actions. One would, therefore, normally express the sentence just given either as "the hero sent by the king, having come to the city, sat down," that is, *aracaṉ aṉuppiya vīraṉ ūrukku vantu uṭkārntāṉ*, or as "as the king had sent him [infinitive], the hero who had come to the city sat down," that is *aracaṉ aṉuppa ūrukku vanta vīraṉ uṭkārntāṉ*. Even more natural than this last sentence is "as the king had sent him [infinitive], the hero, having come to the city [adverbial participle], sat down," that is, *aracaṉ aṉuppa vīran̲ ūrukku vantu uṭkārntān̲.* Even when no ambiguity results from putting more than one adjectival participle before a noun, such sentences are not commonly used in Tamil. It is quite unnatural, for example, to translate "the man who works, eats, and sleeps" as *vēlai ceykir̲a cāppiṭukir̲a tūṅkukir̲a man̲itan̲.* To express the English sense that the man does nothing but work, eat, and sleep, one would have to change the sentence entirely and simply say, "this man does nothing but eat, work, and sleep." The result of this inability of Tamil to modify a noun with many adjectival subordinate clauses is that the language has no tight way of describing one noun in an elaborate compound manner. Thus simple descriptive poetry is rarer in ancient Tamil than in English or Sanskrit.[4] It is true that there are many long passages of description in the anthologies, but their descriptions are generally of an extremely complex type, which fosters suggestion, as will be seen below. Passages that rely for their effect wholly on felicity, conciseness, and simplicity of description, so common in Sanskrit, are almost entirely missing in Tamil poetry.

If Tamil tends to relate nouns and their modifiers more loosely than English, just the opposite is true of Sanskrit. Not only does that language use relative clauses, which are lacking in Tamil (except in a clumsy and unnatural construction using interrogatives and the ending *-ō*), but it can also modify any noun with virtually any number of adjectives, (adjective) participles, and adjectival compounds, because in Sanskrit nouns and the adjectives modifying them (except for relative clauses) must agree in case, number, and gender. Thus it is quite common in Sanskrit poetry to find a noun separated by many lines from some of the adjectives that modify it. A simple example from the *Kumārasaṃbhava* will illustrate this:

(1. avacitabalipuṣpā) (2. vedisaṃmārgadakṣā)
(3. niyamavidhijalānāṃ barhiṣāṃ copanetrī) |
(4. giriśam) (5. upacacāra pratyahaṃ)

[4] The use of compound description is uncommon (or, at least, less common than in most Indo-European languages) in the Tamil poetry of all periods. For example, see the poems from Kampan̲ translated below. A case could be made, I believe, that the difficulty of forming compound descriptions in Tamil is responsible for the currency of elaborate devices for effecting such descriptions in modern political rhetoric.

(6. sā) (7. sukeśī)
(8. niyamitaparikhedā tacchiraścandrapādaiḥ) / / (1.60.)

"(6. She [Pārvatī]) (7. whose hair is lovely) (5. served every day) (4. Śiva), (1. plucking flowers for the sacrifice), (2. careful to keep the altar tidy), (3. bringing *kuśa* grass and water for the nonoptional sacrifices), (8. her weariness dispelled by the rays of the moon on his [Śiva's] head)." It will be seen that the word *sā*, she, is modified by many adjectives spread throughout the verse. To render this in Tamil, it would be necessary to change both the order, putting all of the adjectival phrases before the word *she*, and the construction, by changing the adjectival phrases to adverbial ones so that the verse would read, "Having plucked flowers for the sacrifice, having been careful to keep the altar tidy, having brought kuśa grass . . . , her weariness having been dispelled . . . , she served Śiva every day." In other words, the adjectival relation of each phrase with the word *she* must be replaced by a more nebulous one between the verbs of the clauses and the main verb *served.* Moreover, when the verse is translated in this way with adverbial participles, it sounds rather long-winded and unpoetic. It would be far more satisfactory simply to render each of the phrases into a separate Tamil sentence: "She was careful to keep the altar tidy. She brought kuśa grass." But, while such a translation would sound all right, it would scarcely preserve the sophisticated diction and beauty of the original, which derives much of its loveliness from the way in which the description is given concisely in one sentence.

Thus, while the structure of Sanskrit favors long descriptions in which many elements modify one noun without ambiguity, Tamil favors descriptions in which the different modifiers are not applied to one noun. What, then, happens in Tamil when a poet creates a long description, as in fact he often does? He simply uses a complex method rather than a compound one. Thus in Sanskrit the poet writes, "A, which is B, C, D, E, and F," while in Tamil he says, "A, which is B, which is C, which is D, which is E, which is F." An example of this is Kuṟ. 86, where the heroine separated from her lover grieves:

Are there others who suffer from a sickness hard to bear,
afflicted with loneliness?
Are their others

whose cool eyes, lined with red, well with drops
while they listen to the gentle voice of the uncaring bell,
its clapper striking
every time the cow shakes off the flies,
which buzz close in the winter midnight
whipped by wind and filled with drops?

The result is that the poem is no longer simple enough to produce the effect of delight by conciseness and felicity of expression, as Sanskrit verse generally does. The reader must go deep into the Tamil poem if he is to experience the effect intended, while the effect of the Sanskrit verse is generally achieved in a flash as soon as the reader has realized the grammatical function of each part (or, if the verse is suggestive, determined just what fact or figure is hinted at). In this process of going deeper and deeper into the poem, the Tamil reader naturally begins to become aware of the unexpressed interplay of connotations between different parts of the poem. The more he ponders and analyzes the poem, the stronger does the effect evoked by such discovered interplay become. Thus a good Tamil poem is like a bottomless river, as my Tamil teacher Ramasubramaniam once put it. Even when Sanskrit verses rely on suggestion for effect, they scarcely ever contain as much as interplay as good Tamil verses.

In Tamil, even when there is one phrase that modifies a noun, the exact relationship of the parts to one another is much looser than in Sanskrit or English. For example, *nāṉ aṭitta kiḷai* (literally "the I-hit branch") could mean, according to context, "the branch with which I hit [something]," "the branch under which I hit [something]," "the branch on which I hit [something]," or "the branch that I hit." In Sanskrit, on the other hand, each of these meanings must be expressed differently. This vagueness in the relationship between a noun and its modifiers is well exemplified by Kuṟ. 138, a poem in which the heroine's friend describes how she and her friend waited for the hero to come at night:

Even though this futile city slept,
we did not sleep.
We heard clearly
the fall of blue-sapphire flowers
as they broke
from the soft, lovely branch

of dark-clustered *nocci*
with peacock-feet leaves
beyond the *ē<u>l</u>il* tree
by our house.

As literally as it can be translated, this poem reads, "Even though [the] futile city slept, we did not sleep, having heard well [the] falling of [the] sapphire-like flower[s] [which] broke [from a] soft loveliness-full branch [of] nocci [with] black bunch[es] [with] peacock-feet leaves near [the] ē<u>l</u>il by our house." In Tamil, most of the prepositions that have to be supplied to make the English intelligible are omitted. The result is that words are less clearly and less specifically connected to what they modify than in English or Sanskrit, and hence more meanings and connotations arise when the poem is read in Tamil than in English or Sanskrit translation.

Another property of Tamil that makes it easy to convey suggestion in that language is the ease with which many vaguely related things can be included in the same sentence when in English they have to be put into separate sentences. The poem just given is a good example. By making the words "having heard" subordinate to "we did not sleep," all of the elements in the poem are included in one whole that is impossible to reproduce naturally in English. Moreover, in Tamil the words "having heard" end the poem, so that the entire description looks forward to that end, without which it makes no sense. The result is that, while the relation of each word to what it modifies is looser than in English, the coherence of the whole utterance is greater than in English. Thus the connotations of any one word or phrase can be more easily transferred in the reader's mind to any other word or phrase than in English or Sanskrit.

The ease with which Tamil builds up large sentences is responsible for the most often used formula for suggestion in the poems: the employment of the word *nāṭa<u>n</u>* ("man from a country [where]") or a similar word. This use is demonstrated in Ku<u>r</u>. 193:

In his land
springs with small mouths
seem blue-sapphire vessels
into which liquor has been poured.
Near them frogs croak with mouths wide open

and sound like the beating of snare drums
which frighten birds from the fields.
In the long white light of the old moon
he took my long arms,
and today they smell of budding jasmine.

This poem says literally, "The man from a country where springs . . . near which frogs croak . . . took my long arms in the . . . light of the old moon and today they smell of budding jasmine." The use of nāṭaṉ here enables the poet to state easily an idea that he means to relate to the rest of the poem without the use of any words implying comparison such as *like*, and it is thus an instrument for producing the type of suggestion characteristic of early Tamil.

But why exactly should Sanskrit tend not to use suggestive verse as much as Tamil does? It has been seen, it is true, that Sanskrit is well adapted for compound descriptions of one noun, but surely that fact is not sufficient to keep it from using the sort of suggestion found in Tamil. There is another characteristic of Sanskrit that tends to keep it from producing such profoundly suggestive verse, and that is the extremely refined and concise structures made possible by its grammar. When reading most good Sanskrit poetry (or any other good literature in Sanskrit), the reader feels pleasure at the conciseness and elegance of expression. He experiences the effect of the verse by putting together and relating the various parts of the verse to determine the meaning, which is generally simple and relatively straightforward. In Tamil, on the other hand, the reader rarely feels such pleasure at the elegance and conciseness of expression; to experience the intended effect, he must discover and ponder its meaning. This difference between Sanskrit and Tamil verse is so crucial that it should be exemplified. The reader may compare Kuṟ. 67 with Subh. 742, both typical poems on the heroine parted from her lover. In reading the Tamil poem, which is given first, he should remember that the hero has two conflicting things in his mind: his desire to bring back wealth (in the form of coins) and his longing to make love to his beloved:

Does he not remember me, friend,
who crossed into a wilderness
with milkhedge and blackened earth

where a shining margosa fruit
held in a parrot's beak
resembles a coin for a golden ornament
held in hard, skilled fingernails
by a smith
to push through it a newly made wire?

Your eye is red and swollen from the flowing of the tears,
and slow to move;
the brightness of your lip is injured by your burning sighs;
the curls are ruffled on your brow, and your pallid cheek
rests ever in your hand:
young maiden, tell me who he is
whose past austerities have ripened
to merit this effect.

It is this tendency of Sanskrit to achieve effect by concise and elegant expression rather than by endless interplay of connotations that accounts for the manner in which suggestion was used in the Indo-Aryan tradition. The innate tendency of the Sanskrit and Prakrit languages was to create verses whose simple meaning would appear in a flash as the reader interrelated the various grammatical constructions to create a whole. It was natural, then, to do exactly the same thing with suggestion, to use that technique in such a way that the hidden meaning would dawn upon the reader in a flash, producing a feeling of delight. The interplay, however, would be utterly exhausted in that flash and there would be little use in pondering the poem at length.

The Sanskritist may well wonder at this treatment of suggestion in Indo-Aryan. After all, it was the Sanskrit aestheticians who produced the theory of dhvani, perhaps the most comprehensive statement of literary suggestion ever formulated. The *Dhvanyāloka*, the best and most succinct of the Sanskrit treatises on suggestion, recognizes two sorts of dhvani that are relevant here: *asaṃlakṣyakramoddyotadhvani*, "suggestion whose apprehension occurs without any [intervening] steps being noticed," and *kramoddyotitadhvani*, "suggestion whose apprehension is by [discrete] steps."[5] This latter is also called *anuraṇanarūpadhvani*,

[5] *Dhvanyāloka* 11.2.

"suggestion that takes the form of a resonance." In the first of these two types of dhvani, a feeling or state of mind is suggested, as in the example given by Abhinavagupta in his commentary on the *Dhvanyāloka* called the *Locana*. There, the *sthāyibhāva*, or enduring mood, of *rati*, or sexual enjoyment, is suggested: "My glance, traversing with difficulty her two thighs, then wandering long along the surface of her loins, then becoming motionless on her waist, uneven with the waves of three creases, now, as if thirsty, slowly mounts her two high breasts and looks anxiously again and again at her eyes flowing with drops of water."[6] It is evident that this sort of suggestion, whose apprehension occurs without any intervening steps being noticed, has little in common with the Tamil technique under discussion.[7]

The second type of suggestion is of two types: *śabdaśaktyudbhavadhvani*, "suggestion that arises through the denotative power of words," and *arthaśaktyudbhavadhvani*, "suggestion that arises through the denotative power of meaning."[8] The first of these consists primarily of punning or other such artificial devices and need not be considered here. Examples of the second in the *Dhvanyāloka* are as follows: "The fragrant month [spring] prepares but does not yet give to the god of love his arrows whose points have young people for their targets, whose tips are fresh mango [flowers] and whose feathers are new fronds."[9] Abhinavagupta explains that here the passion of love now beginning and about to increase gradually is suggested. "Respectfully given support by the hand of Youth offered to them and rising up high, your two breasts seemed to rise in salutation to Kāma."[10] Abhinavagupta says that here the girl's desire is hinted at by the stiffening

[6] Ibid., p. 188.

[7] Daniel Ingalls points out that this verse has more connotation than Abhinavagupta mentions. It comes from the *Ratnāvalī* and is the king's description of his emotions as he views a portrait of Sāgarikā. All of the imagery is of *rati* up to the last touch, the tears in the girl's eyes. This turns the mood suddenly, as the reader realizes that the lovers are parted. In his use of this verse to exemplify asaṃlakṣyakramoddyotitadhvani, Abhinavagupta is not concerned with this turnabout, which clearly cannot be characterized as "suggestion whose apprehension occurs without any [intervening] steps being noticed."

[8] *Dhvanyāloka* 2.20.

[9] Ibid., p. 275.

[10] Ibid., p. 276.

of her breasts. "The proud wife of the hunter wanders amid her rival wives, her ear sporting a peacock feather while they wear pearls for their ornaments."[11] The dhvani here, according to Abhinavagupta, is that when the hunter made love to his other wives, he was not very anxious for the pleasures of love and took the time to kill elephants in order to obtain pearls from their temples as presents to them,[12] but when he desired the heroine, he was so overcome by passion that he took time only to kill a peacock. It may remarked that this interpretation is more than somewhat forced. The poem is far more appealing if one sees the heroine's pride as a sign that she wears her husband's peacock feather, the very emblem of the power and occupation of the mountain hunter, while the other wives have been bought with only a few pearls.

In any case, these examples show well that suggestion in Indo-Aryan, even when it is said to have the form of a resonance, is basically just a process of determining a relation or a fact that is not stated in the poems and that stops once the relation or fact has been determined. Thus, while suggestion was borrowed into Indo-Aryan from the South, it was modified in the process to conform to the Sanskritic idea of a good verse: one in which the implication or meaning of the poem suddenly occurs to the reader in a lightninglike flash, while in Tamil the process is one in which the interplay of elements in the poem becomes steadily stronger like a slowly brightening lamp.

This is not to say that ancient Tamil poetry is finer or more profound than Sanskrit verse. The two are so different that such a comparison is not really meaningful. The reader who knows both languages well will find that his preference is determined by his tastes, for in both bodies of poetry the finest poems use their techniques in ways that seem quite impossible to improve upon. The beauty of Sanskrit poetry, as of the Sanskrit language, is its clarity: the reader feels that the idea expressed could not possibly be conveyed more succinctly or more gracefully. Where there is suggestion, the form of the *dyotita*, or hinted meaning, as well as of the *vācya*, or stated meaning, is clear and tightly

[11] Ibid.

[12] See below.

expressed. In Tamil, on the other hand, the various meanings are hinted at entirely without tightness of expression.

Religion as a Factor in the Use of Suggestion

Another reason for the different types of poetry that came to prevail in Indo-Aryan and Tamil was the very different kinds of religion that existed in North and South India when the poetry under discussion was written. In the North, there was and always had been a highly developed mythology about the gods who were worshiped. They were primarily transcendent beings who, if they wished to interfere in worldly events, came in human aspect and acted, like the Greek gods. Even if they did not appear in human form, they were discrete entities that acted upon the world as outside agents. This transcendent nature of the gods was emphasized by the fact that they were invoked at special ceremonies by a special class, the Brahmins. The gods had to be summoned and rewarded before they would interfere in human life. There were of course elements of the sacred present in all areas of everyday life for the ancient Aryans, as for all archaic peoples, but far more important were the transcendent nature of the gods and the special Brahminical rites at which the aid of the gods was invoked.

This outlook is reflected in Aryan poetry. Like most ancient literatures, when it began, Indo-Aryan literature was inseparably connected with the religion of the people who wrote it. The epics, which represent the next step, were still full of stories about the gods and full of religious elements. This approach to literature continues in classical Sanskrit literature, of which almost all works use stories about the gods as their subject material. Even when the subject matter is purely secular, the author generally inserts a large amount of mythological material. In the *Abhijñānaśākuntala*, for example, Kālidāsa has the pregnant Śakuntalā taken away by Indra's charioteer and then has Duḥśyanta find her in a flying chariot in passages filled with famous descriptions of flying through the air.

Thus the religious heritage of Sanskrit has disposed the literature to narrative storytelling and to description, which is, after all, a part of storytelling, rather than to the subjective, anonymous, introspective lyric using mainly suggestion that is found in Tamil. That is why so many Indo-Aryan verses that use suggestion hint at certain situations that the reader is supposed to infer rather than at a complex interplay of connotations such as is suggested in the Tamil poems: even in the use of suggestion, the Indo-Aryan writer clings to his preference for stories and narrative. An example is Sa. 92, given earlier, where the female messenger says to the hero, pretending to be addressing a bee, "O bee, before you never sported among other flowers; yet now that the *mālatī* jasmine is pregnant with fruit, you forsake it." Another example is Subh. 810, where a wanton woman hints that she wishes to make love with a traveler:

> Quicken your step, oh traveler, and be upon your way.
> The woods before you swarm with wild beasts,
> with elephant and serpent, boar and wild ox;
> the sunlight now is fading and you a youth alone.
> I cannot give you room within the house,
> for I am a young girl, and I live unguarded.

Poems such as these are almost entirely missing in ancient Tamil.

In Tamilnad, there was almost no mythology, at least insofar as can be determined from the early poems and the later tradition, where almost all stories about the gods were imported from the North. Rather than being entities about whom stories could be told, the Tamil gods were conceived of as forces that inhered in specific things, as has been seen. These powers were present all the time and were not conceived of as suddenly coming into the world at certain ceremonies or occasions as in North India. Rather, they were omnipresent concentrations of power that could at any moment go out of control and cause trouble. It was to appease these basically dangerous forces that sacrifices and other rituals were performed. The Tamil poets had grown up in an atmosphere in which every action and every object was felt to contain some supernatural power or significance. Indeed, there was a hierarchy of powers for them, and the more important or moving an event, the more impregnated that event and its locus were with potentially dangerous power. Thus the Tamil poets and their audience had become accustomed to seeing beneath the surface of every object and event a sacred power that inhered in it and gave significance to it. It is scarcely surprising that when they described important and moving events in their poetry, they kept their ability to see beneath the surface and created one of the world's finest poetries of suggestion.

An example will illustrate how the habit of seeing sacred power in important events produces suggestion in Tamil. In this poem, the friend of the heroine speaks to the foster mother:

Do not frighten me by saying,
"At midnight, when darkness lay thick
and the rain, after pouring down
from great clouds with thunder and lightning,
had stopped, its noise stilled,
I saw her,
her heavy earrings flashing like lightning on high,
her thick curly hair let loose in the back,
walking very stealthily,
like a peacock coming down from a mountain,
as she climbed the platform in the field
and descended."
Listen, mother.
On the haunted slope where our garden is,
a spirit comes wearing bright flowers,
taking whatever form it wishes.
There dreams delude those asleep,
seeming as if they were actually happening.
This girl trembles even if she is alone without a light.
And if an owl in the courtyard *marā* tree hoots fearfully,
her heart seems to break and she seeks refuge.
And father,
as strong and wrathful as Murukaṉ, is at home
and has let his dogs, like a pack of tigers, run loose.
She is much too afraid to have done what you say.

Here the poet has skillfully described each event in such a way that the sacred power concealed in it is suggested. The first scene is set at the most mysterious time possible: at midnight immediately after it has rained. Because it is cloudy, there is no light at all. To a Tamil, rain is the most indispensable of all natural phenomena and therefore the one most closely connected with sacred power. The heroine meets her lover in a grain field. Of this theme, Eliade writes, "Demeter lay with Iascon on the newly sown ground at the beginning of spring (*Odyssey* V.125). The meaning of this union is clear: it contributes to promoting the fertility of the soil, the prodigious surge of the forces of telluric creation. This practice was comparatively frequent, down to the last century, in northern and central Europe—witness the various customs of symbolic union between couples in the fields."[13] The poet proceeds to identify the heroine with the rain, the source of fertility: her hair, loosened in the back, is by implication like a cloud; her heavy earrings are like lightning. She herself is like a peacock descending from a mountain: a peacock is intoxicated by the rain, and it dances, just as the heroine is intoxicated by having experienced the state of union. The peacock's descending from the mountain into plain sight is comparable to the heroine's descent from the ineffable ecstasy of making love to a more mundane state. The source of the heroine's ecstasy and of the peacock's intoxication is unseen and only its effects can be perceived. Then the poet identifies the heroine with a spirit (aṇañku) on the haunted (*cūruṭai*) slope who deludes those who sleep, making their dreams seem true. The vexing character of the spirit is apparent from the fact that the outcome of its deluding the mother is grief for all concerned. Of course, the intent of the poet is ironic: the heroine in her love-possessed state will cause far more trouble to her family than any mere spirit, whose ability to inflict pain comes to an end as soon as the nature of its illusion is perceived.

The next part of the poem invokes the sacred and threatening aspects of the heroine's actions in going to meet her lover. First she quivers to go alone without a light, showing that she is afraid that she might be the prey of the many spirits lurking outside. This point is emphasized by her fear at the hooting of the owl, a phenomenon that indicates the presence of lurking spirits. Finally, her father with his dogs is compared to Murukaṉ, who punishes all who would go against him. There are potent natural obstacles as well as spiritual ones to her going outside. In fact, the greatest obstacle of all to her meeting her lover is her family, represented by her father. By comparing him to the strongest of

[13] Mircea Eliade, *Cosmos and History: The Myth of the Eternal Return*, trans. Willard R. Trask (New York, 1959), p. 25.

the Tamil gods, the poet is indicating how insuperable an obstacle he represents. The point of the description of these obstacles is to suggest how transfiguring the heroine's experience with her lover must be to enable her to overcome them. Thus Kapilar, the poet, has used a series of hierophanies to create his effect: first, the heroine meets her lover on the field; then she is likened to a cloud; then she is compared to a peacock descending from a mountain; then, she is said to be like a spirit that deludes all who see it; and finally, she is said to be so transfigured in her experience of love that she can ignore the night, filled as it is with dangerous sacred and natural forces, and go to meet her lover. Only in a society such as that of ancient Tamilnad, where sacred powers were thought to inhere to a greater or lesser extent in almost everything, could such means be used as a poetic technique. It is the poet's apprehension of the sacred in the various objects and situations described that enables him to use the technique of suggestion found here and typical of the early Tamil poems.

It is, I believe, chiefly the metamorphosis of the religion of the ancient Tamils under the influence of northern elements that led to the subsequent downgrading of this type of suggestion in their literature. Even by the time of the *Cilappatikāram*, the use of suggestion is far less prominent and generally less subtle than in the anthologies, and stories about the gods that are taken from or modeled on northern sources abound. By medieval times, the Tamils had equaled the North Indians in inventing and retelling mythological stories, and description, mythological and otherwise, comes to occupy as prominent a place as in Sanskrit literature (though even in medieval times the description tends to be complex, rather than compound as it is in Sanskrit). It is true that the medieval writers were influenced by Sanskrit, which they accepted as the language of the gods;[14] yet all Tamil poetry, including that of the medieval period, is very different from Sanskrit. Tamil writers always followed Tamil conventions and took most of their ideas from earlier Tamil literature; the downgrading of the importance of suggestion in Tamil can be attributed

[14] *Kamparāmāyaṇam* 1.10.

only slightly to imitation of Sanskrit.[15] Rather, as mythological stories became more popular and as devotion (whose chief vehicle is story) became the primary ingredient of religion, short lyric poems supercharged with suggestion became less and less common (although such poems have been written to some extent all through Tamil literature). Today, the *Kamparāmāyaṇam* is acknowledged by most Tamils as the greatest work of Tamil literature. In that work, which I feel is as great a composition as can be found in Sanskrit or Tamil, the poetic technique is quite different from that of the ancient Tamil poems. The dramatic sections use a technique of dialogues interspersed with description, which is reminiscent of similar sections in Sanskrit *kāvya*, but which have important differences from their Sanskrit counterparts, while the better descriptions use cosmic imagery in a way that makes the reader aware of the cosmic significance of a small act or object. This latter technique owes much to the suggestive technique of ancient Tamil, but it is not so subtle or complex. A good example occurs in the *Pālakāṇṭam*, where Kampaṉ describes Daśaratha's embrace of Rāma:

> And yet, why do I say he embraced his Son full of goodness?
> No, thinking to measure the earth
> founded on the gathered waters,
> he took his arms and breast
> and measured His broad arms like mountains
> and His garlanded breast, the abode of unfailing good.

In other descriptive verse, Kampaṉ is elaborate and complex in a way that is uncommon in Sanskrit and yet owes little to the suggestive technique of ancient Tamil. For example, in verse 1637, he writes:

> The sharp-filed arrows of the death god [Kāma] spread shame,
> putting all under the spell of desire stronger than blazing fire.
> With the white moonlight and the swift cold wind,
> they afflicted men's bodies and took away their life breath.
> Songs raised in melody were like cobras, hoods raised,
> entering the delicate ears of trembling girls.

The point of such description is more to create a certain mood than to arouse the complex interplay of suggestions.

[15] See *Kamparāmāyaṇam* (Madras, U. V. Swaminathaier Library), *Cuntarakāṇṭam*, p. xx.

8

PROSODY: TAMIL AND INDO-ARYAN PARALLELS

METER

Tamil meter has three important constituents: the foot, or *cīr*, the manner in which different feet are connected, or *taḷai*, and the line, or *aṭi*. As in Western prosody, there are different kinds of feet. The basic component of a foot is called an *acai*, which consists of one *nēr* or *nirai*. Of these, the former may be equated with one long syllable and the latter with two short ones, though the equation does not always hold, as will be seen. The smallest foot consists of one acai and is called *ōracaicīr*. The next smallest and most commonplace consists of two acais and is called *akavaṟcīr* (from akaval and cīr). There are four possible kinds of this foot: nēr nēr; nirai nēr; nēr nirai; and nirai nirai (note that *ai* is short in Tamil, and hence the names have the same rhythms as the feet they represent). The next foot consists of any of the four sorts of akavaṟcīr plus a nēr. Its name is *veṇcīr* and it is obviously of four sorts. Other feet include an akaval plus a nirai; three acai in any combination plus a nēr; and three acai in any combination plus a nirai. These last three are quite rare in the anthologies and need not be considered.

In determining a cīr, the metrical length of the first syllable is always its actual length: long if it contains a long syllable or a short vowel followed by a consonant in the same syllable; short if it contains a short vowel not followed by a consonant in the same syllable. Though this definition of long and short syllables may appear a bit strange, it actually corresponds to the definition used for Sanskrit and Greek meters; for, in Tamil poetry, wherever a vowel is preceded directly by a consonant, that consonant is considered to be in the same syllable as the vowel. Thus the only way in which a vowel can be followed by a consonant in the same syllable is for the next syllable to begin with another consonant or for the syllable in which the vowel occurs to be the last one in the verse. In practice, therefore, a short vowel followed directly by two consonants is long while a short vowel followed directly by only one consonant is short (unless it is the last syllable of the verse). If the first syllable of a cīr is short, the next is considered short whatever its actual length so that the two together constitute a nirai. Thus the second syllable of a nirai may contain a short vowel, a short vowel followed directly by two consonants (or, as a Tamil would say, by a consonant in the same syllable) or a long vowel. If the first syllable of a cīr is long, then it constitutes a nēr. After the first nirai or nēr, this process is repeated to get the second nirai or nēr. If, however, as often occurs, the foot is akavaṟcīr and the only syllable left in the cīr after the first nirai or nēr is a short one, that syllable is considered to be long and constitutes a nēr. The same holds true for the final nēr in a veṇcīr: if after some combination of two acais there is an extra short syllable at the end of the cīr, that is considered to be long and constitutes a nēr. This will become clear when examples are given below. It should be pointed out that the notion of compensatory metrical lengthening or shortening of a syllable is nowhere used in the Tamil definition of cīr. I have used it here in order to facilitate an understanding of the system. Thus to a Tamil a nirai beginning a cīr is (C)V̆CV̆(C), a nēr beginning a cīr is (C)V̄ or (C)V̄̆C, an akavaṟcīr of nirai nēr is (C)V̆CV̄ (C)CV̄̆(C), and a veṇcīr of nirai nēr nēr is (C)V̆CV̄̆(C)C[V̄̆C / V̄(C)] CV̄̆(C).

The most common Tamil meter, in which all of the anthologies except the *Kalittokai* and the *Paripāṭal* are written, is called *āciriyappā* and consists of lines of four cīr that must be either akavaṟcīr or veṇcīr. The taḷai, or connection between different feet in this meter, is mostly antispastic, that is, if one foot ends in a nirai, the next begins with a nirai. This produces a jerky rhythm called *akaval ōcai* ("the sound of akaval"). An example is Aiṅ. 281:

– – ⏑ ⏑ – – – – ⏑ ⏑
veḷḷa / varampi / ṉūḻi / pōkiyum /

– – – ⏑ ⏑ ⏑ ⏑ – – ⏑ ⏑
kiḷḷai / vāḻiya / palavē / yoḷḷiḻai /

⏑ ⏑ – – – ⏑ ⏑ –
irumpal / kūntaṟ / koṭicci /

⏑ ⏑ – – – – – – –
peruntōṭ / kāval / kāṭṭi / yavvē. /

As in most early Tamil poems in the āciriyappā meter, the taḷai is observed only sporadically. In this poem, the next to last line contains only three feet, an optional usage in this meter.

Another important meter, found occasionally in poems of the *Kalittokai* and used frequently in the works of the *Patiṉeṇkīḻk-kaṇakku*, which were composed perhaps two centuries after the anthologies, is the *veṇpā*. These verses (or parts of poems) are generally of two, three, or four lines. All lines but the last contain four cīr, while the last line contains three cīr. The cīr used in this meter may be either akavaṟcīr or veṇcīr, with the exception of the final cīr of the poem,which must be either ōracaicīr (of one acai) or an akavaṟcīr. The taḷai, or connection between feet, should be such that nirai follows nēr, nēr follows nirai, and nēr follows the last nēr of a veṇcīr to produce what is termed *ceppal ōcai* ("a recitative tone"), where *ceppal* is from *ceppu*, to declare. An example is the ninth verse of the *Tirukkuṟaḷ*:

– – ⏑ ⏑ – ⏑ ⏑ ⏑ ⏑ – – ⏑ ⏑ –
kōḷil / poṟiyiṟ / kuṇamilavē / yeṇkuṇattāṉ /

– – ⏑ ⏑ – ⏑ ⏑
ṟāḷai / vaṇaṅkāt / talai. /

In the veṇpā meter, the proper taḷai is more often employed than in āciriyappā. Pope says of the veṇpā meter, "This system may at first sight appear artificial, but its superiority to Sanskrit prosody is very striking. It is admirably adopted to the nature of the Tamil language, and seems naturally evolved from it. The great variety of the melody of veṇpā verse is apparent from the fact that 512 types of the longer lines can be formed." He further says of the veṇpā lines found in the *Nālaṭiyār*, "There are few lines in Pindar, or in any Greek chorus, which will not find a representative here."[1]

There is one final type of meter found in early Tamil that should be mentioned. In the *kali* meter (called *kalippā*), each line contains four cīr, which may be either akavaṟcīr, usually ending in a nirai, or more commonly veṇcīr, usually beginning with a nirai. The rhythm thus produced is called *tuḷḷal ōcai* ("a jumping sound"). An example is the first few lines of *Kalittokai* 3:

˘ ˘ – – | ˘ ˘ – – | – ˘ ˘ | – ˘ ˘
aṟaniṉṟi / *yayaṟuṟṟu* / *mampalai* / *nāṇiyum* /

˘ ˘ – – | – – – | – ˘ ˘ | ˘ ˘ ˘ ˘
vaṟaniṉti / *nī cellu* / *nīḷiṭai* / *niṉaippavum* /

˘ ˘ – – | ˘ ˘ – | ˘ ˘ – | ˘ ˘ – –
iṟai nillā / *vaḷaiyōṭ* / *itaḻcōrpu* / *paṉimalkap* /

It should be remarked that in āciriyappā, akavaṟcīrs predominate and veṇcīrs are rare, while in veṇpā the akavaṟcīrs outnumber veṇcīrs by about five to three,[2] and in kali meter, veṇcīrs predominate.

A poem written according to the Tamil metrical system may be resolved into a series of lines in which each line receives a certain number of beats according to the number of cīrs it contains. This may be seen in the traditional recitation of a four-line veṇpā (see figure 1).

[1] G. U. Pope, *The Naladiyar, or Four Hundred Quatrains in Tamil* (London, 1893), p. xxx.

[2] Ibid., pp. xxxi–xxxix.

Here, for an akavaṟcīr, a nirai is given the time of two eighth notes and a nēr the time of a quarter note. When a veṇcīr occurs, the half note is divided into two triplets of eighth notes; each nirai is given two eighth notes (one for each syllable) and each nēr two eighth notes (two for one syllable). Thus the meter serves to break the poems into units of one cīr, each of which is given the same amount of time in recitation. The structure of the cīr is such that it contains either four or six beats, corresponding to two of the simplest time signatures in western music, 2/4 and 3/4. In other words, each cīr is divided into either a doublet or a triplet rhythm, the two simplest subdivisions that can be made musically.

The inherited meters of Sanskrit, *anuṣṭubh* and *triṣṭubh*, contain respectively eight and eleven syllables to a quarter. In classical poetry, there appear a large number of meters such as *mandākrāntā* in which the number of syllables in each *pāda*, or quarter, is constant and in which the length of each syllable is specified. These classical meters do not appear to have been derived from a popular poetry: they are too difficult for any folksinger or bard to improvise in. Rather, they are almost certainly the artificial creations of the classical poets, fashioned specifically for sophisticated Sanskrit poetry—to which they are very well adapted. In both types of meter, inherited and artificial, the length of a line is determined by the number of syllables it contains, not by the number of time units, or syllabic instants, in it, as in Tamil. Thus it would be pointless to search for Tamil parallels among them.

On the other hand, there appears in the Prakrits a kind of meter based not on the number of syllables in a line, but rather, like Tamil meter, on the total length of the syllables in a line. In this meter (which was later used for Sanskrit as well as Prakrit), the sequence - - - ⏑ ⏑ ⏑ ⏑ would count not as six syllables but as eight *mātrās* or syllabic instants, where each mātrā equals the time it takes to pronounce a short vowel and where a long vowel is exactly twice as long as a short vowel. The *Sattasaī* is written in *āryā*, the most common of these Prakrit meters, in which the first and third pādas must each contain twelve mātrās, the second eighteen, and the fourth fifteen. It is natural to suspect that this meter may be related to the Tamil scheme of meters, which it resembles at least in using the mātrā system, especially as it is not native to Sanskrit.

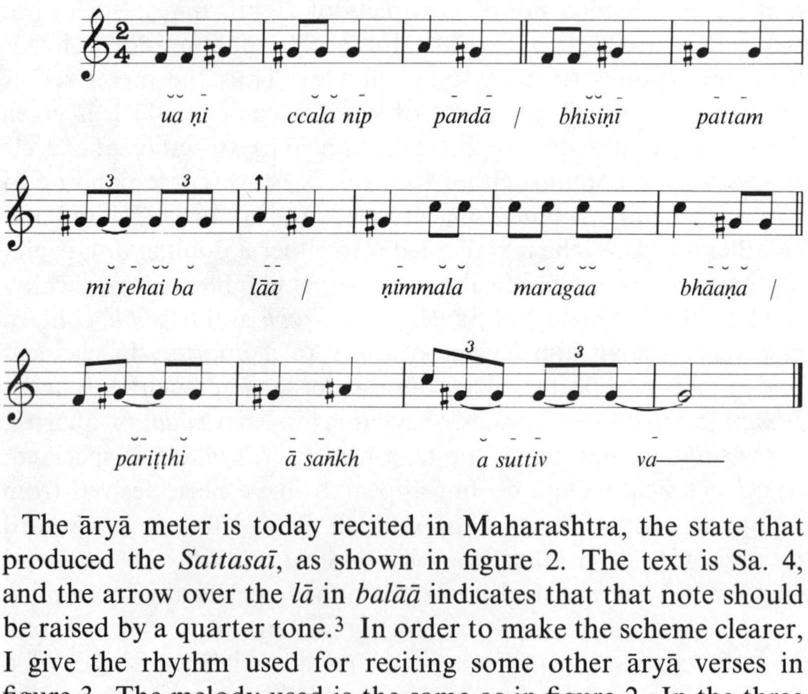

The āryā meter is today recited in Maharashtra, the state that produced the *Sattasaī*, as shown in figure 2. The text is Sa. 4, and the arrow over the *lā* in *balāā* indicates that that note should be raised by a quarter tone.[3] In order to make the scheme clearer, I give the rhythm used for reciting some other āryā verses in figure 3. The melody used is the same as in figure 2. In the three stanzas in figure 3, syncopation between bars is necessary, except in the case of the final syllable. Such syncopation is in fact avoided by the division of the meter into *caturmātragaṇas*, divisions whose length equals four mātrās or syllabic instants. Apte states, "The

[3] I am grateful to Saudamini Bahulikar for demonstrating how this meter is recited.

amıaṃ pāuakavvaṃ padhiuṃ souṃ a je na ā ṇanti /

kāmas sa tatta tantiṃ kuṇanti te kahaṃ ṇa lajjanti / /

sattasa tāiṃ kaıvac chaleṇa koḍī a majjha ā rammi /

Hāleṇ a virai āiṃ sālañ kārā ṇaṃ gāhānaṃ / /

caturmātragaṇas mentioned in this and the next sections must be kept separate by avoiding a long letter at their junction, which thus must not combine the last *mātrā* of an earlier *caturmātra* with the first *mātrā* of a latter one." For āryā, Apte gives the following definition: "[The] first half has seven *caturmātras* and a long letter at the end; [the] second has five *caturmātras* followed by one short letter, one *caturmātra*, and one long letter. . . . In each half the *caturmātras* in odd places must not be *jagaṇa* (⏑ – ⏑), the sixth *caturmātra* in the first half must be either *jagaṇa* or *sarvalaghu* (⏑ ⏑ ⏑ ⏑). But if the seventh *gaṇa* of the first half or the fifth *gaṇa* of the second half are of the *sarvalaghu* type, a new word must begin with the first *laghu*."[4] This may be schematized as follows:

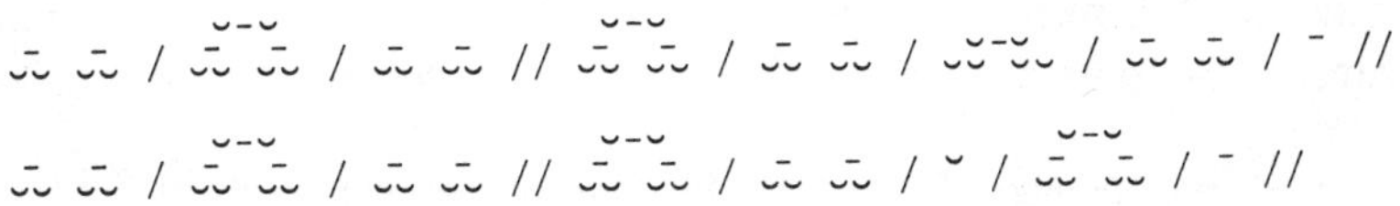

[4] Vaman Shivaram Apte, *The Practical Sanskrit-English Dictionary*, rev. ed. (Poona, 1959), III: app. p. 30.

But while this scheme is adequate to define the meter, it has been seen above that when it is sung (at least in modern Maharashtra), it breaks down differently. The sixth caturmātra of the first line comes together with the first two mātrās of the seventh to make two triplet rhythms that are together given the time of a regular caturmātra, while the last caturmātragaṇa of the second half absorbs the short syllable before and one mātrā of the long syllable after it to produce a similar unit with two triplet rhythms. Thus the grouping of feet according to the number of mātrās in them becomes 4/4/4//4/4/6/4//4/4/4//4/4/6/1//. The short note that stands alone in Apte's scheme is raised when sung (to C in the key used above), producing a nice effect. In order to determine whether in fact this scheme is adhered to in the *Sattasaī*, I have analyzed the first twenty-five poems of that work in appendix 1 below. In all of those poems, there is not one deviation from this system.

It is apparent that this meter is closely related to Tamil meter, whether analyzed by Apte's scheme or by mine. Each line breaks down into a number of feet, each of which is allotted either four or six mātrās, just as in Tamil. There can thus be no question whatsoever that this meter is derived from the same non-Sanskritic source as the Tamil meters. The only real differences are that in Tamil akavaṟcīr the rhythm ⏑–⏑ is not commonly allowed, while in āryā it can occur in half of the feet,[5] and that in Tamil veṇcīr feet must be $\underset{-}{\smile\smile}$ $\underset{-}{\smile\smile}$, while in āryā their equivalent may be any combination of short and long that begins with a short syllable and contains six mātrās.

The reader may wonder whether there is in fact a meter in early Tamil that is identical to āryā as it is sung. There is not, but there are similar meters. For example, the *Nāṉmaṇikkaṭikai*, one of the *Patiṉeṇkīḻkkaṇakku*, is in a type of veṇpā that reads 3/4/4/4, if one takes the true pauses in the verse as the end of each line rather than the conventional place on cīr later; each number indicates the number of feet in a line and each foot is either akavaṟcīr or veṇcīr except for the last one, which may be either aka-

[5] John Marr points out to me that the rhythm ⏑––⏑ is possible for āciriyappā, as in the second cīr in line 106 of the *Tirumurukāṟṟuppaṭai*, quoted in both Pērāciriyar's and Naccinārkkiniyar's commentary on the *Tolkāppiyam, Poruḷatikāram, Ceyyuḷiyal, cūttiram* 325.

vaṟcīr or ōracaicīr. The only differences between this meter and āryā are that the latter has only three feet in the third pāda, that instead of ending in a foot of two or four mātrās, its final foot has only one mātrā, and that the use of akavaṟcīr or veṇcīr is specified for each foot in āryā while in Tamil the use is random. The *Tirukkuṟaḷ* is written in a kind of veṇpā reminiscent of āryā. It is of two lines, of which the first has four cīrs and the second three. A pause or caesura sometimes comes after the third foot in the third line, so that in fact the scheme is often 4/3. If two of these verses are put together, the meter is identical to āryā, except that akavaṟcīr and veṇcīr occur randomly in Tamil and the end of the second pāda may be equivalent to two mātrās in Tamil, while it must contain four mātrās in āryā. An explanation of this is that, in Tamil, this foot represents the final cīr of a veṇpā and hence is given the time of the other cīrs even if it is shorter, while in āryā that cīr is not the end of the verse and so must contain its full complement of syllabic instants. At the end of the fourth pāda, āryā, like some Tamil veṇpās, has a cīr with less than four syllabic instants, which is sung with the syllables held out so that the time it takes to sing is equal to that of the other feet. It should be pointed out that in Tamil āciriyappā meter, the next-to-last line generally contains three cīrs and the last line four, so that its structure is equivalent to each of the two halves of āryā. Thus the only difference in length of lines (or pādas) between most Tamil poems of four lines in āciriyappā or veṇpā and āryā is that in the former, the second line (or pāda) has four feet while in the latter it has three feet. The probable reason for the shape of āryā is that it was influenced by native Indo-Aryan meters, in which the two halves are symmetrical. The melody to which a four-line veṇpā is sung has an important point in common with that used for āryā in modern Maharashtra: in both, the pitch rises by a major third in the third line or pāda, as can be seen in the above examples.

Several other meters common in Indo-Aryan are based on syllabic instants. The number of mātrās in each quarter is 12/18/12/18// for *gīti*, 12/15/12/15// for *upagīti*, 12/15/12/18// for *udgīti*, 12/20/12/20// for *āryāgīti*, and 16/16/16/16// for *mātrāsamaka*. The first four of these meters are defined simply as variations of āryā and so conform to the caturmātragaṇa scheme.[6] Āryāgīti is said to occur when each half of the āryā contains eight caturmātragaṇas (some define each half as being divided into quarters containing three and five caturmātras respectively). Each of the four quarters of mātrāsamaka consists of four caturmātras, the first of which must not be jagaṇa (⏑ - ⏑) and the ninth mātrā of which must be represented by a short letter. It is clear that mātrāsamaka corresponds to the most common of Tamil meters, āciriyappā, the only important difference being that in some feet in the Indo-Aryan meter, the configuration ⏑ - ⏑, not commonly allowed in Tamil, may occur.

The first occurrence of āryā and other related meters in Indo-Aryan is in the Pāli literature of Buddhism. Warder differentiates between "old" meters, in which the number of syllables per line is constant (as in native Sanskrit meters), and "new" meters, in which the number of syllables is variable, but the total quantity of each line is constant. He writes, "a new style of poetry had come into fashion in the 5th or 4th century B.C. which may be called the 'musical' style. In the metres of this style the opposition of long and short syllables, that one long equals two shorts, is exact and inflexible in the same way a note and two notes of half its value [are] in music."[7] Among the "new" meters he describes, only those called *gaṇacchandas*, represented by āryā and gīti meter, are related to Tamil meter.

It seems to me that the dates Warder gives for the first use of the new meters in Pāli are much too early. Winternitz says that the *Tipiṭaka* was written down only in the first century B.C. under the Ceylonese king Vaṭṭagāmini.[8] He says that Pāli, the language

[6] Apte, *Sanskrit-English Dictionary*, III, app. p. 30.

[7] A. K. Warder, *Introduction to Pali* (London, 1963), p. 358. See also A. K. Warder, *Pali Meter* (London, 1968), pp. 138–171. Warder's attempt to derive the Pali gaṇacchandas from what he supposes to be the earlier *mattācchandas* is wholly unconvincing to me. Indeed, in light of the fact that Tamil meter so closely resembles the gaṇacchandas meters, it appears virtually certain that the Pali gaṇacchandas meters must have come from a southern source. Certainly the Tamils did not copy the Pali meters, for if they had done so their meters would be identical or nearly identical to the gaṇacchandas meters. The Tamil meters, moreover, must be quite ancient: they were used for magical formulas even before they were used as poetry, and there is no trace of any earlier metrical system.

[8] M. Winternitz, *A History of Indian Literature*, trans. S. Ketkar and H. John (Calcutta, 1963), II:8.

in which it was written, probably developed during the period after Aśoka when Buddhism had already spread through the whole of Central India and through the Northwest.[9] Thus a reasonable estimate would place the first occurrence of the Tamil-related meters at the third or second century B.C. at the earliest. It is significant that by this time Pāli literature had been exposed to southern elements in Central India and perhaps in Ceylon as well; in any event, there can be no doubt whatsoever that the āryā and gīti meters that Pāli literature uses are closely related to Tamil meter. In light of the diffusion into North Indian culture of many words from Dravidian languages, of elements concerning woman, and of literary conventions at about this time,[10] it is not surprising that a meter closely related to Tamil meter should also appear in popular Indo-Aryan literature at this period.

What is somewhat more surprising is that a meter attested so early in Pāli should not appear until quite late in Sanskrit works. In discussing the plays of Bhāsa, who was perhaps a century earlier than Kālidāsa, Keith writes, "The rarity of the Āryā is remarkable; beside the one Upagīti, which is in Prākrit, there are only eleven, of which five are in Prakrit. Contrast the frequency of the Āryā in Kālidāsa where there are 31 out of 163 in the *Vikramorvaçī*, and 35 out of 96 in the *Mālavikāgnimitra*."[11] Concerning the frequent occurrence of Māhāraṣṭrī verses in āryā and other Prakrit meters, Keith writes, "The Māhārāṣṭrī unquestionably owes its vogue to the outburst of lyric in that dialect, which has left its traces in the anthology of Hāla and later texts, and which about the period of Kālidāsa invaded the epic."[12] In other words, even though Tamil-related meters are attested in Indo-Aryan much earlier than the *Sattasaī*, it is only after that work that they were accepted by Sanskrit writers as proper meters for polished works. Clearly, in about the second and third centuries A.D. there was a large body of poetry composed in Māhārāṣṭrī, of which the *Sattasaī* (or at least some verses of it)

9 Ibid., p. 13.

10 See chapters 5 and 9–10.

11 Arthur Berriedale Keith, *The Sanskrit Drama* (London, 1924), p. 124.

12 Ibid., p. 167.

is the only surviving remnant. This poetry was much finer than the Pāli literature that used Tamil-related meters, and so it came to be imitated by the Sanskrit writers beginning with Bhāsa. The extent to which it was imitated has been suggested above to some extent; it will be seen below that Kālidāsa and later Sanskrit writers took not only meters and techniques from this Maharashtrian tradition, but many conventions as well.

Rhyme

In Tamil, rhyme is called *toṭai.* In the following analysis, "letter" means an initial vowel, a consonant followed by a vowel, or a noninitial consonant—that is, any sound represented by one symbol in Tamil script. Rhyme may be between the first two cīrs of two successive lines or, in the case of end rhyme (*iyaiputtoṭai*), between the last cīrs of two successive lines (both of these are called *aṭittoṭai*, or line rhyme). It may also be between the first and second cīrs of a line (*aṇaittoṭai*), between the first and third cīrs (*po̱lipputtoṭai*), between all four cīrs (*muṟṟuttoṭai*), between the first and fourth cīrs (*orūuttoṭai*), between the first, second, and third cīrs (*kūḻaittoṭai*), between the first, second, and fourth cīrs (*kīḻkkatuvāyttoṭai*), and between the first, third, and fourth cīrs (*mēṟkatuvāyttoṭai*). If the first letter of two cīrs is identical, it is called *mōṉaittoṭai*; if the second letter of two cīrs is identical, it is called *ētukaittoṭai*; if the last letter of two cīrs is the same, it is called *iyaiputtoṭai.* There are two additional kinds of poetic devices described by the Tamil prosodists as toṭai that are not really rhyme. One is *muraṇṭoṭai*, in which two cīrs use words that have opposite meanings; the other is *alapeṭaittoṭai*, in which two vowels, which may be different, of three mātras (as *āa*, *ūu*, corresponding to the Sanskrit *pluta* vowels) occur in two cīrs. By far the most common sort of Tamil rhyme, especially in later works, is beginning rhyme. Ak. 235 is a good example of the various sorts of Tamil rhyme. The rhyming places are underlined.

amma vāḻi tōḻi poruḷ purintu

uḷḷār kollō kātala ruḷḷiyuñ

ciṟanta ceytiyiṉ maṟantaṉar kollō
payaṉilañ kuḻaiya vīcip peyalmuṉintu
viṇṭu maṉṉiya koṇṭal māmaḻai
mañkul aṟkamoṭu poñkupu tuḷippa
vāṭaiyoṭu nivanta āyitaḻt tōṉṟi
cuṭarkoḷ akalil curuñkupiṇi yaviḻac
curimukiḻ macuṇṭaip potiyaviḻ vāṉpū
vicumpaṇi mīṉiṟ pacumputa laṇiyak
kaḷvaṉ maṇṇaḷaic ceṟiya akalvayaṟ
kiḷaiviri karumpiṉ kaṇaikkāl vāṉpū
māriyuñ kurukiṉ īriya kurañka
naṉikaṭuñ civappoṭu nāman tōṟṟi
paṉikaṭi koṇṭa paṇpil vāṭai
maruḷiṉ mālaiyo ṭaruḷiṉṟi naliya
nutaliṟai koṇṭa ayalaṟi pacalaiyoṭu
toṉṉalañ citaiyac cāay
eṉṉaḷkol aḷiyaḷ eṉṉā tōrē.

It should be noted that not all the rhymes fit the definition. In the third from the last line, for example, *liṟai* is rhymed with *laṟi*, where the Tamil letters (*la*, *li*; *ṟai*, *ṟi*) are actually different.

In appendix 1, I have underlined all the rhymes in the first twenty-five poems of the *Sattasaī* that are similar to Tamil rhyme.

Straight lines indicate rhyme exactly analogous to that of Tamil (that is, the occurrence of identical letters in the same position in different caturmātragaṇas), while wavy lines indicate assonance or alliteration used randomly, as in most Sanskrit verses. An infallible criterion for determining whether rhyme in the *Sattasaī* is related to Tamil rhyme is whether the āryā verses use rhyming sounds at the beginnings of successive quarters, since that rhyme is wholly foreign to earlier Sanskrit and Indo-Aryan verse. Appendix 1 shows that such rhyme occurs in the *Sattasaī* in verses 1, 8, 12, 13 (perhaps), 14, 23, 24, and 25. A survey of the rest of the first hundred poems of the *Sattasaī* reveals such rhyme in verses 26 (*ṇa*/*ṇi*; *suṇ*/*suṇ*); 27 (*paṇaa*/*ahaa*); 29 (*a*/*a*; *aṇuhū*/*ahiṇa*); 32 (*aha*/*suha*; *eṇ*/*aṇ*); 35 (*diarassa*/*diaham*, pādas 1 and 3); 37 (*da*/*ḍa*); 44 (*a*/*a*); 46 (*taha*/*jaha*); 50 (*suha*/*laha*); 51 (*ahava*/*suha*); 53 (*dhiassa*/*uassa*/*alassa*); 63 (*ua*/*ṇia*); 64 (*ṇi*/*ni*); 66 (*ha*/*ha*); 73 (*jaṃjaṃ*/*aṃgaṃ*; *pacchā*/*icchā*); 79 (*ha*/*hi*; *a*/*a*); 81 (*a*/*a*); 84 (*taha*/*jaha*); 86 (*ekkaṃ*/*hatthaṃ*); 88 (*jāṇa*/*aṇuṇa*); 89 (*eāṇa*/*aṇṇāṇa*); and 99 (*aṇṇo*/*puṇṇe*). From a survey of ten poems of the *Akanāṉūṟu*, the frequency of beginning rhyme in Tamil appears to be about 20 percent. That may be compared to 10 percent for the first hundred poems of the *Sattasaī* and 2 percent for the first hundred verses of the *Meghadūta*, used for a control.

Even more peculiar to Dravidian poetry than beginning rhyme is the rhyming of the second syllable, called *dvitīyākṣaraprāsa* in Sanskrit. Of this, Sambamoorthy states, "The *dvitīyākṣaraprāsa* is a distinctive feature of the poetry and musical compositions in South Indian languages. It is definitely a South Indian concept. The *Dēvāram* and the *Tiruvācakam* are the earliest musical compositions wherein we come across this type of *prāsa*. We do not come across this variety of *prāsa* in the *Aṣṭapadīs* of Jayadeva, although they contain *antyaprāsas*."[13] In the first hundred poems of the *Sattasaī*, such rhyme (counting only occurrences between the beginnings of successive pādas) occurs no less than twenty-three times. There can be little doubt, then, that Tamil and Māhārāṣṭrī derived not only their meters from the same non-Sanskritic source, but also their rhyme.

[13] P. Sambamoorthy, *South Indian Music*, 2d ed. (Madras, 1954), IV:280.

9

TAMIL POETIC CONVENTIONS AND INDO-ARYAN PARALLELS

In this chapter I discuss Tamil conventions that have close Indo-Aryan parallels only after the *Sattasaī*; conventions that occur in the *Buddhacarita* or in the epics are considered in chapter 10. In appendix 2, the reader will find a list of all the Tamil conventions discussed that have Indo-Aryan parallels and the Indo-Aryan works in which they occur.

Puṟam Conventions

The puṟam poems are categorized by the *Tolkāppiyam* and by the colophons to the poems themselves according to the *tiṇai*, or poetic situation, they treat, and, within each tiṇai, according to the poetic theme, or *tuṟai*, they contain. The tiṇais of puṟam are seven according to the *Tolkāppiyam*: *veṭci* (cattle raid and recovery of cattle); *vañci* (invasion); *uḻiñai* (siege and defense of fort); *tumpai* (pitched battle); *vākai* (victory); *kāñci* (transience); and *pāṭāṇ* (praise of kings). These tiṇais each have eight to twenty-one tuṟais associated with them; the total number of tuṟais is 138.[1]

[1] K. Kailasapathy, *Tamil Heroic Poetry* (London, 1968), pp. 187ff.

Only a few of the puṟam themes have Indo-Aryan parallels. In many poems, a bard asks a king for a gift (Puṟ. 3, 135, 136, 138, 139, 154, 158, 159, 160, 167, 204). Some poems in this group describe the wilderness the bard has had to traverse in order to arrive at the king's palace or camp; then they speak of the suffering of the bard and his family; and they end with an appeal for a gift (Puṟ. 3, 136). A good example is Puṟ. 135: "As my bangled Viṟali behind me suffered from climbing small paths on hard crevices in high tiger-haunted mountains, I came, Lord, bent over and staggering, thinking of your good fame, embracing at my side, with a modest heart, my small yāḻ. . . . Whenever it is, if you see suppliants in your court, you give them herds of elephants." Subh. 1435 is a similar poem:

The sprout grew at my first resolve
and formed its leaflets as I left;
the twigs upon my journey grew,
the mighty branches as I reached the town.
The buds appeared at morning audience,
and now that Your Majesty is seen,
this tree of my true heart's desire
has flowered and has borne its fruit.

A large number of puṟam poems in Tamil are concerned with the praise of kings (pāṭāṇ tiṇai), as are a large number of Sanskrit verses. Both use similar means. They often tell of the king's valor in battle, describing the sad condition of his enemies (Puṟ. 31, 51, 54, 73, 299; R. 4.21, 6.63, 15.97, 18.5, 18.25; Subh. 1431), his enemies' wives (Puṟ. 25, 41, 78, 97; R. 6.28, 9.14, 12.78, 18.44; Subh. 1405, 1453), or his enemies' lands (Puṟ. 341, 350, 355; Patiṟ. 13; Subh. 1401, 1409, 1412). Often they include passages that relate the beauty or extraordinary fertility of the king's land (Puṟ. 7, 13, 18, 22, 28, 38, etc.; compare the passages in the first *sarga* of the *Raghuvaṃśa*). Such poems may also describe the king's generosity (Puṟ. 3, 27, 32, 35, 54, 55, etc.; Bu. 2.40; R. 1.7, 3.16, 5.15, etc.), his wives (Puṟ. 3, 6, 24, 56, 68, 71, 73, etc.; Su. 8.29, 8.30; R. 8.27; Kum. 4.5; Subh. 1008, 1420, 1438), and his mercy or benevolence (Puṟ. 5, 27, 38, 42, 50, etc.; R. 4.37, 6.21; Subh. 1392).

Another common way of praising a king is to contrast his cruelty toward his enemies with his generosity toward suppliants and others dependent on him (Puṟ. 12, 40, 49, 53, 68, 73, 94, 104, 128, 142, 156, 177, 226, 337, 380, 390, 398). This theme is treated in many different ways in Tamil. In Puṟ. 40, the poet describes how the detractors of the king hang their heads while his praisers are resplendent (see also Puṟ. 12, 54, 142, 156, 380). In Puṟ. 59, the poet tells the king, "You are like the sun to your enemies, but like the moon to us." In Puṟ. 73, the king says that if his enemies would come as suppliants and beg for his kingdom and even his life, they could have them, but that they will never get either if they try to take them in war (see also Puṟ. 177, 226, 337). In Puṟ. 177, 390, and 398, the poet says that friends can easily enter the king's city, but enemies will never be allowed in (see also Puṟ. 128). In one interesting variation on this theme, the king is compared to a crocodile that can kill an elephant and that lies in shallow water, which is muddied by children from the town playing there (Puṟ. 104). This theme occurs twice in the Sanskrit sources surveyed. In R. 1.16, Dilīpa is said to have been both fearful and gentle, like the ocean with monsters and jewels, and in Subh. 1438, the poet tells the king that to enemies, to scholars, and to women, by his bravery, humility, and grace, he brings severally their suffering, their affection, and their love. A related idea is found in Subh. 1219, which compares good men to *puṇḍra* sugar cane, which bends if it chooses but breaks if twisted by someone who would bend it, and in Subh. 1244, where the poet asks, "Who can understand the hearts of the truly great, which are harder than diamonds and softer than flowers?"

In both traditions, the king is supposed to be inscrutable. Puṟ. 30 says that the king's actions can in no way be surmised beforehand by even the wisest of men, for he possesses hidden strength like a rock that an elephant conceals in his cheek (and that he will later throw with his trunk). In R. 1.20, Dilīpa's actions are said to be inferred only from their fruit, like previous *saṃskāras*, and in R. 17.53, the undertakings of the king are said to have ripened secretly like rice in its husk.

It is common to say of a king that he does not rule the earth in common with others. In Puṟ. 8, the poet says of the king, "He does not deign to possess anything in common, always spurred on by the thought that his land is small." In Puṟ. 363, the poet says,

Benevolent kings who have ruled this vast earth
surrounded by the black sea
so that not even a part of the center of one *uṭai* leaf
belonged to another—
even they have gone to the ground of burned corpses
as their final home,
more of them than there is sand heaped by the waves.

(See also Pur̠. 357.) The notion that a king rules the world alone and does not share his authority over it with other kings is found in Sanskrit in R. 1.30, 2.47, 4.7, 8.27, 9.15, and 18.4.

In Tamil, a king is often praised by saying that he is unaffected by bad omens, a theme whose purport is that the king's greatness and sacred power are so extraordinary that the disposition of other sacred powers makes no difference to him or his kingdom (Pur̠. 20, 68, 105, 117, 124, 204, 384, 386, 388, 389, 395, 397). For example, in Pur̠. 124, the poet describes the king's generosity by saying that even though suppliants go at a wrong time full of bad omens and talk without respect, the king gives to them. This same theme is found in Subh. 1391, where the dust of the king's feet is said to wipe away the syllables written by fate on the foreheads of men who receive the dust by obeisance.

Akam Situations: A General Consideration

All of the Tamil akam poems are put in the mouth of some person involved in the situation. These include the hero, the heroine, the real mother (*nar̠r̠āy*), the foster mother (*cevilittāy*),[2] the heroine's girlfriend, who is sometimes the daughter of the foster mother, the hero's friend, the hero's bard, who is sent as a messenger, onlookers who see the couple eloping, neighbors, the courtesan, and the courtesan's girlfriend. Curiously, the girl's father and the boy's relatives are not the speakers of any of the poems. These conventions appear first in Indo-Aryan in the

[2] In *Kur̠untokai*, comm. U.V. Swaminathaier, 4th ed. (Madras, 1962), p. 73 of the introduction, Swaminathaier writes about the function of the foster mother (*cevilittāy*): "The foster mother is a friend of the real mother and the mother of the heroine's girl friend, according to the grammar books. She loves the heroine very much, protects her, gives her the food she needs, lets her sleep next to her at night, guards her [from going out to meet her lover], is distressed and searches for her when she elopes, and rejoices when she sees her [happy] domestic life."

Sattasaī, though they are not observed in all the poems of that work, the speaker often being the poet himself. In Sa. 9 and 30, the heroine's friend talks to the heroine, trying to console her; in Sa. 17 and 29, a woman whose husband has left for a journey laments; in Sa. 51, the heroine speaks angrily to her husband; in Sa. 78, the hero, who is absent on a journey, remembers his beloved; in Sa. 110, the heroine addresses her mother; in Sa. 220, the female messenger describes to the hero the state of his beloved after he left her. These are only a few of many examples in which the Tamil conventions, or close parallels, appear in the *Sattasaī*. The conventions of Prakrit appear later in Sanskrit. Section 18 of the *Subhāṣitaratnakośa* consists of poems in which the female messenger speaks to the hero, telling of her mistress's love for him. In many of the poems of section 22, the lady parted from her lover grieves. In some poems of section 23, the hero grieves, separated from his beloved. In section 24, the courtesan or adulteress is described, often speaking in the first person. In Subh. 675, the heroine speaks to her mother telling her how she loves the hero. These themes are found also in Kālidāsa to some extent. Thus, in the *Abhijñānaśākuntala*, Śakuntalā is surrounded by her two female friends, Priyaṃvadā and Anusūyā, while in the *Kumārasaṃbhava*, Parvatī's friend responds to Śiva when that disguised god asks why she is practicing austerities (5.52, 5.61), and the same girl is sent as a messenger to Śiva to inform him that Pārvatī's father has agreed to their marriage (6.1).

The speakers are the same in Prakrit and Sanskrit, but differ somewhat in those traditions from those of Tamil. Thus, in Indo-Aryan, there is no foster mother and the messenger is always a woman, usually the heroine's friend, rather than the husband's bard as in Tamil. It should be noted, however, that one of the chief functions of the female messenger in Sanskrit is to apprise the hero of her friend's love for him (Subh., section 18), the same office that is often performed by the heroine's friend in Tamil (for example, Aiñ. 51–60), though in Tamil she is not thought of as a messenger. The Tamil messenger, usually a bard, has a more specialized duty: he comes to conciliate the heroine either when his master is away or when he is with courtesans. There is no one to whom these two functions are allotted in Indo-Aryan poetry. The function of the courtesan in Tamil is taken over by the rival wives of the heroine in Indo-Aryan, while many of the Indo-Aryan poems attributed to loose women and harlots have no real Tamil equivalents. That is because in the Tamil poems where the courtesan appears, the chief emotion expressed is jealousy, while in the Indo-Aryan poems about the *asatī*, the chief emotion is sexual enjoyment. In some poems of the *Sattasaī*, however, the harlot appears in the same role as the parattai (courtesan) in the Tamil poems (for example, Sa. 53, 417).

If these Indo-Aryan conventions had been borrowed directly from Tamil, they would resemble the Tamil conventions much more closely than they in fact do. It should be remembered that between the earliest of the Prakrit poems and the Tamil anthologies there can scarcely be a hundred years, too little time for the borrowed conventions to have been as radically altered as they were. Probably, then, the two sets of conventions were both borrowed from the same source; this hypothesis will be considered below, after the treatment of related themes and situations in Tamil and Indo-Aryan love poetry. In all cases in the following treatment, the earliest occurrences of the themes in Indo-Aryan are given so that the reader may judge for himself when they first appear in the northern tradition.

Kuṟiñci Poems

Akam poems, like their puṟam counterparts, are divided into tiṇais, of which five occur in the poems of the early anthologies. Each of these is described below, and those situations and conventions in them that occur in Indo-Aryan are given. Kuṟiñci is a mountain flower that has given its name to the tiṇai, which concerns secret love before marriage. The setting for such poems is the mountains, whose flowers, animals, birds, grains, and inhabitants are often mentioned in the poems.[3]

A common theme is the lovers' rendezvous. In Tamil, the meeting is usually either in the day as the heroine guards the

[3] For a chart giving the various conventional elements associated with each akam tiṇai, see A. K. Ramanujan, *The Interior Landscape, Love Poems from a Classical Tamil Anthology* (Bloomington, Ind. 1967), p. 107. Kamil Zvelebil has reproduced this chart with a few additions in *The Smile of Murugan: On Tamil Literature of South India* (Leiden, 1973), p. 100.

millet from parrots (Kuṟ. 141, 142, 198; Ak. 28, 32, 38; and others) or at night, often in the rain (Kuṟ. 244, 266, 312, 321, 335, 360; Ak. 2, 22, 58, 68, 102, 122; and others). Both of these themes are illustrated in Kuṟ. 141, where the heroine addresses her friend, asking her to tell her lover to come during the day as she guards the millet and not at night:

What harm, friend, if you tell him what mother said,
to go and keep from the high millet
small parrots with curved beaks?
And what harm if you say to him,
"At midnight you come, with its difficult darkness.
Then a tiger with small paws
suffers at the hatred of a long-trunked elephant
and, skilled at killing,
looks for a chance to catch a wild dog with hungry eyes.
Man of the slopes, do not come then."

In Sa. 691, the theme of meeting while the heroine guards a grain field appears: "Day by day, worried because she will be deprived of her place of rendezvous, the girl protecting the *kalama* [the December rice crop] holds her ever-paler head lower just like the rice." This theme appears also in Sa. 9, where the friend asks the heroine, "Why do you weep because the paddy fields are white [that is, cut]? The hemp field is like a dancer, her face ornamented with *haritala* [and you can meet him as you guard that]." The theme of a night meeting occurs in Sa. 385, 412, 653, and Subh. 890. Of these, Sa. 385 is a good example: " 'You will come!' Thus the first half of the night spent awake passed like a moment. The next half went like a year for her, as she was overcome by grief."

The meeting at night also occurs in Indo-Aryan in a convention in which the heroine, called an *abhisārikā*, goes out secretly to meet her lover, often in the rain. Thus, in Sa. 445, the heroine tells her lover, "O ingrateful one! I still see the village mud I went through to get to you on rainy nights." (See also Sa. 607; R. 6.75, 16.12; Kum. 6.43; Subh. 233, 261, 816, 817, 825, 826, 829–832, 896.) This theme appears often in Tamil. For example, in Ak. 162, the hero describes how his beloved came to him:

At midnight when skies were pouring down without respite,
spreading swift drops, as thunder roared cruelly,

and lightning, like banners of fire, flashed,
splitting the sky like the thick black ocean,
its measureless depths filled with conchs
that never diminish no matter how many are taken,
I was standing at one side of her father's high house,
as the wind pricked, swirling with cold,
and I was waiting for the guards hard to elude
to slacken their vigilance
when she came, her hair shining like black sand,
her lovely petaled rain eyes wandering on her face
as brilliant as a flower . . .
and embraced me continuously
so my afflicting pain left.

This theme also occurs in Kuṟ. 312, where the hero speaks after having met his beloved:

My beloved has cunning that knows two things.
In the middle of the night
she comes
as fragrant as Muḷḷūr forest
in the land of Malaiyaṉ
whose sword is red, whose strength is inimical,
and she is fit for me.
Then she shakes out the mixed flowers
I put in her hair,
rubs sandal and oil in her tresses,
and with a new face
she is fit for her family when day comes.

In Ak. 198, the heroine comes to the rendezvous "scared, keeping her dense anklets from rattling, bent like a cocked bow and wearing cool flowers so bees followed behind her at a time when the city slept." (See also Ak. 58, 158.) This may be compared to Subh. 829:

These beauties, silencing their anklets by knotting their skirts
and binding up the jeweled clasps within the extra fold,
attempt to render silent their amorous expeditions.
Alas, to no avail, for they are marked upon their way
by the jingling swarm of bees
that seek the honey of the flowers in their hair.

Similarly, in Subh. 834, the abhisārikā has to silence her anklets. In Kum. 6.43, abhisārikās in Alakā find their way on cloudy nights by the light of herbs. This may be compared with Ak. 192, in which the heroine's friend tells the hero, "if you say you will come in the middle of the night, the jewel dropped by a snake and brought by the water of a rushing falls as it goes through black caves of a great hill will light up the street of the mountain village." Usually in Tamil, the hero's hard way to the meeting is described, as in this poem, rather than the heroine's (Kuṟ. 268, 324, 336, 340, 355; Ak. 2, 12, 18; and others), a convention not found in Indo-Aryan. Unlike the Sanskrit convention, which makes the abhisārikā go to the house of her lover (Subh. 816), in the Tamil tradition, the meeting is either near the heroine's or, less often, actually in it (Ak. 102). Another important difference is that in Indo-Aryan the abhisārikā is a wanton woman (Subh., section 24), sometimes even married (Subh. 825), while in Tamil she is an unmarried girl meeting the man with whom she is in love.

Also present in the two traditions is the theme of the heroine or her friend suggesting an appropriate place for a rendezvous. In Tamil, the suggestion is rarely explicit. Thus in Kuṟ. 113, the heroine's friend says to the hero,

> Near the town there is a pond.
> And not far from the pond is a small forest river.
> Except for a little white heron searching for prey
> nothing comes near the grove there.
> We will go to that place
> taking clay for our hair,
> and she also will come,
> the innocent girl.

(See also Kuṟ. 114; Ak. 18, 148; Aiṅ. 174.) There are several poems in the *Sattasaī* in which the friend or the heroine hints to the hero that a certain place would be suitable for a rendezvous without actually stating that fact. In Sa. 4, for example, the heroine says, "A crane appears motionless on a lotus leaf like an oyster in a vessel of pure emerald." Here, according to the *Kāvyaprakāśa*,[4] she means that, since the place is lovely and

[4] *Kāvyaprakāśa*, comm. V.R. Jhalakīkar, 7th ed. (Poona, 1965), p. 30.

uninhabited, it would be ideal for a meeting place (see also Sa. 171, 175). In the Tamil tradition, and in Kuṟ. 113 just given, the heron searching for prey is a symbol of sexual intercourse; it is almost certain that the same symbolism is intended for the crane in the Prakrit poem.

There are several poems in the *Sattasaī* in which the heroine worries that her meeting place may soon be destroyed by the changing season. In Sa. 104, for example, the poet describes her despair: "Look, she gathers the fallen flowers of the *madhūka* as if they were the bones of relatives on the burning ground." Since spring is over, the cover provided by the madhūka is no longer sufficient for it to be a rendezvous (see also Sa. 103, 626, 691). This theme appears in Aiṅ. 207:

Your millet will not dry out,
my friend.
Look there:
his high blue-sapphire mountain
wreathed in clouds
looks like a croquette
covered with fat.

Even though the millet seems to be dead in the drought so that the heroine cannot meet her lover while guarding it, her friend consoles her that rain is at hand. Similarly, in Ak. 192, the friend says, "Her forehead . . . has become the color of gold. What will become of her? The millet is bent over [and will soon be cut so that she can no longer guard it and meet her lover]."

Sa. 635 describes an ideal village for a rendezvous: "Fortunate are they who live in a village with fences of many leaves and retreats in bamboo bowed over by the wind where one can make love without worrying." In Sa. 636, a similar idea is stated: "I like villages with thick *kadambas* [to excite love], clean rock surfaces [to make love on], happy peacocks [for amusement after love], and descending falls [to make noise so that no one can hear]." Bamboo, peacocks, and waterfalls are all characteristic of mountains and appear in many Tamil poems on this same theme of secret love.

In several Tamil poems, the hero tells how hopelessly in love he is. According to the colophons, most of these poems are addressed to a male friend who is trying to dissuade the hero from his folly. An example is Kuṟ. 119:

As the child
with lovely stripes
of a little white snake
afflicts a forest elephant,
that young girl,
her teeth as bright as sprouts,
her wrists bangled,
afflicts me.

(See also Kuṟ. 58, 78, 95, 129, 132, 136, 156, 184, 206, 222, 286, 337; Ak. 130, 140; Aiṅ. 171, 174, 256, 259.) This may be compared to Subh. 483:

The maiden left,
with face upon her turning neck like lotus on bending stem.
The glance she cast from curling lashes,
ambrosia mixed with poison,
cut deep within my heart.

(See also Subh. 478, 480, 482, 485–488, 496.)

In Tamil, the heroine is often kept at home by her mother so that she cannot see her beloved (Kuṟ. 244, 246, 262, 292, 294, 343, 361, 401; Ak. 7, 20; and others). This theme appears once in the *Sattasaī*, in poem 497: "The Malaya wind blows hard and mother[5] forbids me to go out; but whoever dies by the fragrance of the *aṅkoṭa* [a plant kept in the house] really dies!" She means that if she cannot go out to meet her lover but must stay at home and smell the sweet fragrance of the aṅkoṭa plant, which reminds her of love, she does not know how she will bear it.

Pālai Poems

Pālai is a desert tree that has given its name to the tiṇai of poems that concern the travels of the hero (sometimes accompanied by his beloved) across the wilderness. Concerning such barren land, Eliade writes:

[5] The Prakrit word used is *attā*. According to the *chāyā*, its Sanskrit equivalent is *śvaśrū*, mother-in-law. But attā, a Dravidian loan, may also mean mother (D.E.D. 121). It seems to me more likely that the girl is unmarried and her mother is keeping her inside than that she is married and is kept from her illicit affair by her mother-in-law.

> The world that surrounds us . . . , the world in which the presence and the work of man are felt—the mountains that he climbs, populated and cultivated regions, navigable rivers, cities, sanctuaries—all these have an extraterrestrial archetype, be it conceived as a plan, as a form, or purely and simply as a "double" existing on a higher cosmic level. But everything in the world that surrounds us does not have a prototype of this kind. For example, desert regions inhabited by monsters, uncultivated lands, unknown seas on which no navigator has dared to venture, do not share with the city of Babylon, or the Egyptian nome, the privilege of a differentiated prototype. They correspond to a mythical model, but of another nature: all these wild, uncultivated regions and the like are assimilated to chaos; they still participate in the undifferentiated, formless modality of pre-Creation. That is why, when possession is taken of a territory—that is, when its exploitation begins—rites are performed that symbolically repeat the act of Creation: the uncultivated zone is first "cosmicized," then inhabited.[6]

In many of the Tamil poems, the hero decides to leave the heroine and go searching for wealth, usually in the summer; in his quest, he must cross over the pālai wilderness. Thus, in Ak. 187, the heroine says, "He is ashamed of the secret meetings with me, which have stretched over many days, . . . and, his heart urging him to get wealth in a far land, he has gone and thinks of raising my position." In some poems, he leaves after marriage (for example, Aiṅ. 309). The poems describe the dangers through which he must travel, making the other-worldly character of his way quite clear. In Kuṟ. 283, for example, the heroine says, "He went, friend, on a way where there is no water, full of ancient places where vultures wait for the flesh of wayfarers, killed, as they stopped for the night, by robbers [Maṟavaṉs] with murderous spears who are always like Death." It is common in many societies for the man to have to wait to marry until he can support his wife.[7] Thus among the Erava villagers, a jungle tribe in Cochin state, "A young man is never allowed to marry unless he is able to support a wife." Similarly in Orissa one has to show his man-

[6] Mircea Eliade, *Cosmos and History: The Myth of the Eternal Return*, trans. Willard R. Trask (New York, 1959), pp. 9–10.

[7] Edward Westermarck, *A History of Human Marriage*, 5th ed. (London, 1921), I:46–47.

hood before his marriage among some peoples.[8] There is, however, more to the poetic convention of pālai than simply an instance of this widespread and sensible custom. Eliade describes initiation as symbolic "death to the profane condition followed by rebirth to the sacred world, the world of the gods."[9] Initiation usually comprises a threefold revelation: revelation of the sacred, of death, and of sexuality.[10] For the ancient Tamils, the central manifestation of the sacred in life was marriage. It was only natural that an initiatory ordeal should have been associated with the entrance into that state, and in fact the man's journey through wilderness for gold is exactly such an ordeal (of course, it is only a literary convention, not a custom that was actually practiced). Thus the man goes out into the other world and almost dies many times from attacks by robbers, from the heat of the sun, from lack of water, or from acts by other agencies. The theme of return is put under the category of mullai, described below, and takes place during the monsoon, the time of new creation after the death and sterility of summer. After the hero has gone through the desert and undergone symbolic death, he finds gold, that is, he completes his task and by so doing symbolically overcomes death and returns reborn. Gold is the magic talisman that he brings from the other world and that is the symbol of his changed condition.

The true character of this theme is made clear from a comparison with similar stories in other literatures. At the beginning of the *Odyssey*, Telemachus undergoes a symbolic initiation: he sets off from Ithaca across the waters to the other world, Greece. There he visits Menelaus and Helen, eats food that has been drugged by Helen, and falls asleep, thus undergoing a symbolic death. Finally he returns to Ithaca accompanied by a prophet, Theoclymenus, whose purpose is evidently to help the young initiate negotiate his way back through the world of death. Concerning this story, Lord writes:

> The pattern of the tale of the youthful hero setting out on his first adventure sometimes contains the rescue of someone from

[8] Ibid., pp. 48–50.

[9] Mircea Eliade, *The Sacred and the Profane* (New York, 1959), p. 157.

[10] Ibid., p. 188.

> the hands of an enemy, often by killing the enemy, who is possibly a supernatural monster. Sometimes the journey takes the hero into the other world and as such entails experience with the guardians, entrances, and exits of that world. Sometimes, too, the purpose of the journey is to obtain power-bestowing knowledge or information to be used on the return of the hero, or perhaps, if not used in a specific situation, to make a powerful magician or simply "a man" of the hero. This last is actually Athena's avowed purpose in sending Telemachus to the mainland.[11]

It was to become "a man," to become one who could do all that society expected of him, that the Tamil hero was supposed to make his journey: "To keep from ruin my kin, to feed my family, to be close to kin who are not kin [that is, guests], I wished to undertake with resolve manly action. Because I have finished my hard task . . . , gotten valuables as hard to get as Uṟantai city . . . , I will embrace her." (Ak. 93; see also Ak. 173, 231.)

In the *Pauṣyaparva* of the *Mahābhārata* (1.1–9), a story occurs that is even closer to the Tamil theme than the episode of Telemachus. There, Uttaṅka asks his guru what he wishes as payment. He is told to ask the guru's wife, who tells him to get and bring to her the two earrings of King Pauṣya's wife. After much wandering, he manages to obtain the earrings and finally returns, after having been imprisoned for a time below the earth in the land of the snakes. It is significant that in this story an ornament is the magic object for which he goes to the other world. In the *Odyssey* too Telemachus brings back many presents from the palace of Menelaus, chief among them a gown given by Helen "for his future wife" (book 15). Similarly in Aiṅ. 463, the heroine says, "Our lover is tarrying so that he can bring an ornament he has gotten in the enemy's land." It is also significant that in the Pauṣya story, it is a woman who sends Uttaṅka on his task to the other world, for in Tamil the hero undergoes his ordeal for a woman. Similarly, in the epic of *Gilgamesh*, the goddess Ishtar is indirectly responsible for Gilgamesh's journey to the land of immortality, in the *Odyssey*, Circe sends Odysseus to the underworld (books 10, 11), and in the *Iliad*, the Greeks cross over the ocean for the sake of Helen.

[11] Albert B. Lord, *The Singer of Tales* (Cambridge, Mass., 1964), p. 162.

In Tamil, if it seems as if the hero will never receive permission from his beloved's relatives to marry her, she often accompanies him on his journey to find a home. The initiatory character of that journey is clear in Aiñ. 395, where after going through the world of death the hero describes to his beloved how they are about to enter into a paradise:

We have crossed
through the desolate wasteland
where long creepers of sharp flames
shoot out their radiance,
born in dry bamboo
and strengthened by the wind,
and roar in caves inside rock fissures.
Go now
very gently,
little girl,
to our hilly land
with shining groves
where falls mixed with flowers
descend
with roaring music.

Often, too, the deflowering of the heroine on that journey is described as an initiatory ordeal. In Kuṟ. 343, for example, the heroine's friend tells her:

Think, friend, of a way to go with the man
on whose tall hill
a mighty tiger is impaled
on the handsome face of a lord elephant with rutting temples
and then, his mouth split open
after bloodying the white tusks with red spots,
lies like a branch of black-stemmed *vēṅkai*,
its flowers withered,
blown down by the summer wind
in a cave full of crevices.

In Indo-Aryan the journey of the hero and his subsequent separation from his beloved are common themes, appearing first in the *Sattasaī*. In these poems, as in Tamil, the purpose of the journey is often to get money. Thus, in Sa. 76, the heroine says,

"I do not mind his being away so much as his returning without what I want." (See also Sa. 537.) In Subh. 1314, the poet says,

"Come, little one, weep not so long to see the other boys
in their fine dress. Your father too will come,
bringing a jeweled necklace and a suit of clothes."
Close by the wall a penniless traveler stood
and heard the mother's words. Sighing and with tears
upon his lowered face, he left his land again.

Another common theme in Tamil is the traveler who is comforted in the midst of the most terrible heat by the cool thought of his beloved:

In the wilderness where bamboo towers
are groves dessicated by the heat of the sun,
there, small-eyed elephants fear
that their round trunks, dotted and lined,
will be burned, and walk
so they do not touch the earth.
Yet even in such fearful places
the virtue of this woman keeps me cool.

This theme appears in Sa. 399: "Even though it is the middle of a summer day, the traveler is cool by the flood of moonlight from the face of his beloved who stays in his heart."

Another theme the two literatures share is that of the traveler who does not want to leave his beloved. In Sa. 500, the poet says, "The traveler, as he saw the face of his wife grow pale as he took leave of her, overcome by sorrow, did not want to go." In Sa. 261, the traveler is happy at the bad omens that make him stay at home. In Ak. 43, the hero says, "I lie on the lovely breast of my gentle-natured woman who has ample black hair and a fragrant forehead that smells of the black forest as fertile budding jasmine mixes in the wind. Eternally wretched, wretched are those foolish men who have left their sweet companions, going away without mercy for useless wealth, impelled by greed." (See also Kuṟ. 267, 323; Ak. 51, 149, 199.)

Another common theme in Tamil is the foster mother who laments when her daughter elopes, asking how her girl, so delicate and weak, will bear the difficulties of an arduous journey through the wilderness. In Ak. 17, the foster mother says, "If she threw a ball a little in her wealthy home or played with molucca beans with her young girlfriends, then tired out, she would say, 'My body aches, mother!' . . . That time is gone. Now she does not think of her friends with fine bangles or of me. Evading the hard guard of her father who took an oath, my little girl has grown up, has given her heart away to a stranger, and has become his. Are her little feet with jingling anklets able to go in the wasteland blocked by dark clouds?" (See also Kuṟ. 356, 396; Ak. 89, 105, 117, 145, 153, 207, 219; Aiñ. 377, 382, 385, 386, 389.) The theme of high-born people going into the wilderness occurs in the *Rāmāyaṇa*. In the *Ayodhyā Kāṇḍam* 55.4–6, for example, Kausalyā says of Sītā: "How will Maithilī, young, dark, very delicate, used to pleasures, now bear the heat and cold? After eating fine food, with soups and pungent morsels [*daṃśa*], how will long-eyed Sītā eat forest food of wild rice? After hearing the auspicious sound of singing and instruments, how will she hear the evil sounds of vultures and lions?" (See also *Ayodhyā Kāṇḍam* 36.9, 52.7, 54.7–16, 60.8.) In the *Buddhacarita*, when Gautama is about to renounce the palace for the forest as an anchorite, Aśvaghoṣa emphasizes his lack of fitness for such an arduous life, just as the Tamil poets emphasize this about the girl who has eloped. In Bu. 8.55, for example, he describes Gautama's soft feet and asks, "Shall they tread on the hard ground of the jungle?" He continues to describe Gautama's body: "Accustomed to sitting or lying on the palace roof . . . , adorned with priceless clothes, aloes, and sandalwood, how will it fare in the forest in the heat, the cold, and the rains?" Gautama, he says, "has been sleeping on a spotless golden bed and awakened at night by the strains of musical instruments. How, then, shall he lie in accordance with his vows on the ground with only a piece of cloth interposed?" In the *Kumārasaṃbhava* the poet comments in similar fashion on Pārvatī's becoming an ascetic: "Her hand, no longer busied with her lips that have now renounced rouge nor busy playing with a ball [once] reddened by the rouge of her breast, is now wounded from plucking sharp kuśa grass and has become a close friend of the rosary" (5.11); "[Pārvatī] who would get tired from playing ball submitted herself to the austerities of the ascetics" (5.19). The theme of the girl who would get tired playing ball but who has gone to the wilderness occurs in no less than five Tamil poems (Kuṟ. 396; Ak. 17, 153, 219; Aiñ. 377).

Sometimes the foster mother asks that the elements be kind to her eloped daughter; for example, in Kuṟ. 378, she says, "May the sun not burn; may there be rich shade; may sand be spread abundantly on little paths over mountains; and may a cool rain fall in the wilderness where my innocent black girl has gone with the warrior whose long spear has a glistening point." (See also Ak. 15, 203; Aiṅ. 371, 398.) Reminiscent of this verse is the blessing of Kaśyapa when Śakuntalā sets out from the hermitage for Duḥṣyanta's home: "May her path be blessed, its distance lovely with ponds green with lotuses, the rays of the sun intercepted by shadow-giving trees, [covered] with a soft dust of lotus pollen, and [cooled] by a pleasant, peaceful breeze" (4.10).

Many of the Tamil pālai poems are soliloquies in which the speaker addresses his heart. Most common is the hero, traveling in the wilderness to get wealth, who speaks to his heart, either blaming it for making him go in search of wealth leaving his beloved behind (Ak. 3, 19, 21, 33, 51, 79, 123, 212; Aiṅ. 455), or addressing it before he sets out, rebuking it for making him wish to leave his beloved to get wealth (Ak. 77, 131, 191, 193, 199, 225). Elsewhere he addresses his heart in the wilderness, telling it how happy it would be if his beloved were with him (Kuṟ. 347; Ak. 121; Aiṅ. 323, 329). Sometimes the hero's heart actually leaves him as he is away from his beloved to go to see her (Kuṟ. 142; Ak. 9, 29, 47, 181). In Ak. 181, for example, the hero says, "You are not brave enough to stay in the forest. Since you lag behind and wish to return, tell her how I am, heart." In some poems, too, the heroine's heart may leave her to go to her lover (Kuṟ. 153; Aiṅ. 295, 334).

Similar themes appear in Indo-Aryan. In Su. 36.55, Hanumān is said to have remained where he was with his body but to have gone to Rāma with his heart (*hṛdaya*). In Bu. 3.7, as Śuddhodana takes leave of his son, "With his voice he bade him set forth, but out of affection did not let him go in his mind." In Sa. 105, the hero addresses his heart: "O heart, like a big branch carried by a small river, in place after place you are caught and burned by someone." In Sa. 658, the heroine says, "When my lover is away, my eyes are somehow still, but my heart even now goes with him." This may be compared with Aiṅ. 334: "Friend, he . . . left me so my innocent heart would follow through forests." In other examples in Indo-Aryan, the mind or thoughts of a lover go after his beloved (R. 12.59; Megh. 98).

In other themes concerning the heart, lovers take possession of their beloved's heart: "She has taken my heart and hidden it" (Aiñ. 191; see also Kuṟ. 280); "Hearts pawned [with her] are not ever gotten back" (Sa. 154). Sometimes the two hearts mix or join: "Like rain that falls on red fields, our hearts, filled with love, have mixed together" (Kuṟ. 40); "Those . . . whose hearts are joined, not they whose bodies only join, are truly joined" (Subh. 1648). In both traditions, desire stays in the heroine's heart: "My heart, full to the brim with desire, is at rest" (Ak. 141); "Full of shame, her desire for you . . . grows ripe only in her heart" (Sa. 610).

Mullai Poems

Mullai, or jasmine, grows primarily in fertile forests in the monsoon, and hence it is to that tract of land that it has given its name. Poems on this theme describe several situations: the grief of the hero or heroine in separation; the happiness of the hero as he returns home; and the foster mother's description to the real mother of the happiness of the married couple, whom she has just visited. The season invoked in these poems is invariably the monsoon.

When the heroine grieves because her lover is away, she often says that the monsoon season, when he promised to come, is at hand, but her lover has not yet come (Kuṟ. 24, 158, 188, 194, 200, 216, 221, 254, 287, 380; Ak. 23, 139, 229; Aiñ. 252, 457–461). Typical is Kuṟ. 200: "He does not come, friend. Certainly he has forgotten, but I will not forget him. In the evening of the time of showers, black clouds thunder out sweet music. He gave his word to come before that when he left." In Indo-Aryan, the promise of the hero to return by the monsoon is implicit in many poems. Usually the poet describes the distraught state of the heroine during the monsoon. For example, in Sa. 538 he says, "As the traveler's wife saw the clouds, she looked at her son, her face full of weeping." (See also Sa. 315, 336, 540, 621, 673; Subh. 249, 708.) Often the very life of the traveler's wife is in danger. In Sa. 29, for example, she says, "As I hear the thunder, it is like the executioner's drum." In Sa. 336, the mother-in-law "protects, doing nothing else, her daughter-in-law as if she were the herb of life for her son as that girl's life comes to her throat at the sight of new clouds." (See also Subh. 708.) These poems may be compared with Kuṟ. 216: "not knowing I am so much to be pitied, the black clouds still roar and rain and send lightning, friend, aiming at my sweet life." (See also Kuṟ. 65, 103, 108, and others.)

In Sanskrit it is common to describe the pain of the traveler, apart from his beloved, in the monsoon. In R. 13.27, for example, Rāma points out to Sītā Mount Mālyavān "where I, separated from you, could not bear the smell from ponds rained on by showers and the kadamba with its half-grown stamens and the cries of peacocks." Similarly, the whole of the *Meghadūta* describes the longing of the hero separated from his beloved; in verse 3, he says:

> Somehow, he stood before that cloud
> that makes the *ketaka* blossom,
> and, keeping his tears inside him,
> that attendant of the king of kings
> began to remember.
> Even the fortunate when they see a cloud
> feel a change in their mood—
> what, then, must one feel
> when the person who longs to bend her arms around his neck
> is far away? (My translation.)

(See also Subh. 131, 228, 240.) Descriptions of the hero's grief in the monsoon are rare in Tamil; rather, his suffering in separation is usually in the pālai tract in the summer. There are, however, some poems that describe how he grieves for his beloved during the monsoon in the king's camp. In Aiñ. 448, for example, the hero says,

> The rattling royal drum sounds in the morning
> and the king, fierce in his wrath,
> has begun the business of war.
> On soft lowlands jasmine flowers blossom
> and the monsoon has begun
> with pattering drops from seething clouds.
> And I,
> every time I think of her

whose hair is thick,
have begun sleepless confusion.

(See also the other poems in the decad of Aiṅ. 441–450.)

In both traditions, the monsoon is evoked by dancing and crying peacocks (for example, Kuṟ. 251, 264; Aiṅ. 413; Bu. 7.5; Sa. 559; R. 6.51; Subh. 215, 222, 236, 243, 253). This theme occurs in Sanskrit as early as the *Rāmāyaṇa* (4.27.18). Another common way of describing the monsoon is to picture flowers laughing in it. Thus, in Kuṟ. 162, the heroine complains:

The evening is empty.
Many cattle enter the broad field
full of water given by the clouds.
Jasmine, O jasmine,
you are smiling
with your little white buds.
Is it fitting to mock those who are alone
with this semblance of laughter?

(See also Puṟ. 117; Kuṟ. 126, 186, 220; Ak. 54.) Similarly, in Sa. 537, the heroine says, "Now that the traveler, his weighty business finished, returns, the new monsoon seems to laugh, aunt, with the laughter of the *kuṭaja*."[12] In Subh. 162, "laughing jasmine" is mentioned, and in R. 9.42, the new jasmine (*navamallikā*) is said to have "a smile of flowers, a lower lip of shoots, and a smell like wine." (See also Subh. 754.)

There are several poems in both traditions that describe the sad state of the traveler's wife in spring: "He said clearly he would come now, in the sweet spring[13] when a red-eyed black *kuyil* [Sanskrit *kokila*] calls lovingly from the swaying top of a mango tree with lovely shoots, . . . but he has not come" (Ak. 229). This may be compared with Subh. 741:

[12] According to the *Sanskrit-Wörterbuch*, *kuṭaja* is *Wrightia antidysenterica*. It is derived from a Dravidian word (D.E.D. 1375) whose Tamil form is *kuṭacam*, which can mean either *Holarrhena antidysenterica* or *Millingtonia hortensis*, also called *malaimallikai* ("mountain jasmine") in Tamil (pictured in color in Charles McCann, *100 Beautiful Trees of India* [Bombay, 1959], p. 168). Mallinātha on Megh. 4 glosses kuṭaja by quoting Halāyudha, who identifies it as *girimallikā* ("mountain jasmine"). It seems likely therefore that the Prakrit word used here means mountain jasmine, or *Millingtonia Hortensis*.

[13] *Iḷavēṉil*, literally "young summer." Tamil has no other word for spring.

When her friends ask her why she wilts
like a crushed jasmine, the shy young wife,
saddened by absence, still does not speak out;
holding the tears within her eyes,
she only manages a glance
at the mango tree just budding in the courtyard.

In Subh. 1678, where the same theme occurs, spring is evoked by a kokila. (See also Subh. 160, 176; Sa. 97.)

A theme that occurs several times is that of the heroine who scratches marks in the wall to count the days until her husband's return. In Ak. 61, the heroine's friend reassures her by saying, "Do not be plunged in grief, friend, sad as you look at the long wall marked with the days." (See also Kuṟ. 358.) Similarly, in Sa. 170, a traveler tells the heroine's husband, "That good woman [*āryā*] protects with her hands the marks on the wall telling [when you will] return from the streams of water coming in through openings in the hut." (See also Sa. 208.) In Sa. 307, the heroine uses up her fingers and toes counting the days and then cries, "What can I count with now?" In Megh. 83, the wife of the exiled Yakṣa "counting, tallies on the ground with blossoms set on the threshold the remaining months of the term that began with the day of [her lord's] going." (See also Megh. 10; Subh. 558.)

Another common theme is the pretense by the heroine or by her friend that the rain at hand is only an untimely shower, not the monsoon, and thus that the hero has not failed to keep his promise to return by the rainy season. In Aiñ. 462, for example, the heroine's friend says:

Why, girl, should you be troubled
as you see the garlanded state of the naive *koṉṟai*,
which thinks in its delusion
that this untimely shower is the monsoon?
He will not let your beauty wither
who crossed a land where meadows unfold their buds.

(See also Kuṟ. 251, 289, 382.) Similarly, in Sa. 70, the heroine is consoled: "Take heart, traveler's wife! These are not clouds of the monsoon but smoke from the Vindhyā's forest fires," and in Subh. 704, her mother-in-law says, "My child, these are not clouds, but elephants on which the gods do ride. . . . Why, then, sweet innocent, defile your face with tears as though the rains had come?" (See also Subh. 190.)

The time evoked in most mullai poems is evening. Indeed, the idea of evening as the time when pain is most intense for separated lovers has been used so often in Tamil that the poet can say,

The sun leaves the reddening sky,
pain grows sharp,
and jasmine flowers open in the dwindling light.
Then is evening the deluded say.
But for those without their lovers
evening is the great brightening dawn
when the crested cock crows all through the tall city;
and even the day is evening
for them. (Kuṟ. 234.)

(See also Aiñ. 183.) For the Tamil poet, the sadness of the lonely lover is best evoked in the evening, when the activity of the day has suddenly ceased, and the sudden change to introspection is dramatized by the reddening sky and dwindling light (evening is much shorter and comes on much more suddenly in South India than in more northerly latitudes). The agony of night is foreshadowed by evening and is not directly described; the most poignant time of suffering is its beginning, filled as it is with foreboding:

Light dwindles,
jasmine flowers open,
the rage of the sun is spent
and activity comes to an end.
Though I swim the whole of evening, friend,
toward the dark,
it is no use.
The night is vaster than the flood of the sea. (Kuṟ. 387.)

In Indo-Aryan, I have found only one poem in which evening is clearly used to evoke the pain of a woman separated from her beloved:

At day's end as the darkness crept apace
the saddened traveler's wife had gazed
as far as eye could reach along the quiet road.
She takes one step returning to the whitewashed house,

then thinking, "At this very moment he may come,"
she turns her head and quickly looks again. (Subh. 728.)

It may be noted in passing that the idea of the traveler's wife looking in the direction from which her beloved will return is found also in Tamil (for example, Ak. 163). There are a few other Indo-Aryan poems where evening is a time of sadness. In R. 16.11, for example, deserted Ayodhyā is described: "This city [is] like the end of day when the sun has sunk to its home and clouds are blown by a strong wind." Similarly, in Subh. 881, the poet describes "the pain in the closing of full-blown lotuses [at sunset]."

Usually in the Indo-Aryan tradition the suffering of the separated lover is at its worst at night: "The night that passed like a flash with me in the joys she yearns for she now finds long in her solitude and spends in burning tears" (Megh. 85). In Sa. 315, "lightning illuminates the traveler's wife as she sits helpless in the hut whose straw roof has been blown off." (See also Sa. 252, 502; Megh. 84, 104; Subh. 220, 228.) Night as a time of suffering also occurs in Tamil. In Kuṟ. 261, for example, the heroine says, "The buffalo, hating the muddy fields, cries out 'ai!' in the thick midnight. At this time, full of fear, my eyes do not sleep, friend, grieving as they count time like watchmen because my heart has been wounded." (See also Kuṟ. 6, 11, 28, 91, 136, 145, 163, and others.)

In Tamil the return of the hero takes place during the monsoon season. Invariably he returns in a chariot, and in many poems he addresses his charioteer. A typical example is Aiṅ. 489:

Pull the strong reins twisted from tiny strands,
and drive your chariot swiftly
with its fast-gaited horses.
Drive so that my woman,
her heart despondent,
may rejoice
as in the evening
striped bees swarm with lovely wings
and jasmine creepers flower on soft fields.

(See also Kuṟ. 189, 227, 246, 247, 275, 301, 338, 345, 400; Ak. 4, 9, 14, 34, 44, 64; and others.) Often the hero describes the sights along the way to his beloved after he has returned; for example, in Aiñ. 492, he says,

Peacocks danced like you.
Jasmine flowered
as fragrant as your lovely face.
Deer glanced about, startled, like you.
I have come remembering you,
lovely-faced woman,
more swiftly than the rains.

(See also Aiñ. 494–498.) This theme is absent in Sanskrit, but many verses contain elements reminiscent of it. In the first book of the *Raghuvaṃśa*, for example, King Dilīpa and his wife Sudakṣiṇā travel in a chariot "whose sound was deep and smooth [*snigdha*]; they were like lightning and Airāvata riding a monsoon cloud" (1.36). Hearing their chariot, peacocks think it is the thundering of a cloud portending rain, and they cry (1.39). The monsoon season is the time when the traveler returns in Indo-Aryan as in Tamil. In Megh. 93, the cloud says, "I with deep yet gentle sounds speed on their way the throngs of weary wanderers who yearn to loosen the wifely braid." (See also Sa. 537, 694.) The sound for which the wife listens in the *Sattasaī* is that of her returning husband's bow: "O you who wait for the sound of your lord's bow, this is only the sound of thunder" (Sa. 55; see also Sa. 54). In Tamil, on the other hand, it is the sound of the bells of his returning chariot for which she listens: "Is that noise from the bells tied to the cow . . . or is it from the bells of the chariot coming on forest roads [covered] by wet sand, its sides protected by young bowmen [of my lord], his heart full after having finished his work?" (Kuṟ. 275).

There are several Tamil poems in which according to the colophon the foster mother of the heroine describes to the real mother the happy married life of the couple, whom she has just visited (Kuṟ. 167; Aiñ. 401–410). In several other poems, other people describe the couple's happy life together (Kuṟ. 178, 193, 229). In Kuṟ. 167, for example, the foster mother says,

Wearing the unwashed dress
with which she wiped her fingers
soft as *kāntaḷ* flowers
after mixing the curdled yogurt,

she stirs and cooks a sweet tamarind sauce,
as smoke from the seasoning gets in her eyes.
Then her husband tries it,
says, "It is good,"
and her bright face seems even happier.

This may be compared to Sa. 13: "The face of the wife, touched by her hand dirty with soot from working in the kitchen, is [compared] laughingly to the moon by her husband [in other words, like the moon, her face now has a spot on it]." In Sa. 507, the joy of the heroine's mother as she sees the teeth marks on her daughter's thigh as her dress is lifted by the wind is as great as if she had seen the lid (*mukha*) of a treasure. (See also Sa. 264.) Sometimes the description of the couple shows them with their little son, as in Aiṅ. 409:

The father embraced his son,
and the child's mother of gentle words
embraced the two of them.
As they lay there it was sweet.
Indeed, it was the equal of all this earth
with its wide expanses.

(See also Aiṅ. 401–406, 408, 410.) Similar is Sa. 409: "One breast flows with milk, the other's hairs stand on end as she sits between her husband and son."

Marutam Poems

Marutam is a flowering tree of the agricultural tract where paddy is grown. It has given its name to the category of poems concerning the infidelity of the husband after marriage, usually after the heroine has given birth to a child.

In many poems the heroine or her friend scolds the hero for his philandering, as in Aiṅ. 65:

In your town full of water
a lily flourishes in a field
planted with sugarcane
and satisfies the hunger of bees.
Do not embrace my body,
which has given birth to your son.
Your chest might be spoiled.

In this poem the hero is compared to a bee that occupies itself with a lovely weed (his courtesan) rather than with the productive but odorless sugarcane (the heroine, no longer exciting to him, who has produced his son).[14] (See also Kuṟ. 258, 295, 384; Ak. 36, 46, 116, 176, 196, 226; Aiṅ. 24, 48, 68, 70, 83, 85.) Sa. 92 is similar: "O bee, before you never sported among other flowers; yet now that the *mālatī* jasmine is pregnant with fruit, you forsake it." (See also Sa. 182, 294, 453, 469; Subh. 1660.) Sometimes the heroine or her friend blames the hero for making so many women unhappy:

> His town
> has spotted crabs whose mothers die bearing them
> and crocodiles that eat their young.
> Has he come?
> Why, friend, does he spoil girls,
> embracing them so their gold bangles jingle,
> and then leave them?

Similarly, in Sa. 147, the heroine says, "They do not sigh or weep or get thin—they are lucky whose lover you are not, O you with many mistresses."

Often the hero's harlot abuses the heroine, as in Aiṅ. 87: "O man of a prosperous city where cowherds, who wear *pakaṉṟai* garlands and who have many cattle, shake mango fruits down with sugarcane sticks! Your wife dislikes everyone; why shouldn't she hate me?" (See also Kuṟ. 80, 364; Ak. 76, 106; Aiṅ. 88.) This theme appears only once in the Indo-Aryan poems surveyed, in Sa. 417: "Oh—we are bad women. Go away, chaste one! Your name [*gotra*] has not been dirtied. And what's more, we do not love the barber [a polluted, low-caste man] as much as the wife of a certain person [meaning "you"] does."

In one of the commonest Sanskrit conventions, the angry heroine, or *māninī*, is described. She is usually irate because her

[14] In his commentary on the *Tolkāppiyam*, *Poruḷatikāram*, *Uvamaiyiyal* 30, Pērāciriyar says of this poem (using the reading *lotus* rather than *waterlily*), "She [the heroine] speaks of the man in whose city a lotus growing spontaneously in a field whose purpose is for planting sugar and not lotuses satisfies the hunger of bees. The meaning of this is that in a palace made for concubines [*iṟparattaiyar*] and courtesans [*kātaṟparattaiyar*] I too live, keep house [*illaṟam pūṇṭu*], and give hospitality." There is nothing in the poem or its colophon to justify this rather forced interpretation.

lover has taken up with another woman, often a rival wife, but sometimes a harlot. This theme occurs as early as the *Rāmāyaṇa*, where in Su. 12.30–31 the poet describes a river with flowering trees whose branches touch the water, which they hold back briefly "like an angry woman being held back by her relatives." Then the water comes around (the branches) "like a woman [*kāntā*] who is again calm in front of her lover [*kānta*]." This theme appears also in Sa. 302: "The lover [of the girl] washes the moonbeams mixed with the rays of her *indranīla* earrings from the face of the māninī thinking them tears mixed with collyrium." (See also Sa. 129, 539, 634, 653.) In the *Subhāṣitaratnakośa*, section 21 is devoted to this theme. The jealousy of rival wives first appears in Indo-Aryan in the *Sattasaī*, as in verse 106: "The redness of her lower lip, taken at night by her lover, is seen in the morning in the eyes of her rival wives." (See also Sa. 79, 449, 638; R. 10.57, 19.21, 19.22; Subh. 603.) In Tamil, poems in which the wife scolds her husband for taking up with courtesans often resemble Indo-Aryan verses that describe a wife's jealousy. For example, in Aiṅ. 118, the heroine says, "Friend, when I saw that wicked man [*aṟaṉilāḷaṉ*], I left angrily, determined to refuse; but pondering afterwards, I repented and went back." (See also Kuṟ. 93, 177.) Conciliation sometimes is accomplished in the presence of the couple's child, as in Kuṟ. 359: "he, victorious, embraces in affection his son, breathing like a sleeping elephant. The mother of his son puts her arms around him from behind [and makes up their quarrel]." (See also Ak. 5, 66.) Similarly in Sa. 11, "The wife, though angry, laughs as her son climbs the back of her husband who has fallen at her feet."

It has been seen that the heroine often scolds or abuses her lover when he takes up with courtesans in the Tamil poems. The theme of the heroine's anger occurs also when she quarrels with the hero over his intended or completed journey. In Kuṟ. 43, the heroine says, "I scorned him, thinking he would not go; and he scorned me, thinking I would not agree [to his going]. From that fight my heart is confused . . . as if bitten by a cobra." (See also Ak. 5, 225.) In Ak. 39 the hero tries to conciliate his beloved after his return: "You say, 'With a heart that spurned giving up [your quest for wealth] you went on your way. Did you not think of me and realize [your mistake]?' as your smile, revealing sharp teeth, goes away on your coral lips, showing your grief. Do not say things that [show] indifference [to my suffering]. . . . Far away, thinking of you . . . I saw you standing [before my mind's eye]. I said, 'O you with sweet laughter, why are you fighting with me while I am like this?' and I caressed your round forehead with high curving eyebrows and stroked your fragrant hair. At that wonderful time, the false dream ended leaving only emptiness, and I grieved wearily. If you do not consider that, you are cruel [*pulatti*; literally "sulking"] to me." In Sa. 273, the heroine angrily importunes her lover not to go: "How could you want to go already? My hair bent [from being tied in a *veṇī* braid when you were last away] is not yet even straight." (See also Sa. 143.) Sa. 17 describes how a traveler's wife is angry when her lover returns from his journey: " 'He will come, I will be angry, and he will plead.' Thus a woman's wish garland bears fruit for her lover." Similarly, in Subh. 738, the poet says,

"Time and time again you play me false.
What use are words? Begone."
Thus silencing you, in her wrath
she raised her weakened arm.
From it the bracelets slipped—
such was her thinness from your absence—
as witness now the crow that flies about the city
wearing them about his neck.

Sometimes the woman is coy in the Tamil poems. In Ak. 32, the heroine describes her first meeting with her lover:

Yesterday a man appeared in the millet field
wearing a glittering ornament set with a lovely sapphire.
Changing his kingly demeanor,
he repeated the obsequious words of a suppliant:
"O you who chase parrots from the tiny millet,
beating weakly your pleasant-sounding rattle over and over,
standing like a goddess,
who are you?
You have bewitched me—I will eat you up!"
and he embraced me from behind.
At that my heart was afflicted,
melting like mud in pouring rain.

Afraid he might know, I said harsh words I did not mean
and loosed the grip of his hands.
As I stood my ground,
he stood away like a frightened doe,
overcome by my strength of will,
and he did not dare to say anything else.
He left sadly
like an elephant separated from his herd,
and even today he has not recovered.
He does not know that he is faultless,
and the right to these ample arms with curving joints is his.
Come, let's go, friend,
to laugh at him as he comes
trying to get what he wants,
begging as I turn my back.

This may be compared to Subh. 494:

She wanders freely through her courtyard
but hides herself from my sight.
To others, fortunate, she gives full glance,
but gives half glance to me.
With others she converses
but with me she silence keeps.
My love has set me far apart
from even common folk.

(See also Subh. 482.)

The poems also describe the coyness of the newly married woman. For example, in Ak. 86, the hero remembers their marriage and the marriage night: "that night when [we were] together in one house, she cowered in her ornamented garment, which covered her hunched back. I touched her back and, wanting to embrace her, uncovered her face. Frightened, she breathed hard, and I, laughing sweetly, told her, 'Say everything you wish in your heart.' The ear where her earring hung shining with red jewels moved slowly and, her heart full of joy, she lowered her face and quickly looked down, that black woman with cool, thick hair whose glance had the proudness and timidity of a doe's." (See also Ak. 136.) In Sa. 645 the poet says, "She does not look at you, she will not let you touch her, she does not speak—yet, even so, being with one's new wife is pleasant." In R. 8.7, Kālidāsa writes that Aja enjoyed the earth compassionately "lest she become afraid, as if she were a new wife." In R. 13.28, Rāma describes his stay on Mount Mālyavān to Sītā: "As I remembered how you would hide yourself, making me tremble, I somehow suffered through the thundering of clouds echoing in caves." In Subh. 469, the poet says,

When seen, she drops her glance, and though addressed
she makes no conversation.
Brought to the bed, she turns away,
and when embraced by force she trembles.
When her companions leave the bridal chamber
she would fain leave with them.
My new-wed darling by her very forwardness
brings all the greater joy.

It is common for the Tamil poet to describe how the hero plays in the water with his harlots, causing jealousy in the absent heroine, while in Indo-Aryan the hero often plays in the water with his many wives. In Ak. 6, the heroine says, "in the flood of the Kāviri, where poles [pushing boats] can never be still, yesterday you played in the water with her whom you desire, with shining ornaments and earrings, embracing the white raft of sugarcane . . . so the flower garland on your chest withered." (See also Ak. 116, 166, 226; Aiñ. 64, 71, 75–80.) The girl in the water usually wears flowers in her hair, and she may wear a pearl necklace (Ak. 116). Sometimes the harlot speaks, inviting the hero to come play with her in the water (Aiñ. 77–78). In Kuṟ. 222, the hero sees the heroine and her friend playing in the water and falls in love:

If her friend goes to the front of the raft,
she also goes.
If her friend goes back to the rear,
she follows.
And, it seems, if her friend were to leave the raft
and slip into the water,
she would follow then too,
she whose cool eyes with their luscious corners
are like the red backs of fat jasmine buds
streaming with water in the rains,
she who resembles a shoot drenched with drops.

(See also Aiñ. 72–74.) In some kuṟiñci poems the hero plays with his beloved in water descending from a falls (Kuṟ. 353; Ak. 228), while in some neytal poems, he plays with her in the sea, causing his courtesan to be jealouṣ (Aiñ. 121, 123, 126). In Sa. 58, wives bathe with their lovers: "Just today he has gone, and all his wives stay awake [ostensibly out of fear, but actually to meet their lovers]; and just today the shores of the Godāverī are colored with turmeric." It is notable that in this poem the roles of the man and woman are the opposite from what they are in Tamil, where the married man makes love to his harlots as he bathes. In Sa. 79, one wife shows that she is her lord's favorite by ducking her rival wives as they bathe for a festival. Here too the Tamil connection of bathing with jealousy is present, though in a somewhat altered form. In Sa. 299, the wife "puts on the breast of her tired husband who has sported with her for the summer afternoon her wet hair, flowers falling from it and fragrant after bathing." In Kālidāsa the theme of a hero's bathing with his wives occurs often (R. 6.48, 16.13, 16.57–68, 19.9, 19.10). As in Tamil they play on a raft, and the women wear pearl necklaces and flowers in their hair.

There are two situations in Tamil that come under marutam in which the courtesan does not figure. In one of these, suitors come to see the heroine, who is already in love with the hero, a situation that may be put under marutam because it involves the potential jealousy of the hero. In Kuṟ. 171, the heroine asks,

Look, my friend,
just who are these strangers,
these animals caught in a fish net
spread across a stream
filled to its banks with productive waters?

(See also Kuṟ. 385.) This may be compared with Sa. 492: "The glance of the poor girl, excited, wanders as if in a forest searching for the sight of you even in [a place] full of handsome men." (See also Sa. 676.)

The other situation occurs in only one Tamil poem, and even there can be inferred only from the colophon:

Ku koo crowed the cock,
and my heart was frightened
that, like a sword

to separate from me
my lover sunk in my arms,
the dawn had come. (Kuṟ. 157.)

The colophon remarks, "What the heroine said when her menstrual period began." If it is correct (and there is no reason to believe that is not), then the dawn is a figure for the beginning of her menstrual period, the redness and sudden onset of both being the obvious points of comparison. To this may be compared several poems in the *Sattasaī* in which the hero, beside himself with desire, makes advances to the heroine in spite of her menstruous condition, as in Sa. 480: "Even though it is blamed by the world, it is inauspicious and indecent, still the sight of that menstruous girl is pleasure for my heart." Similarly, in Sa. 528, the poet describes how "the rival wives of the menstruous girl wept when they saw his shoulder smeared with the ghee from her head." (See also Sa. 481, 528.)

Neytal Poems

Neytal, or the blue waterlily, is a flower that grows near the seashore and has given its name to the tiṇai of poems that take place in that setting. Often such poems express the complete despair of the heroine; sometimes they describe the heroine's meeting with her beloved as he comes at night, usually in a chariot along the beach. Actually, the first of these conventions might also be included under mullai and the second under kuṟiñci, were it not for their surroundings. For this reason, it appears that neytal is the least specific tiṇai in the akam poems, and that it was probably the last to take shape.

The only neytal situation found also in Indo-Aryan is that of the heroine who in her distress cannot sleep, as in Kuṟ. 5:

My friend, is this the affliction of love?
On his gentle shore full of sweet water
a *puṉṉai* tree whose shadow is pleasant
buds in the spray of breaking waves
as birds who have made it their home sleep in it.
He has left,
and my blackened eyes with their many petals
do not close in sleep.

(See also Kuṟ. 6, 11, 28, 138, 145, 163, 186, 261, 301, 329; Ak. 45, 50; Aiṅ. 107, 142, 172, 173, 195.) Sa. 412 may be compared to this: "Why do you tell me, 'Sleep, the third watch has passed,' friends? The fragrance of the *śephālikā* does not let me sleep —you sleep." Similarly, in Subh. 723, the heroine says,

Unhappiness comes over me, not sleep;
I count his virtues, not his faults.
The night slips by but not my hope of union;
my limbs grow thin but not my love.

(See also Sa. 252, 385; Subh. 717, 726.)

Messenger Poems

In the messenger poem, which occurs in one puṟam example as well as in akam verses, someone asks an animal or insentient thing to convey to another person a message of consolation or to look after him or her. In Puṟ. 67, Picirāntaiyār sends to Kōp-peruñcōḻaṉ, whom he has never seen, a message by means of a gander:

Listen, gander:
in the evening, which brings sadness and inactivity,
when the budlike light of the moon,
its horns come together,
shines like the bright face
of the warrior of killing battle
showing mercy on his land,
if, after eating *ayirai* fish in the great bay at Kumari,
you go to the northern mountain,
then stop on your way
at the good land of the Chola king
and go to the high palace at Kōḻi with your mate.
Without pausing at the door, enter that palace
and say for the great king Kiḷḷi to hear,
"Āntai of Picir is your humble servant."
If you will do that, he will give
for your beautiful mate to wear and rejoice
a fine ornament that is beloved to him.

The old commentary states that the northern mountains mean the Himālayas. It is interesting that the goose is going north to the Himālayas just as the cloud in the *Meghadūta*, the most famous of all Indian messenger poems, travels from the Vindhyās to those mountains.

In Kuṟ. 235, the hero advises the north wind (*vāṭai*) to look after his beloved, telling it where to find her village. Similarly, in Ak. 163, the heroine asks the north wind to go to where her beloved is and to wear his heart away "like a hillock of fine sand in a channel full of water" so that he will return. In Ak. 170, the heroine says,

The grove will not tell him,
the backwater will not tell him,
the *puṉṉai* tree, its fragrant flowers humming with bees,
will not tell him. Except for you
I have no one to tell that man
in whose bay bees swarm,
attracted by the scent of the redolent petals of waterlilies
flowering like eyes in the dark backwater,
and eat the cool pollen,
and get so drunk that they cannot fly.
You must tell him, sand crab.
Say, "Will she cross over the grief she feels
who many times dispelled your sadness
on midnights, when a little crow
sat languishing on the low branch of a screw-pine bush
by the sea with his loving mate,
unable to hunt in waters infested with sharks,
and dreamed of white shrimps?"

In Kuṟ. 392, the friend of the heroine asks a bee to go to the hero's mountain to tell him that the heroine is always with her relatives, and the only way in which he can see her is to marry her. In Naṟ. 54, the heroine asks a heron to go tell her lover how she suffers. In Naṟ. 70, she rebukes a crane (*veḷḷāṅkuruku*), saying, "You came to my city, searched through our bay, and ate schools of *keṭiṟu* fish. Then you went back to his city and had such lack of love that, forgetful, you did not tell him of my great grief."

In Sanskrit the most famous use of this theme occurs in the *Meghadūta*, where a Yakṣa exiled on the Vindhyā mountains asks a cloud to take his message of suffering and consolation to his beloved on Mount Kailāsa in the Himālayas. In verse 5, he says,

What does a cloud,
a collection of smoke, light, water, and wind,
have in common with messages,
which must be conveyed by living beings
skilled at their task?
Yet in his anxiety
the Guhya [Yakṣa] considered none of this,
but made his request to the cloud,
for those afflicted by desire
are by nature pitiful
whether the thing they address is sentient or not.

(My translation.)

In Kum. 4.16, Rati, lamenting the destruction of her husband, Kāma, asks him to take back his form "and instruct the kokila in the words of love messages." In Subh. 718, the heroine asks an assortment of birds what news they have to tell her of her lover, and Subh. 1695 mentions "a message carried by the monsoon wind." It is notable that this convention, which in later times became one of the most often used conventions in both Sanskrit and Tamil (as well as in most of the other Indian languages) occurs nowhere in Indo-Aryan before Kālidāsa. It is unrepresented even in the *Sattasaī*, the closest approach to it appearing in Sa. 16, where a traveler's wife asks the moon, "Touch me with the same rays [*kara*] with which you touch him." Thus the messenger poem is well documented in Tamil about two hundred years before it appears in Indo-Aryan, and there can be little doubt that it originated in the southern tradition.

Poetic Ideas that First Appear in Indo-Aryan in the Sattasaī or Later

One of the most common conventions of classical Sanskrit is the Malaya breezes, "which blow from the South, especially from Mount Malabar (*malayagiri*: Subh. 1126, 1133, 1140, 1143), where the cooling and refreshing sandalwood grows. Perfumed by sandalwood (Subh. 1138, 1144) and by other southern scents, by cloves, the *lodhra*, and the *lavalī* (Subh. 1132), the spring breeze earns its epithet of 'scent bearer' *(gandhavāha)*. . . . On reaching the north, the south wind fills the cuckoo's throat (Subh. 1128, 1145), opens the spring jasmine (*kunda*, Subh. 1129, *mallikā*, 1135–1136), and brings forth the bees (Subh. 1134)."[15] (See also R. 9.33; Kum. 3125; Sa. 97, 443, 497.) It is noteworthy that the word *malaya* itself is of Dravidian origin, being related to Tamil *malai* ("mountain").[16] In the Tamil poems surveyed, the south wind (*tenṟal*) appears twice: in Ak. 21, the hero journeys to where "the south wind is redolent from shaking *marā* trees, touching them so flowers fall from their branches," and, in Ak. 237, the heroine's friend describes the season: "[It is] summer [*vēṉil*] when the kuyil birds learn to sing as the south wind makes its way through the fragrant branches buzzing with bees of *Kuravu*, its buds like serpents' fangs about to open, and decorates the fine sand with [flowers] from slender *atiral* creepers and with striped bunches of blossoms from empty-stemmed *pātiri* bushes." The description in this poem makes it clear that the season meant is spring, called young summer (*iḷavēṉil*) in Tamil, since elsewhere that is the time when kuyils (kokilas in Sanskrit) sing (Ak. 25, 97, 229; Aiñ. 341, 346, 369). The adjective "young" (*iḷam*) qualifying "summer" has simply been omitted.

It is common in classical Sanskrit for poets to describe refreshing breezes charged with drops from streams or rivers. In R. 2.13, for example, the poet describes how when King Dilīpa was oppressed by the heat of the sun, "the breeze charged with the spray of mountain streams, scented with the gently shaking flowers of trees, served [refreshed] him." (See also R. 4.73, 5.24, 16.36; Kum. 1.15; Megh. 31, 94.) This theme occurs in Ak. 133, where the hero asks, "Will she be able to come with me as we drink drops raised up to the sky and brought by the wind from the forest river whose sweet water supports lovely flowers?" (See also Ak. 186.)

Classical Sanskrit verses also describe breezes scented by passing through flowers. In R. 1.38, for example, as Dilīpa and his wife go on their chariot, they are touched by winds "smelling of forests, wafting pollen, and fragrant from blowing through

[15] Daniel H. H. Ingalls, *An Anthology of Sanskrit Court Poetry: Vidyākara's "Subhāṣitaratnakośa"* (Cambridge, Mass., 1965), 34.1.

[16] D.E.D. 3882.

śāla trees." (See also R. 1.43, 4.55, 5.42, 5.69, 8.34, 9.45, 10.49, 11.11, 13.16, 16.36; Kum. 1.15; Megh. 31, 42, 103.) In Ak. 43, the heroine's forehead "smells of the great black forest where fragrant budding jasmine mixes in the wind," and in Kuṟ. 273, her forehead is said to be "as cool and fragrant as the swirling wind moving through a great forest where buds bursting with pollen shine in the night." (See also Ak. 21, 186, and 237, quoted above.)

In several poems, natural phenomena are compared to musical instruments. The most elaborate Tamil example of this theme occurs in Ak. 82:

he from a land
where the summer west wind makes flute music
in the shining holes bored in swaying bamboo by bees,
where the music of the cool water of sweet-songed falls
is the thick voice of gathered concert drums [muḻavu],
where the harsh calling voices of a herd of deer
are the brass tūmpu,
where the bees on the flowering mountainside are the lute [yāḻ],
and where
as a court of monkeys looks on entranced,
loud in their appreciation as they hear the melodic music,
a peacock swaying in dance on that slope thick with bamboo
looks like a Viṟali entering the stage.

In Ak. 225, "the wind blows in a narrow hole penetrated by a bee in swaying bamboo among bushes and makes a lovely sound, like music from the flute of a cowherd with a long staff driving his herd to water." In Ak. 219, the blowing of the summer wind is mistaken for a cowherd's flute by a stag, while, in Aiṅ. 215, bees trying to enter closing flowers are said to "hum more sweetly than the sweet-voiced flute of players behind the *taṭṭai* and *taṇṇumai* [drums]." This is a favorite theme of Kālidāsa. In R. 2.12, he describes how King Dilīpa "heard songs describing his own glory sung loudly by the nymphs of the forest accompanied by humming bamboos whose holes were filled with wind and who provided as it were the music of flutes." Similarly, in R. 4.73, Kum. 1.8, and Megh. 56, the wind blowing through bamboos is said to produce a sound like that of a musical instrument.

Sometimes animals listen entranced by a woman's singing. In Ak. 102, "On a platform in a field where millet is high a forest man drinks wine until he is happy and stays there as his wife . . . sings kuṟiñci so that a young elephant slumbers." (See also Puṟ. 374; Kuṟ. 291.) In Subh. 197, the poet describes how in summer "a herd of innocent gazelles has gathered close at the singing of the girl who tends the well, charmed by its sweetly rocking lullaby."

In Tamil the young heroine often plays with her friends in the sand, making sand houses, playing ball, and playing with dolls. In Ak. 60, for example, she "makes toy houses with her garlanded friends on the shore heaped high with sand by the north wind," while, in Aiṅ. 377, her mother laments that she has eloped "leaving her ball, her doll, and her molucca beans for me." (See also Puṟ. 53; Ak. 17, 20, 110, 153, 219, 230; Aiṅ. 115, 181.) Similarly, in Kum. 1.29, Kālidāsa describes how Pārvatī would play in her youth "making altars [*vedikā*] in the sand of the Ganges, with balls, and with dolls." (See also Kum. 5.11.)

In both the Tamil and Indo-Aryan traditions clouds are described to evoke a man's generosity. In Puṟ. 159, for example, the poet says, "[I] praise your generosity, which is like a cloud's as it rains down with lightning and roars with thunder on millet that has not yet produced its grain." (See also Puṟ. 34, 54, 55, 160.) In Puṟ. 203, the poet exclaims, "If clouds, thinking, 'We have rained in the past,' should stop, there would be no life for any creature. If people like me beg, saying, 'Give more,' it is cruel of people like you to refuse saying, 'You took before.'" Megh. 109 is similar: "I hope you will do this for me [that is, take my message to my beloved]. Clearly I need no reply to know you are worthy of my trust. Without a word you give water on request to *cātaka* birds; for the noble make answer to suppliants simply by fulfilling their desires." (See also Subh. 1094, 1098, 1207, 1362, 1379.) In Subh. 1087, the poet exclaims, "While others, desirous of its properties, will water the noble sandalwood, if the useless thorn tree would have a savior, it must be the great-souled cloud." Similarly, in Puṟ. 142, the poet Paraṇar praises his patron Pēkaṉ: "Pēkaṉ . . . is like clouds whose endless race fills dry tanks, falls on wide fields, and rains on salt places rather than where it is of use. Though he is ignorant as far as giving is concerned [in other words, though he gives to all, regardless of merit], if he meets an enemy army, he is wise indeed!" In Puṟ. 205, the sea from which the cloud takes its water is invoked for generosity: "Just as thundering clouds, which to get new wealth lower themselves and gather by the ocean, do not go without water, so the families of suppliants do not leave [you] without elephants with high shining tusks and chariots." Similarly, in R. 17.72, Kālidāsa describes a king's generosity: "Virtuous suppliants in great need received generosity from the king as clouds from the sea." Other examples of clouds drinking from the sea are found in Puṟ. 17, 161, 365, R. 1.18, and Subh. 1207; in R. 13.9, Megh. 13, 46, and 51, clouds drink from rivers. It should be pointed out that as early as the *Buddhacarita* clouds were invoked in Indo-Aryan for their qualities. Thus in Bu. 1.93, it is prophesied at the birth of Gautama that "like a mighty cloud with its rain at the close of the summer heat, he will give relief with a rain of *dharma* to men burnt with the fire of passions." However, it is here the coolness of the cloud's rain that is invoked rather than its generosity in giving water so that crops can grow, as in later Indo-Aryan and Tamil.

One of Kālidāsa's most famous similes occurs in Kum. 8.54: "The west holds up a red line of the evening sun that has almost set just as a battlefield might hold a curved scimitar, discarded and smeared with blood." A similar figure appears in Puṟ. 4: "Swords as they bring victory are changed and take on the loveliness of the red [evening] sky."

In both Tamil and classical Sanskrit, pearls are thought to come from the heads of elephants (Puṟ. 161, 170; Patiṟ. 32; *Murukāṟṟuppaṭai* 304–305; *Kuṟiñcippāṭṭu* 35–36; *Malaipaṭukaṭām* 517–518; R. 9.65; Kum. 1.6; Subh. 948). In Tamil, they are said to come from the tusks, while in Sanskrit they are supposed to be from the elephant's temples (see Mallinātha on R. 9.65). In *Malaipaṭukaṭām* 518, a mountain is said to have "many bunches of tusks that have pearls [torn from] elephants of great strength, suffering from hard wounds after fighting with striped tigers." To this may be compared Kum. 1.6, which describes how hunters in the Himālayas find the trails of lions that have killed elephants by the pearls (which the lions took from the dead elephants, holding them in their claws, and which then) have fallen from their claws, since the blood they left in their tracks has been washed away by the snow (and cannot be used to trail them).

It occurred to me that the so-called pearls in the tusks of elephants might be excrescences that grow there. The Tamil word *muttu*, unlike the Sanskrit word *muktā* (which is of Dravidian origin and is related to it[17]), may mean grain of rice, pomegranate seed, and oil seed in addition to pearl, so that a globular piece of ivory could well be denoted by it. Unfortunately, I have nowhere been able to find any reference to such growths in books on elephants or on ivory, and I have been forced to conclude that the Tamil "pearls" are as imaginary as their Sanskrit counterparts. In his commentary on Puṟ. 170, Duraicami Pillai remarks that pearls are produced on the tip of the tusks, but that statement appears to be contradicted by *Kuṟiñcippāṭṭu* 35–36, which speaks of "elephant tusks filled with muttu[s]." In any case, only very strong and mature elephants were thought to produce pearls in their tusks, for Puṟ. 161 mentions elephants with "tusks that are mature [*muṟṟiya*] so that they produce pearls."

In Tamil, as in Sanskrit, pearls were also thought to be produced by bamboo, for, in Ak. 173, the desert over which the hero must travel is described as a place "where the west wind spreads, stays, and feeds on tall bamboo so that it dries up, its joints split, and unpolished muttus burst forth looking like molucca beans and fall into an old pit." That this belief was current in Sanskrit is clear from the verse quoted by Apte from Mallinātha (unfortunately, without exact reference) under his definition of *muktā*:[18]
Karīndrajīmūtavarāhaśaṃkhamatsyāhiśuktyudbhavaveṇujāni /
Muktāphalāni prathitāni loke teṣāṃ tu śuktyudbhavam eva bhūri //
"It is commonly said that pearls come from elephants, clouds, boars, conchs, fish, serpents, oysters, and bamboo, but those that come from the oyster are the largest."[19] I have attempted to find some explanation for the Tamil notion that muttus come from bamboo. At the node of the culm (the joint) of bamboo, there is a hard bud that could conceivably burst forth when the

[17] D.E.D. 4062.

[18] Vaman Shivaram Apte, *The Practical Sanskrit-English Dictionary*, rev. ed. (Poona, 1959), II:1273.

[19] Daniel Ingalls tells me that the earliest instance he has found of the belief that pearls come from the heads of elephants is Bhāsa's *Ūrubhaṅga*, verse 5.

plant dies and the joints crack, but I was unable to determine for certain whether the Tamil muttu is indeed such a dried up bud. Certainly the Tamil verse quoted above appears to be describing a real phenomenon, not an imaginary one, while the Sanskrit pearl that comes from bamboo is clearly imaginary (since the Sanskrit word has only that one meaning). It would appear that this is a case of borrowing in which too narrow a meaning was assigned to the Dravidian word by the Indo-Aryan languages appropriating it.

Conclusions

Of the situations given above that are common to the Tamil and Indo-Aryan traditions, there are few that appear in Indo-Aryan before the *Sattasaī*. With only one or two exceptions, the shared themes described in this chapter first appear in or after that anthology. The *Sattasaī* is, on the other hand, filled with so many extremely close parallels to Tamil verses that their close relationship cannot be questioned. Furthermore, because of the Dravidian meter and Dravidian rhyme that first appear in Indo-Aryan in the *Sattasaī* and show how dependent that anthology is on the Dravidian tradition, there can be little doubt that the themes and situations that first appear in the *Sattasaī* come from a southern tradition of poetry and not a northern one. And yet the agreement between situations and themes in ancient Tamil and the *Sattasaī* is not great enough for one to have borrowed directly from the other. It has been pointed out above that the Tamil anthologies and the *Sattasaī* are too close in time for the Prakrit tradition to have borrowed from the Tamil one and then to have gradually reshaped the themes; moreover, there is no evidence of cultural contact between Tamilnad and Maharashtra in or before the second century A.D. that would be extensive enough to account for the vast amount of borrowing.

Rather, both poetries appear to be refined developments of a common popular, and undoubtedly oral (that is, unlettered[20]), tradition. This tradition must have flourished all over the Deccan in a culture that was extraordinarily conservative. The Allchins

[20] See chapter 6.

remark of this civilization, "Certainly the excavated settlements do not give much indication of any major change in the way of life accompanying the arrival of iron (c. 1000 B.C.). One is left with a feeling of remarkable conservatism among the population of South India throughout the period. There can be little doubt that many of the traits already established in the Neolithic period persisted right through the iron age."[21] In such a conservative and homogeneous culture, it is not surprising that literary forms were quite uniform. Thus it is quite plausible that one literary tradition spread all over the Deccan should have been drawn upon to produce remarkably similar bodies of poetry in Maharashtra, where Aryan and Deccan culture mixed, and in Tamilnad, whose civilization evidently developed from Deccan culture with little outside stimulus, Aryan or other.

The *Sattasaī* took this tradition and reinterpreted it in light of the new mores prevailing because of Aryan influence. Emphasis on chastity was dropped, and as a result many of the poems describe the adultery of the wife, a situation wholly absent in Tamil. Adultery was probably missing as well in the tradition from which both poetries were derived and in which the Dravidian value of chastity must certainly have prevailed. With the shift in values away from chastity, Prakrit poetry came to emphasize purely erotic elements more and more—for example, in the poems in which the hero desires his menstruous beloved. There were in addition other elements that influenced the Maharashtrian poets to modify the inherited Deccan tradition. It has been seen that earlier Sanskrit poetry stressed description rather than suggestion. As a result the use of suggestion, which must have been quite prominent in the tradition from which Prakrit poetry developed, was greatly reduced, replaced by often stark description, such as that in Sa. 314: "Her house drenched by the storm, the lonely woman sunk from exhaustion is as if lit up by the lightning from the clouds." There is not one example of this sort of vivid description in the Tamil akam poems surveyed, and I do not believe that Prakrit could have taken it from the original southern tradition. Nevertheless, the extent of the indebtedness of the *Sattasaī* to the Deccan poetic tradition is indicated by the above analysis of

[21] Bridget Allchin and Raymond Allchin, *The Birth of Indian Civilization: India and Pakistan before 500* B.C. (Baltimore, Md., 1968), p. 232.

themes and situations common to the *Sattasaī* and early Tamil. Keith was well aware of the fact that the *Sattasaī* was the product of something other than the Sanskrit tradition, for he wrote, "Prakrit lyric as we have it in the *Sattasaī* of Hāla comes before us with a definite character of its own which is not reproduced in Sanskrit, though Govardhana in his *Saptaçatī* deliberately attempts to imitate it."[22]

Tamil did not keep unchanged the original southern poetic tradition, either. Rather, as a written tradition, it was refined considerably, making each word count and each figure the source of extremely complex suggestions. The situations used in the original tradition must have been categorized to a considerable extent by the Tamil poets, who came to use certain tracts of land to evoke certain situations. Such associations are lacking in the *Sattasaī* and must have been absent in the original tradition as well. Even Tamil does not invariably adhere to their use, but commonly mixes two or more categories, a practice termed *tiṇai mayakkam* by the grammarians. Situations are sometimes placed in the wrong tiṇai in Tamil, as in Aiṅ. 120–128, where the hero's courtesan is described amidst the seaside scenes appropriate for neytal poems, not for marutam. On the other hand, some rudimentary associations must have already been present in the original tradition, for they have come into both Prakrit and Sanskrit: separation with the monsoon season; meeting and suffering with night; and traveling with the heat of summer, to name the most obvious.

In spite of the changes that Tamil made in the original Southern tradition of poetry, I believe that, unlike Prakrit, it preserved that tradition in its essentials. Among archaic peoples, most poetry has religious significance. That is to say, such peoples are so accustomed to giving religious interpretations to all that occurs, to relating all events and all creation to a cosmic prototype or purpose, that they rarely if ever compose what could be called purely secular literature. As such peoples grow more "sophisticated," they become what Eliade has called desacralized—that is, they think less and less in terms of cosmic prototypes and more and more in terms of pure history. In their literatures,

22 Arthur Berriedale Keith, *A History of Sanskrit Literature* (London, 1920), p. 223.

they cease to relate all things to religious notions and describe things in and of themselves. It is the conformity of the Tamil lyric poems with the religious beliefs of ancient Tamil culture that makes me believe that they must represent essentially the southern tradition. It has been seen that for the ancient Tamils the most important contact with the sacred for a man or woman was in marriage and that as a result a woman's chastity was believed to be extremely important. It is exactly such a view that is reflected in the ancient Tamil poems. An unchaste married woman, commonly described in Indo-Aryan, is nowhere so much as mentioned; moreover, the connection of marriage with initiation, the strong association of union with a sacred state, the theme of mistaking the heroine's sickness from love for possession by Murukaṉ, and the evocations of the married state for its fertility and sacred fulfillment all fit perfectly with the religious preeminence accorded by the ancient Tamils to marriage. In one of the only myths about Murukaṉ that is as old as the poems, that god meets Vaḷḷi as she guards the millet and then marries her (Naṟ. 82), thus playing the part of the hero of a kuṟiñci poem. Thus the kuṟiñci poems have a mythical prototype and are in a real sense religious. In the *Sattasaī*, on the other hand, the view of love has been desacralized to a great extent, even though several poems describing suttee show that the Indo-Aryan view of chastity could not have been too different from that among the Tamils.

Another reason why Tamil must have preserved the older tradition of South Indian poetry in its essentials is that Tamilnad did not come under the influence of outside civilizations to any great extent between the time of the megalithic culture and the anthologies. There were, it is true, many immigrants and ideas arriving from the North in that period, and the old religious notions were already beginning to change. But the language is still quite uninfluenced by Aryan borrowing in the anthologies, and the old Dravidian customs still held sway for the most part, as has been seen in chapter 3. Maharashtra at the time of Christ was, on the other hand, the southernmost outpost of the Aryan culture. There, elements of Dravidian and Aryan culture must must have mixed freely. It is only natural that any poetry surviving from the Dravidian tradition in Maharashtra would be profoundly altered as a result of Aryan influence.

It has been seen that many themes that are of great importance in Kālidāsa and classical Sanskrit poetry first appear in the *Sattasaī* (see appendix 2). Is it possible that Kālidāsa derived these themes from the Prakrit tradition? Both Keith[23] and Winternitz[24] believe that, in spite of the similarities between Prakrit and Sanskrit lyric poetry, they developed separately (with the exception of some Sanskrit works that are conscious imitations of Prakrit). Neither of these writers, however, gives any real evidence for such a belief. The presence in Kālidāsa of Prakrit lyrics that use the technique of the *Sattasaī*, as shown above, proves beyond question that that poet was intimately familiar with the Prakrit tradition. Is it not extremely likely that themes that first appear in Indo-Aryan in the *Sattasaī* and subsequently recur in Kālidāsa were taken from the Prakrit tradition by that poet, or perhaps by his immediate predecessors whose works have not survived? It is true that many elements of Kālidāsa's poems are quite foreign to the Prakrit tradition; he was, after all, following epic and other Sanskrit models. But, where common elements do occur that are found first in Indo-Aryan in the *Sattasaī*, it seems to me that those elements may be considered to have been taken by the great classical poet (or his predecessors) from the popular Prakrit tradition.

It will be seen in the second appendix that a substantial number of Tamil themes first appear in Indo-Aryan literature in Kālidāsa or later. It seems highly likely to me that most of these themes came into Indo-Aryan through Māhārāṣṭrī, even though they are not attested in the *Sattasaī*. It must be kept in mind that the *Sattasaī* contains only seven hundred extremely short poems of limited subject matter. One can scarcely expect all or even most of the themes that were used in Maharashtrian poetry to have found their way into it.

In Sanskrit, these themes, ultimately of Dravidian origin, came to be even more modified and even more desacralized. In Kālidāsa's time, South Indian notions that stressed the sacred nature

[23] Keith, *History of Sanskrit Literature*, p. 223.

[24] M. Winternitz, *A History of Indian Literature*, trans. H. Kohn (Calcutta, 1959), III:100.

of marriage were becoming popular in North India. Kālidāsa accepted such notions to a large extent, and his poems rarely describe immoral, purely erotic love; rather his heroines are chaste women who find fulfillment in marriage, just like the heroines of the Tamil poems. Other Sanskrit poets, however, did not stress the sacred nature of marriage to such an extent; they wrote poems, often quite beautiful, describing the erotic delight of forbidden and immoral love. The Tamil situations are changed to accommodate this new view. Thus there are poems in the *Subhāṣitaratnakośa* in which the heroine scolds her friend for having made love to the hero when she should have been giving him a message, and poems in which the traveler's wife asks a stranger to stay with her (a situation found also in the *Sattasaī*). There are many poems in Sanskrit that describe love-making in extremely frank terms, as for example the poems about *viparītarata* (intercourse in which the woman takes the man's part). Because Tamil society was primarily monogamous, in order to evoke jealousy the poet had to describe the hero's infidelity with a courtesan. In Aryan society, on the other hand, prominent men had many wives, and it was natural for the poet to describe the jealousy of rival wives. It may be that the institution of polygamy was largely responsible for the desacralization of Dravidian values concerning marriage in Aryan literature It is scarcely reasonable, after all, to expect a woman who must share her husband with many other wives to show the devotion and self-sacrifice that was expected of a woman in the Tamil tradition.

10

TAMIL ELEMENTS IN INDO-ARYAN BEFORE THE *SATTASAĪ*

Many poetic elements have been described in chapter 9 that are common in Tamil and that enter Indo-Aryan only in the *Sattasaī* or afterward. Such elements, it is clear, were originally common to a Deccan tradition of poetry that embraced all of South India and entered Indo-Aryan through the southernmost Prakrit, Māhārāṣṭrī. But other common elements are found in Indo-Aryan before the *Sattasaī* as early as the *Mahābhārata*, the *Rāmāyaṇa*, and the *Buddhacarita*. These cannot be traced by an analysis of situations shared by the two traditions, for there are few situations common to Tamil poetry and Aryan poetry before the *Sattasaī*. Rather, they consist of similar treatment of such things as flowers and animals. In order to come to some conclusion regarding the nature and origin of such elements, several of them are analyzed below.

Figures of Speech Involving Eyes

It is quite common in both traditions for a woman's eyes to be compared to a blue waterlily (Sanskrit *nīlotpala*, *kuvalaya*;

Tamil *kuvaḷai,* to which *kuvalaya* is etymologically related,[1] *nīlam, neytal*). In Su. 11.16, Sītā is said to have eyes like the petals of a waterlily (*utpalapatrākṣī,* where *patra* means petal[2]). In Bu. 3.10, the road along which Gautama passed with his entourage is said to be spread "with halves of blue waterlilies like eyes." In R. 11.93, as Rāma enters Ayodhyā, "the eyes of women anxious to see Sītā changed the windows to waterlilies [kuvalaya]." (See also Sa. 5, 140, 323; Kum. 1.46, 7.20; Megh. 91; Subh. 390, 409, 506, 1383.) In Tamil a typical occurrence of this simile is in Aiṅ. 299, where the hero says,

> Even the dark waterlily [kuvaḷai]
> with its mouth opening wide
> as it blooms in the fresh spring
> on the slope of the hill man
> cannot bloom
> like the eyes of the mountain girl
> with a swaying walk.
> Even the peacock
> cannot be as lovely
> as she.

In Ak. 27, the heroine's glance is said "to defeat the great worth of waterlilies, their stems gathered together, in clear water." (See also Kuṟ. 9, 13, 29, 339; Ak. 10, 149, 150, 188; and others.)[3]

It is significant that in early Tamil a woman's eyes are nowhere compared to lotus flowers, one of the most common comparisons in early Sanskrit. Sharma writes as follows concerning the day-blooming lotus in the *Mahābhārata*:

1 D.E.D. 1574.

2 Otto Böhtlingk and Rudolf Roth, *Sanskrit-Wörterbuch* (St. Petersburg, 1855–75), IV:414.

3 In *An Anthology of Sanskrit Court Poetry: Vidyākara's "Subhāṣitaratnakośa"* (Cambridge, Mass., 1965), 16.2, Daniel H. H. Ingalls says that the point of this comparison is the color of the waterlily and the eye, both of which are very dark. He suggests that "the Sanskrit poet refers to the pupil or sometimes to the white and the pupil, never as we do to the iris." The iris of most Indians, especially in the South, is very dark brown, so dark indeed that it is indistinguishable from the pupil except in bright light. Conventionally, the pupil and iris together are said to be black, and a woman with black eyes is thought to be lovely. Such a standard would have no meaning if only the pupil were meant, for then all women would have black eyes. The occasional South Indian with blue irises is said to have "cat's eyes," the unusual color of his eyes being considered a defect.

> The lotus as a comparison for male or female eyes is more common in compounded epithets, as follows:
>
> (a) (*kanyāḥ*) *kamalalocanā*(*ḥ*), "lotus-eyed girls"; 1.60.11; 68.13; 3.12.16. (b) *kamalapatrākṣ*(*ā*), "lotus-petal-eyed"; 1.1.7; 61.67; 93.27; 113.10; 3.147.24; 186.12; 275.3; 6.33.2; cf. 3.61.1. . . . (c) *kamalekṣaṉ*(*a*), "lotus-eyed"; 1.113.23; 3.292.23. (d) *puṇḍarīkākṣa*, "lotus-eyed"; for Kṛṣṇa, 1.213.22; 3.13.42; 19.27; 6.102.49. . . . (e) *puṣkarekṣaṇa*, "lotus-eyed"; 1.112.24. . . . (f) *rājīvalocanā*(*ḥ*), "lotus-eyed"; 1.46.34. . . . (g) *vanajapatrākṣ*(*īm*), "lotus-petal-eyed"; 1.160.40. (h) *padmāyatākṣ*(*ī*), "having long eyes like a lotus"; 1.61.96. . . . (i) *śatapatrāyatekṣaṇīm*, "having long eyes like a lotus"; 3.65.20.
>
> It would appear that *puṣkara*, *rājīva*, and *vanaja*, which have dark blue flowers, are used because of the color resembling that of the eyes. But *padma* and *kamala*, which have red flowers argue against this. In all probability, the comparison is based on the shape and beauty of the lotus rather than on its color. As passages such as 1.61.96 and 3.65.20 clearly show, the shape of the lotus (its petals?) is to be regarded as the *tertium comparationis* in this context.[4]

In later Sanskrit the red lotuses are scarcely ever likened to women's eyes, at least in the sources surveyed. This indicates that the color rather than the shape came to be the quality compared, perhaps because of the influence of the South Indian tradition, where in early Tamil poetry it is always the color of a waterlily and not its shape that is compared to the eyes. Another difference between Tamil and early Indo-Aryan is that in the *Mahābhārata*, lotus flowers are compared to the eyes of men as well as women, while in Tamil waterlilies are compared only to the eyes of women. In this respect also, later Sanskrit resembles Tamil more than earlier Sanskrit literature.

Another common simile for a woman's eyes is a doe's or fawn's eyes. Thus, in Su. 12.45, Sītā is said to have eyes like those of a fawn (*mṛgaśāvākṣī*). In R. 8.60, Aja addresses his dead wife, "you left your rolling eyes with the does." (See also Sa. 25; R. 1.40; Kum. 1.46, 5.13, 5.15; Megh. 78, 91, 100.) In Tamil, women's eyes are compared to a doe's eyes, but never to those of a fawn. In Ak. 74, the hero thinks of his beloved "every time

[4] Ram Karan Sharma, *Elements of Poetry in the Mahābhārata* (Berkeley, Calif., 1964), pp. 86–87.

he sees the glance of the timid young doe of the black-horned stag." (See also Puṟ. 354, 361, 374; Ak. 86, 91, 195.) This simile does not occur in the parts of the *Mahābhārata* studied by Sharma. It is notable that, in the sources surveyed, it is only in the *Sattasaī* and afterward that the Tamil comparison, that of a woman's eyes to those of a doe (and not of a fawn), occurs in Indo-Aryan.

In Sanskrit the eyes of a proud or angry woman or of an angry man are said to be red. In Mbh. 1.68.21, Śakuntalā is said to have eyes red from anger as she is insulted by Duḥṣanta, while, in Mbh. 2.58.36, Draupadī is said by Yudhiṣṭhira to be red-eyed (*tāmrākṣī*), by which he evidently means that she is proud and aristocratic, and that he should not use her for a stake in the game of dice. In Sa. 106, the rival wives of the heroine have eyes red from jealousy. In Puṟ. 349, a girl over whom a war is about to be fought is said to have proud red-lined eyes. (See also Puṟ. 350.) In Mbh. 1.140.20, an angry person is said to have red eyes, while, in Su. 45.13, the eyes of Akṣa as he fights are compared to blood. (See also Mbh. 1.78.24, 1.73.31; Su. 1.54, 24.33.) Similarly, in Puṟ. 100 and 300, the eyes of a man in war are red, while, in Puṟ. 311, the red eyes of a hero in battle are said to smoke.

Beautiful eyes are long or extended in both traditions. In Su. 25.35, Sītā's eyes are as long (*āyata*) as a lotus petal. (See also Mbh. 1.61.96; Bu. 5.84; Sa. 252; Subh. 351.) In the *Sattasaī* and later Sanskrit, the eye is said by hyperbole actually to extend to the ear (Sa. 338; R. 4.13; Subh. 100, 466). In Tamil, the epithet "long-eyed" (*neṭuṅkaṇ*) is twice applied to a woman, in Aiṅ. 200 and 498.

A woman's eyes are compared to arrows in Indo-Aryan in and after the *Sattasaī*. In Sa. 504, for example, the hero asks, "Whom could you not kill, naive one, with the *bhalla* glance sent by your bow-like brow?" (A bhalla is an arrow with a scimitar-like blade). (See also Subh. 796.) In Megh. 70 and Subh. 324, women's glances are likened to Kāma's arrows. In Kuṟ. 272, the hero laments,

> Tell me, do I dare to touch her arms?
> This mountain girl
> has hair that is fragrant and dark.
> Her eyes,
> striving with one another,

are like arrows extracted with welling blood
from the breast of the swift stag
who cried out when his foolish doe
ran near her brothers,
flushed from her herd
by rocks thrown by whistling bowmen.

In Ak. 27, the heroine has "blackened eyes with red lines like a sword that has prevailed in battle." (See also Ak. 77.)

In classical Sanskrit the dark part of a woman's eye is compared to a bee. In R. 7.11, for example, as ladies watch the procession of Aja, the windows from which they watch are likened to "lotuses with eyes for bees." (See also Megh, 35; Subh. 100.) Similarly, in Ak. 59, the heroine is said to have "eyes like flowers where bees land." (See also Ak. 149.)

In Subh. 506, the tremulous side glances of a woman are likened to garlands of full-blown jasmine sewn with blue waterlily, the point being that jasmine is like the whites of the eyes. Similarly, in Ak. 42, the corners of the eye of the heroine are compared to the "red underside of a fragrant bud brought out by the rain of *pittikam* [a kind of jasmine]." (See also Kuṟ. 222.)

Usages in which Flowers Figure

In Tamil the bee in conjunction with the flower it visits is used as a symbol for the male part in lovemaking or in courting. In Kuṟ. 370, for example, the courtesan says, "In his city there is a cool harbor where a bee opens the mouth of a luxuriant bud of a pond lily. . . . If I lie with him, we are united like [fingers] holding a bow." In Ak. 71, the heroine separated from her lover says,

Like the loveless people
who search out the prosperous with their hearts
and forsake all attachment to the deficient
because they are of no use,
the swarm of bees
has left the flowers in the spring
and gone to the flowers of the branches.

(See also Kuṟ. 2, 3, 21, 175, 211, 220, 239, 306, 370; Ak. 21; and others.) In Su. 7, where the harem of Rāvaṇa is described, several verses mention bees in a way that makes their use as sexual symbols clear. In verse 35, the women's mouths are said to be surrounded by intoxicated bees that beseech them, while, in verse 60, Rāvaṇa's women embracing one another are compared to a garland bound on a string (swarming with) intoxicated bees. (The notion of a garland swarming with bees is found in Kuṟ. 321, Ak. 131, and many other poems in Tamil.) The use of bees as sexual symbols becomes quite common in the *Sattasaī* and in classical Sanskrit. In Sa. 139, for example, the heroine says, "That the bee wants to drink from flowers with taste [*rasa*] is the fault of tasteless [*nīrasa*] flowers, not of the bee [and so I do not blame my man for seeing other women]." (See also Sa. 37, 92, 128, 366, 387, 422, 444, 495, and others.) In a famous verse of the *Abhijñānaśākuntala*, Duḥśyanta addresses a bee with jealousy:

> Ever and again you touch the moving corner of her trembling eye;
> as if telling secrets you softly graze her ear
> and as her hands tremble drink her luscious lip.
> Here we are dying at the gates, oh bee, while you have entered heaven.[5]

(See also Kum. 3.56; Subh. 272, 409, 651, 760; and others.)

In both traditions the destruction of flowers is used as a symbol of sexual enjoyment. In Su. 7.44, for example, the women of Rāvaṇa's harem "have torn or dirty garlands, like blooming creepers dirtied by elephants in a forest." This may be compared to Puṟ. 73, where the king declares, "[If I do not defeat my enemies], then may my garland wither in the unresponsive embraces of women with thick black hair who have no love in faultless hearts." (See also Puṟ. 6, 347; Kuṟ. 36; Ak. 5.) The sexual symbolism of an elephant destroying plants is also found in Tamil. In Kuṟ. 179, for example, when the heroine's friend invites the hero to spend the night in their village she says,

> You torment stags in the noisy forest.
> But now the sun's light grows dim,
> and your dogs have tired.
> Do not go, lord!
> Over there is our town,
> among the hills where green bamboo is stunted,

[5] *Abhijñānaśākuntala* 1.20. This translation is by Ingalls.

eaten with relish by stupid elephants with deep mouths
who tear sweet honeycombs
from the slopes of towering mountains.

(See also Ak. 8, 12, 148; Kuṟ. 37, 112, 180.) In Bu. 5.32, the sleeping women of Gautama's harem are described as "presenting the appearance of a lotus pond whose lotuses have been blown down and broken by the wind." In Sa. 56, the hero makes love to the heroine "so that her limbs become like faded *śirīṣa*." (See also Sa. 422, 632.) Similarly, in Kuṟ. 343, a woman who has been deflowered is compared implicitly to "a branch of black-stemmed *vēṅkai*, its flowers withered, blown down by the summer wind in a cave full of crevices." (See also Ak. 8, 12, 36, 56, 58, 68, 80, 148, 160; Aiṅ. 91, 93, 99, 101.) One of the most common occurrences of the sexual symbolism of ruined flowers in Tamil is the description of how plants are mutilated by the wheels of the hero's chariot as he comes at night to meet his beloved, as in Ak. 160: "He would come at night, bringing his horses with lovely gaits . . . across the cool salt pan filled with productive waters. Budding waterlilies, their tips cut off by his wheels, would rise [back] up, withered, like the rising hood of a cobra." (See also Kuṟ. 189, 227, 336; Ak. 80; Aiṅ. 101.) The reader of this poem must know that a woman's pubis is conventionally compared in Tamil to a cobra's hood (Naṟ. 366; see also Subh. 630).

In both traditions a woman suffering in love is compared to a ruined plant. In Su. 23.8, for example, Sītā apart from Rāma is said to have trembled like a plantain (*kadalī*) fallen in the wind. (See also Mbh. 3.275.14, 3.144.5, 3.297.27.) In R. 14.54, Sītā, on hearing that Rāma has renounced her, falls to the earth "like a creeper toppled by a strong wind." In Subh. 741, a traveler's wife wilts like crushed jasmine (see also R. 8.47; Kum. 4.31). These poems may be compared to Ak. 78, where the heroine's friend asks the hero whether he remembered his beloved while he was away "in the autumn [*muṉpaṉikālam*] when cold comes and the north wind shakes cooly so the long petals of *kāntaḷ* break." In Aiṅ. 170, the heroine asks the bard who was sent as a messenger by the hero, "When you say the man of the bay where a white-necked crow destroys waterlilies . . . is good, why should my blackened eyes, like many-petaled flowers, become pallid?"

(See also Kuṟ. 112, 180, 327, 336, 348, 349, 381; Ak. 84; Aiñ. 21, 25, 26, 29.)

Ruined plants may also evoke the valor of a wounded or dead hero in battle. In Mbh. 3.255.14, Jayadratha's soldier, his chest broken, vomiting blood from his mouth, is said to have fallen down in front of Arjuna like a tree severed at the root. Mbh. 3.12.58 says, "Through the rubbing together of the arms of those two strong warriors (Bhīma and Kurmīra), there arose a terrible noise in the battle like that of the splintering of a bamboo." In R. 4.33, the king's path is said to have been "characterized by his depriving the [hostile] kings of their wealth and by dethroning and routing them in various ways, like the path of a tusker, which is marked by trees shorn of their fruits, uprooted, and destroyed in various ways." In R. 18.5, the king is said to have destroyed the power of his enemies as an elephant destroys a place full of reeds. (See also R. 9.63; Subh. 1412.) In Tamil, the king killing and destroying in battle is twice compared to an elephant crushing bamboo (Puṟ. 73, 80). While the Tamil simile seems certainly related to the figures given from Sanskrit classical literature, it is rather far from the figures cited from the *Mahābhārata*, and it may not be related to them.

Another theme that is related in the two traditions is the falling of flowers. In the *Rāmāyaṇa* this is used for purely descriptive effect. In Su. 1.11–12, as a mountain is taken and picked up by Hanumān flowers fall from its trees so that it seems made of flowers. In Su. 1.47, Hanumān covered with many flowers looks like a cloudlike mountain covered with fireflies. (See also Su. 2.2, 12.11; Bu. 1.24; Subh. 1189.) In Tamil falling flowers are often described in the wilderness, where they remind the traveler of rain or other phenomena associated with richness or fertility. Sometimes they symbolize his distraught state of mind, as in Ak. 199: "Elephants wander to assuage their thirst, thinking rain the ripe flowers of *marā* falling down many together as the wind comes in waves like the white waves rising in the sea." (See also Ak. 9, 95, 101, 107, 211, 225; Aiñ. 320.) In Su. 12.10, the poet describes how trees in a grove are struck by the wings of birds so that many-colored flowers rain down. This may be compared to Ak. 205, where "proud monkeys climb high in the great branches of a *vēṅkai* tree and call and frolic so that fragrant flowers, like striped skins flayed from tigers, drop down."

Sometimes an empty plant evokes bereavement or sorrow. In Su. 12.15, trees that have shed their flowers are compared to defeated gamblers who have shed their garments and ornaments. In Su. 15.24, Sītā in her separation from Rāma is compared to a creeper without flowers. (See also R. 3.7.) In Ak. 19, the absent hero thinks of his beloved who stays at home: "Her soft-jointed wrist, a few bangles hanging from it, moves slowly, empty like a creeper whose flowers have fallen." (See also Ak. 227.)

Several themes involving falling flowers first occur in Indo-Aryan in or after the *Sattasaī*. Sometimes the falling of flowers suggests the end of love, as in Sa. 10, where the poet writes, "Look, she gathers the fallen flowers of the *madhūka* as if they were the bones of relatives on the burning ground [since she can no longer meet her lover hidden by the flowers of that tree]." (See also Sa. 104.) In R. 14.69, as Sītā, renounced by Rāma, grieves in the forest, trees abandon their flowers. In Kuṟ. 282, the hero is said to grieve in the wilderness as he thinks of the heroine's bangles, "which will grieve like the fresh tube-shaped flowers of white *kūtaḷam* . . . that fall from their stems, unloosed." (See also Kuṟ. 51, 110, 282, 329, 397.)

The wind blowing down flowers is so much of a convention in classical Sanskrit that Kālidāsa can write, in R. 10.49, "The gods followed Vishnu [to be born on earth] just as trees follow the wind with their flowers." (See also R. 1.10, 5.69, 9.56.) This theme is quite common in Tamil, as in Ak. 1, where in the wilderness "swift whirling winds take bunched white flowers of fiberless *muruṅkai* trees making their branches wave so the scene resembles a seashore boiling with spray from waves roaring as they break." (See also Ak. 21, 125, 199.)

In Sa. 469, *pātala* flowers are said to blow down and rest on the hero's head, showing that he has been unfaithful with the woman who lives in the only house in the village with a pātala tree. Similarly, in Ak. 21, "the south wind is redolent from shaking marā trees, touching them so flowers fall from the branch, as if hit by a strong man, so they come to rest on the heads of brave men going in the wilderness." (See also Puṟ. 307.)

Falling flowers are compared to weeping in both traditions. In R. 8.35, as flowers are blown from the garland on Nārada's *vīṇā* surrounded by bees, the vīṇā seems to weep tears mixed with collyrium. Similarly, in Aiñ. 458, the heroine, seeing that the time has passed at which her lover promised to return, says,

The bunched fruits of the *koṉṟai*
have ripened and resemble tresses of hair.
Its cold flowers
streaming down through the violent rain
are like my eyes,
which have lost their beauty
since the man admired by bards left.

In both traditions the shaking of a plantain tree is used to evoke a person's trembling. In Su. 17.2, Sītā is said to shake like a plantain tree in the wind when she sees Rāvaṇa. In Mbh. 3.275.14, the poet says, "Sītā, having heard those frightening words, trembling, suddenly fell down like a felled plantain." (See also Su. 23.8.) In Aiñ. 460, the heroine asks, "as the whole trunk of the broad-leafed plantain shakes, the north wind afflicts. What will become of me, pitiful as I am?"

In Su. 27.2, the trembling of Sītā's left eye, a good omen, is compared to the shaking of a lotus hit by a fish. Similarly, in Megh. 91, the Yakṣa says to the cloud, "Her fawnlike eye will leap and tremble, I surmise, at your approach, rivaling in charm the blue waterlily stirred by the darting of fish." In Naṟ. 310, the heroine's friend describes the hero's city as a place where "as a *vāḷai* fish in a deep-water tank jumps, the green leaves of a lotus, emitting lamplike radiance, wave like an elephant's ears, and girls [bathing in] that tank are frightened away." (See also Ak. 186.) In Aiñ. 40, the hero's city is said to be a place where "the lily that longs for bees opens because the *keṇṭai* fish jumps."

Sometimes the waving of a plant is compared to the motion of a woman's arms or hands. In Bu. 8.28, Aśvaghoṣa describes Gautama's renounced wives: "As creepers waving in the wind strike themselves with their own tendrils, so these noble women beat their breasts with jewelless lotus hands." (See also Bu. 4.30, 8.29.) In R. 13.24, Rāma tells Sītā, "The creepers, unable to talk, showed me where you had gone with branches whose fronds were bent." In Tamil one of the stock images for a woman's arms is bamboo, the chief likeness between the two being the graceful motion of each. Thus, in Kuṟ. 364, the hero's concubine (*iṟparattai*) says, "the time of the *tuṇaṅkai* [dance] has come for girls who have supple-jointed bamboo arms [to hit on their sides in the dance]." (See also Kuṟ. 185, 226, 268, 279, 318, 326, 338, 357; Ak. 18; and others.) In Ak. 19, the journeying hero thinks of his beloved, "her soft-jointed wrist hanging with a few bangles moving slowly, empty like a creeper whose flowers have fallen." (See also Ak. 196; Aiṅ. 25.)

A beautiful woman is often compared to a blossoming or moving plant. In Su. 4.20, Sītā is compared to a flowering creeper. (See also Su. 7.44, 15.24; R. 3.7, 8.47, 14.1, 14.54.) Similarly, in Ak. 54, the returning hero says to the charioteer, "We will see the state of my beloved [who is like] a flowering creeper in the evening, laughing with buds." (See also Puṟ. 139, 316, in both of which poems a woman's waist is compared to a creeper.) In Bu. 8.59, the forsaken women of Gautama's harem "clasp one another with their arms and let fall tears form their eyes as shaken creepers drop honey from their flowers." In R. 9.33, the mango creeper in the spring (*sahakāralatā*) is said to move in the Malaya wind as if it were a girl practicing *abhinaya* (dancing movements). In Kum. 5.13, Pārvatī is said to entrust her movements to creepers (for safekeeping) as she becomes an ascetic. (See also Subh. 175.) Similarly, in Aiṅ. 400, creepers are said to shake, dancing like girls.

In both traditions the embrace of man and woman is likened to the clinging together of two plants. In Bu. 4.46, for example, one of the women of Gautama's harem tries to attract his attention by saying, "Behold this *tilaka* tree embraced by a mango branch like a man in white garments embraced by a woman with yellow body paint." In R. 7.21, Kālidāsa writes that Prince Aja, "holding his bride's hand in his own, looked still more handsome, like a mango tree after it has reached [and touched] the tender leaf of a neighboring *aśoka* by means of a corresponding leaf of its own." (See also R. 8.47, 14.1; Kum. 3.39, 4.31.) A Tamil example of this theme is Aiṅ. 14, in which the heroine says,

In his sapphire bay
fertile shoots
of a mango with small green fruits

tremble
when a *vḻam* with long flowers
is so close it touches.
His breast, sweet and gentle,
brings cool sleep.

Similarly, in Aiñ. 400, creepers are said to shake, dancing like girls, and to embrace marā trees, which are like warriors. (See also Aiñ. 11, 454.)

In both traditions the closing of certain flowers in the evening is described to evoke pain or loss. In Bu. 5.57, for example, Aśvaghoṣa, describing Gautama's harem, writes, "Other [women], though really large-eyed and fair-browed, showed no beauty with their eyes shut, like lotus beds with their flower buds closed at the setting of the sun." In Subh. 881, the closing of lotuses is described:

At first the thick slow-moving filaments
drooped at the tip;
the inner petals then, each separately
shrank a bit together;
at last the outer leaves effected
some measure of contraction;
such was the pain there was in the closing
of the full-blown lotuses.

These examples may be compared to Kuṟ. 122: "Like the small backs of green-legged herons, the lilies in deep water are folding up. The evening has come; only he is not here." (See also Kuṟ. 310; Ak. 116, 183.)[6]

If the closing of a flower at night evokes pain, its opening in the morning signifies a return of fertility. In R. 5.69, bards awakening Prince Aja say, "The morning breeze, as if desirous of obtaining by means of borrowed properties the natural fragrance of the breath of your mouth, bears away the flowers of trees loosened from their stalks and comes in contact with lotuses opened by the sun." In Kuṟ. 168, the hero describes his beloved: "Like the opening at dawn in the rain of lush jasmine, all closed at once in the green shelter of a palmyra tree and flowing with

[6] The lily meant by the word *āmpal* is the red lily, which blooms in the day, and not the white lily (*veḷḷāmpal*, Sanskrit *kumuda*), which blooms at night.

water, she is fragrant and cool." (See also Ak. 213). The opening of flowers in the evening may evoke the time of love that is at hand, as in R. 19.34: "The king [Agnivara], finding pleasure only in touching women, became like a lily [kumuda] that is awake at night and sleeps in the day." In Ak. 150, the heroine's friend tells the hero how she pines for him: "The day you left, she grieved . . . every time she saw the grove and the salt pan blooming coolly with waterlilies that smell like liquor, where in morning the lovely petals of *cerunti* close and in evening the mouths of their buds open, along with the dark flowers of thick blue waterlilies, like eyes."

It is fairly common in Sanskrit for night-blooming flowers to be contrasted with day-blooming ones. In R. 6.86, Kālidāsa describes the *svayaṃvara* of Indumatī after she has chosen Aja: "That assemblage of kings, having on one side the party of the bridegroom transported with joy and on the other, looking sad [the losers], was like a lake at daybreak with full-blown lotuses in one place and night lilies gone to sleep [that is, closed] in another." (See also R. 6.36, 6.66, 17.75.) This may be compared to Naṟ. 300, where a bay is described "where a waterlily, assailed by the wind, closes [*olki*] and bows [*iṟaiñcum*] to a lotus, just as naive girls clasp their hands in supplication before a princess when she is angry." Here *olki* could simply mean "shrinks" or "cringes"; but the point of the figure is the likeness of the closed flower to the clasped hands of the girls (a figure that occurs also in Bu. 4.2). In Aiṅ. 68, the heroine speaks of the courtesan: "O man from a city where the strong-stemmed waterlily flower blooms like a lotus in the virgin dawn [*kaṉṉi viṭiyal*], does your woman [that is, your harlot] have no manners? Even though I restrain myself, she does not [that is, she talks about me]." The heroine means that though the harlot looks like a majestic lotus, her conduct shows that she is no better than a waterlily.

In classical Sanskrit it is fairly common for a bee to be caught in a flower that closes at night (Sa. 495; Subh. 867, 868, 958, 960, 962, 967). This idea does not appear in Tamil, but, in Aiṅ. 215, bees are said to hum sweetly "as they try to enter the contracting holes in flowers," a notion that is so close to the Sanskrit idea that it is probably related to it.

Usages in which Animals Figure

A weak animal attacked by a strong one is used in both traditions to evoke pity. The animal attacked is most often a deer, as in Su. 23.5, where Sītā, threatened by Rākṣasīs, trembles "like a doe, separated from her herd, afflicted by wolves." In Su. 56.52, Sītā surrounded by Rākṣasīs is likened to a doe in the midst of tigers. (See also R. 12.37, 16.15; Subh. 203.) Similarly, in Ak. 97, the dreadful way over which the hero must travel is a place "where the stench is strong after a tiger [smelling of] flesh ruined the strength of a lovely spotted deer so that its horns fell off and left its joints broken." (See also Ak. 3, 107; Aiṅ. 373.) In Aiṅ. 354, the hero's compassion in returning soon is evoked by describing the wilderness he crossed as a place where "a wild brown dog [*ceṉṉāy*] who has made love to his mate leaves the doe and her fawns without taking them." In Aiṅ. 216, the animal used to evoke pity is a baby elephant:

In his land
a male tiger skilled at taking prey
hides in rich shadows where jack fruits hang
and waits to catch the cub of a simple elephant,
just born and trembling as it walks
in a forest of tall thickets.
Why, friend, should your limbs fade for him
withering like a plucked-off sprout?

(See also Aiṅ. 397.) Similarly, in Su. 26.1, Sītā is said to tremble "like a lord elephant's daughter [*gajarājakanyā*] on whom a lion comes." In R. 12.27–29, a lion attacks a cow in a cave, while in Puṟ. 323, and old cow takes for its own calf the offspring of a cow caught by a tiger.

Suffering may also be evoked by the description of a deer or other animal afflicted by a hunter's arrow. In Mbh. 3.117.1, for example, Jamadagni, killed by the kinsmen of Sahasrārjuna, is likened to a deer killed in the forest by an arrow. In Bu. 5.1, Gautama, though tempted by objects of sense, "obtained no relief, like a lion pierced in the heart by a poisoned arrow." (See also Bu. 4.103.) These examples may be compared to Kuṟ. 272, where the love-stricken hero compares the eyes of his beloved to "arrows extracted with welling blood from the breast of a swift stag."

In both traditions a lion or tiger is often said to fight and defeat an elephant.[7] In Mbh. 6.57.1, young Abhimanyu encountering five warriors is likened to a lion cub fighting with five elephants, while, in Mbh. 6.97.38, Sātyaki pierces Śāradvata with arrows as tigers kill an elephant. Elsewhere in the Indo-Aryan sources surveyed, it is always a lion and not a tiger that kills an elephant (see Su. 15.22, 26.1, 34.35; R. 17.52; Kum. 1.6, 6.39; Subh. 864, 930, 948, 1655). In Tamil it is always a tiger, not a lion, with one exception in Ak. 73. Occasionally (for example, Kuṟ. 343) the elephant wins the encounter, but it is clear that proverbially the tiger was supposed to win. Thus, in Puṟ. 100, a king's anger is said to be like that "of an elephant mighty enough to fight a tiger." Similarly, in Kum. 6.39, the city of Alakā is supposed to have elephants that have conquered the fear of lions. A typical Tamil example of this theme is Ak. 119, where the wilderness the hero must traverse has a mountain "where a tall elephant, his knees bent so they touch the ground, his head split into pieces from fighting with a brave tiger, puts his head in a dry spring and sighs." (See also Puṟ. 100, 237; Kuṟ. 88, 141, 215, 343; Ak. 12, 20, 22, 30, 45, 72, 73, 88, 92, 112, 118, 145, 148, 168, 169, 202, 227; Aiṅ. 218.)

Often an animal staying happily with its mate is described to evoke the happiness of a human couple. In Mbh. 1.185.4, Draupadī follows Arjuna as a cow elephant follows her mate. In Sa. 460, the poet hints that the heroine and not some other woman has won the love of the hero by saying, "Look, the cow shows her good fortune in the corral, scratching her eyes on the bull's horn." In R. 16.68, the king playing with his wives in the water comes down from his raft, his necklace swinging, "like a wild king elephant surrounded by his mates with an uprooted lotus on his shoulder." (See also Mbh. 3.262.39; Sa. 683; R. 3.24, 19.11; Subh. 1154.) In Su. 9.8.9, Hanumān in the midst of Rāvaṇa's wives is compared to a bull in the midst of corralled cattle and to a bull elephant in the midst of his mates. Here the purely descriptive approach of the epic poet is evident: he is not concerned

[7] See Ingalls, *Anthology of Court Poetry*, 33.10.

with whether Hanumān is the husband of the women he is with, but is content with a figure based entirely on similarity of appearance. In Kum. 3.36–37, the mating of different animals in spring is described to indicate that the time of love is at hand: "The bee followed his mate and drank from the same flower; the antelope scratched his beloved with his horn as she closed her eyes at his touch; the elephant gave to his mate the water in his trunk smelling of lotus pollen; and the *cakravāka* bird gave his mate half-chewed lotus stems." In Tamil the description of an animal with its mate evokes the appropriateness of love in a given situation. In Aiṅ. 416, for example, the hero says, "The male elephant embraced his mate. . . . I also embraced my bangled woman." In Ak. 121, the hero expresses his happiness that his beloved has agreed to accompany him on his journey: "We are happy, heart. They say that she . . . will come with us where a strong elephant . . . washes the soft head of his young mate." (See also Puṟ. 200, 266; Kuṟ. 65, 85, 332, 338; Ak. 14, 134, 139, 146, 154, 189; Aiṅ. 94, 333, 414, 419.)

The suffering of a lover in separation is often compared to the grieving of an animal in the same situation. In Su. 15.22, for example, Sītā separated from Rāma is compared to a cow elephant separated from her herd by a lion. In Su. 17.17, she is compared to the wife of an elephant king captured and tied to a post as she sighs without her mate. (See also Mbh. 3.61.23; Su. 14.30; Bu. 8.23, 8.50, 9.27; Sa. 383, 594; Megh. 79; Subh. 756.) Similarly, in Kuṟ. 183, the heroine asks of her absent lover, "Will he see a straight-horned deer who, like him, has left his small-headed mate?" In Ak. 137, the way the hero must traverse has "a forest river where an elephant yearns for the footprints of his mate." (See also Aiṅ. 238.) The animal separated from its herd also occurs in Tamil, as in Puṟ. 157, where the poet praises a king by comparing him to a tiger in a cave "who listens [without going out to kill the stag] while a stag, separated from his herd in a forest where he cannot see the place where he lives, calls to his young, foolish mate." (See also Ak. 32.)

There are several themes concerning animals and their mates that Tamil shares with the *Sattasaī* and classical Sanskrit but that are absent in the epics and the *Buddhacarita*. A hunter unable to attack an animal who is staying with his mate sometimes evokes the hero's condition separated from his beloved, as in Sa. 618: "As the doe gazed lovingly at the stag, the bow fell from the hand of the man who loved his wife." (See also R. 9.67.) In Aiṅ. 354, the hero is said to have returned quickly to his beloved from the wilderness "where a wild brown dog who has made love to his mate leaves the doe and her fawns without taking them." (See also Aiṅ. 397.)

In Sa. 454, the efforts of the heroine to help her lover are compared to those of a cow elephant trying to help her mate, in a rather obscure verse: "The cow elephant goes about, suffers, and puts out her trunk to help her mate get up as he sinks in the mud; she is caught [? Sanskrit *nigaḍita*] through her love for him." In Ak. 8, the heroine uses similar imagery to suggest that she could help her lover in the wilderness if he would elope with her: "an elephant to save her mate caught in a deep pit towering with plantain and *vaḻai* breaks with her trunk a huge tree with a crash that resounds in caves that scrape the sky." (See also Ak. 68, 165.)

Sometimes in classical Sanskrit the happy condition of an animal with its mate is contrasted to the sad state of a separated lover, as in R. 13.31, where Rāma tells Sītā that when he was apart from her he "saw with envy the cakravāka birds giving each other waterlily filaments." In Kuṟ. 37, the heroine's friend assures her that her absent lover has not forgotten her: "Where he went, to keep their mates from being hungry, bull elephants with huge trunks strip soft-branched *yā* trees snd thereby show their affection." (See also Kuṟ. 174, 308, 313, 319; Ak. 23, 59, 197, 201; Aiṅ. 445.)

The love of a man for a woman is sometimes compared to the affection of an animal for its offspring, as in Su. 64.3, where Rāma on seeing Sītā's jewel says, "My heart is like a cow that gives [milk] from love, loving her calf." Similarly, in Kuṟ. 344, the heroine says, "They must have done mortification, friend, who see their lovers coming back after they stayed away to get . . . wealth in the evening when cows . . . their udders swollen up . . . leave their herd thinking of their calves and go to the city, their udders dripping [with milk they will feed their calves]." In Kuṟ. 132, Aiṅ. 44, and Aiṅ. 268, the heroine is compared to the animal's young, the hero to the mother.

The love of a mother separated from her child is sometimes compared to that of an animal in the same condition. In Bu. 9.26, for example, envoys to Gautama tell him that his mother "weeps piteously and incessantly in distress like a loving cow who has lost her calf." (See also Bu. 8.25, 8.51, 8.86.) In Ak. 49 the foster mother describes how she would embrace the heroine "like a cow . . . tied to a tree who [embraces] her bent-legged calf." (See also Kuṟ. 181; Aiṅ. 401.) All of the examples of this theme in the *Buddhacarita* describe the suffering of a mother separated from her child. Such a description is used to enhance the dread of the forest through which the hero must travel in Ak. 83: "the country Vēṅkaṭam [ruled by] Puḷḷi, the lord of unlearned young men who . . . separate a baby elephant from its foolish mother . . . so that she goes crying through the forest."

Bhrāntimadalaṅkāra

Kuṟ. 127 contains a typical Tamil example of a figure called *Bhrāntimadalaṅkāra*, in which one thing is mistaken for another. The heroine talks to her husband, who has taken up with courtesans and has sent his Pāṇaṉ to conciliate his angry wife:

In your town of *kāñci* trees and ricefields,
a *keṇṭai* fish dives as a heron tries to seize it
and then is frightened
of the white buds of a shapely lotus nearby.
Since your bard tells lies,
it seems to those you have left
that all bards are thieves.

Like the fish that has escaped from the heron and thereafter mistakes all white things for that predator, the heroine, once cheated by the hero's bard, is in no mood to believe him again. In all the Tamil occurrences of *bhrāntimadalaṅkāra* animals are involved. In Puṟ. 283, otters and crocodiles mistake a snake for a shrimp and fight over it; in Puṟ. 319, children mistake the calf of a wild cow for an ordinary calf; in Ak. 21, elephants mistake wells for traps and cover them over; in Ak. 68, thunder mistakes a swing for a snake and roars;[8] in Ak. 111, elephants think spider

[8] In Tamil, thunder is said to break the heads of snakes willfully.

webs are clouds and trumpet; in Ak. 121, a deer thinks the whistling of the wind through palmyra umbrellas is the calling of its mate; in Ak. 138, a cobra mistakes a bee for the jewel that has fallen from its head; in Ak. 199, elephants mistake falling marā flowers for rain; in Ak. 219, a stag mistakes the blowing of the summer wind for a cowherd's flute; in Ak. 227 and 228, an elephant mistakes a vēṅkai tree for a tiger; in Ak. 232, an elephant thinks that thunder at midnight is a tiger roaring; in Aiṅ. 106, a conch thinks that a goose with webbed feet is its mate; in Aiṅ. 166, a crow mistakes a cowrie for a net and is afraid; and in Aiṅ. 239, an elephant mistakes a rock for his mate.

Bhrāntimadalaṅkāra occurs twice in the sections of the *Mahābhārata* surveyed by Sharma: "People living in the forest mistook king Pāṇḍu for a god, having shining armor, brave, conversant with the best missiles, as he roamed about" (1.106.10); and "Having heard the sound of [Nala's] chariot, those elephants and peacocks, with their faces turned upwards, trumpeted and screamed as if having seen the rising of clouds" (3.71.7). It becomes far more common in the *Sattasaī*, where, as in Tamil, all examples of it involve animals. In Sa. 531, "the monkey runs off, shakes, makes sound, and again scratches [the ground? *samullikhati*]. He does not eat the *jambu* fruit thinking it the bee he bit before." In Sa. 532, a monkey mistakes his mate's hand for a nettle; in Sa. 641, the mistake of a bee that leaves a lotus and goes to a *kapittha* flower is compared to a villager's touching a painting of a *laḍḍuka* (a kind of sweet; a *laḍḍu* in the modern South Indian languages); in Sa. 551, a buffalo mistakenly licks a serpent thinking it a mountain stream, and the serpent mistakes the spittle of the buffalo for a waterfall over black rocks; and in Sa. 640, an elephant tries to wet its head with a snake hanging over it, thinking it a waterfall. It is notable that the comparison of a snakeskin to a waterfall also occurs in Kuṟ. 235.

Bhrāntimadalaṅkāra occurs several times in the classical Sanskrit sources surveyed. In R. 13.32, Rāma thinks that an aśoka bent by clusters as lovely as (women's) breasts is Sītā. In Subh. 157, parrots mistake bees for berries and bees mistake the red beaks of parrots for *kiṃśuka* flowers; in Subh. 199, a parrot parched with thirst sips at the necklace pearls on a girl's breast, thinking them water; in Subh. 409, a bee mistakes the heroine for flowers, since each part of her body resembles some flower; in Subh. 471, the heroine grasps a wild goose, thinking it a lotus bud as its head is under water eating lotus roots; and in Subh. 1355, "a goose seeking lily stems at night bit a star's reflection in the pool, and now by day refuses the shining buds fearing they may be the stars."

Conclusions

From the foregoing, it is evident that there exists a relationship between the southern tradition, which produced Tamil poetry, and pre-*Sattasaī* Sanskrit poetry. There are three possible explanations of this relationship: Tamil could have borrowed from Sanskrit; the themes in question could have been of pan-Indian extent even before the Sanskrit epics; or Sanskrit could have assimilated them from the southern tradition, at a date not much before the composition of the epics.

Of these alternatives, the first may be completely discounted. It is true that the Sanskrit epics were known in Tamilnad at the time of the anthologies; however, the form in which the themes common to early Sanskrit and Tamil poetry occur in the anthologies precludes the possibility of their having been borrowed recently from the North. First, they fit too well with the conventions and techniques of Tamil poetry for them to have been recent innovations. Thus the reader will observe that in the Tamil examples of the various flower and animal themes, those themes are invariably used in the suggestive way peculiar to Tamil. Secondly, they are used quite differently in Tamil from the epics, where their use is for the most part purely descriptive. Thirdly, they are less common in the epics and the *Buddhacarita* than they are in Tamil; had they been borrowed by Tamil, one would expect them to be more common in early Sanskrit. Finally, the themes appear to be more at home in early Tamil culture than in the culture of the Indo-Aryans. It has been seen that flowers were used for many different purposes in ancient Tamilnad, performing some function by their presence in almost every significant facet of Tamil society. On the other hand, the relative unimportance of flowers in early Indo-Aryan life may be inferred from the fact that they are mentioned far less often in the Sanskrit epics than in the Tamil anthologies. As for animals, it has been seen that in early Tamil society, marriage is the central sacred event. It is entirely in keeping with that view that the Tamil poets should have seen in the world of nature many examples of perfect love between male and female, whether in intertwined creepers or in loving pairs of animals. In early Indo-Aryan society, on the other hand, marriage was not given the central importance it had for the Tamils. Thus it seems impossible that the themes should have been borrowed by the Tamils from the Aryans.

Could these themes have been of pan-Indian extent at a very early time, then, so that neither tradition borrowed them from the other? Such an explanation cannot be entirely ruled out, but circumstantial evidence renders it unlikely. First, it has been seen in chapters 5, 6, and 8 that at the time of the Sanskrit epics, there was a considerable influx of Dravidian elements into Aryan India—of words, of customs, and of meters. It is likely that popular poetic conventions accompanied that influx. Further, an examination of the use in early Sanskrit of the themes it shares with Tamil shows that the writers of the epics and the *Buddhacarita* used them in the least sophisticated ways imaginable, always specifying exactly what was supposed to be compared and limiting the comparison to only one aspect. Such usage cannot be attributed to lack of skill on the part of the poets; the *Mahābhārata*, at least, contains much sublime poetry. Rather, such usage is, I submit, exactly what one would expect to find if the themes were only just entering Aryan India from a foreign source. The writers, unfamiliar with the themes and the suggestive technique employed for their treatment in the South, simply adopted them in the most straightforward manner possible. In the *Rāmāyaṇa* and the *Buddhacarita*, these southern themes become quite prominent, a fact partly responsible, I believe, for the *Rāmāyaṇa*'s conventional position as the *Ādikāvya*, the first Sanskrit kāvya. In my opinion the relative newness of the southern poetic elements in the *Rāmāyaṇa* and the *Buddhacarita* accounts for their clumsy treatment in those two works, and, since they are quite important for the effects the authors wish to achieve in those works, this accounts at least in part for the inferior poetic quality of those poems.

By the time of Kālidāsa many new elements had entered Sanskrit poetry from the southern tradition, as has been seen. The number of southern elements in Kālidāsa and classical Sanskrit is, in fact, far higher than is indicated by the few shared themes described above. There is scarcely a verse in which some element cannot be found that can be traced back to the southern tradition. Kālidāsa's achievement was to use the southern elements in a fully natural and sophisticated manner and to combine them harmoniously with elements native to the North. He was, as far as is known, the first Sanskrit poet to do this. Partly because Kālidāsa was such a great poet and partly because he synthesized in such a perfect manner elements from the two preeminent cultures of India, his work set the standard for all future Sanskrit poetry and for much poetry in languages other than Sanskrit, though unfortunately the quality of his verse was rarely if ever equaled by his imitators.

With one exception, little occurred in Sanskrit poetry that was really new after Kālidāsa. The poetry grew convention-ridden and unnecessarily difficult. Writers after Kālidāsa seem to me to be lacking in sensitivity, though occasionally one finds a truly fine verse in the later writers. The exception, who had no worthy imitators, is the anonymous author of the *Bhāgavatapurāṇa*, who took his inspiration from the works of the Tamil Vaishnava saints and their tradition.[9]

In general after the time of Kālidāsa, it is to languages other than Sanskrit, languages that had living traditions to draw upon, that one must look for India's great literature. Among those literatures, Tamil has a preeminent place: it is the oldest and the least dependent on Sanskrit. Some may find it cause for regret that Tamil poetry did not retain the use of suggestion in the elaborate and exquisite form found in the anthologies. I believe that the technique of suggestion had been perfected in the anthologies. It could not be improved upon, and imitation of it could

[9] There are some who claim that the *Bhāgavatam* was not written by a Tamilian; yet anyone familiar with the *Divyaprabandham* finds so many similarities that there is little question regarding the matter. There is much other evidence as well. For example, the word *avamocanam*, meaning an inn, occurs in 10.5.20, its only recorded occurrence in Sanskrit literature. It makes sense only as a neologism coined by a Tamilian with the word *viṭuti* ("inn") in mind, as both words are from roots that mean "to leave"—*muñc* and *viṭu*.

lead only to stagnation. Thus I feel that it is fortunate that Tamil poetry found a new direction in the *Cilappatikāram*, which imitated oral epic poetry, and then in the *Cīvakacintāmaṇi* and the *Kamparāmāyaṇam*, which used North Indian stories but relied on South Indian tradition for their style, figures, and techniques. Indeed, the *Kamparāmāyaṇam* is the culmination of medieval Tamil literature. It may lack the depth of suggestion found in the anthologies, but it more than makes up for that by its dramatic treatment of the story and by its treatment of the incarnated god that is Rāma.

While writers who lived after Kampaṉ were influenced by him, the best of them, like Villipputtūrār, who wrote the most popular version of the *Mahābhārata*, were strongly influenced as well by the living folk literature of Tamilnad, and that kept their works from becoming lifeless rehearsals of what had gone before. Modern Tamil poetry has come half circle from the time of the early anthologies. It is a poetry of declamation, which sounds wonderful when read from a platform, but cannot be enjoyed by a reader who likes to pore over every line to discover suggested meanings. Today the Tamil anthologies are not much read by Tamil writers. Perhaps if the Tamils rediscover their most ancient literature and understand correctly its techniques, a new dimension will be added to the works of Tamil writers that will make Tamilnad once again the home of one of the world's finest literatures.

APPENDIX 1

AN ANALYSIS OF THE METER AND RHYME OF THE FIRST TWENTY-FIVE POEMS OF THE *SATTASAĪ*

For a discussion of the meter and rhyme of the *Sattasaī*, see chapter 8.

⏑ ⏑ ⏑⏑ /- -/- ⏑ ⏑//⏑ ⏑ -/- -/ ⏑ - ⏑ ⏑ ⏑/- - //

pasuvaiṇo rosāruṇapadimāsaṃkaṃtagorimuhaandaṃ

⏑ ⏑- / ⏑ - ⏑/- ⏑⏑ //- -/⏑ ⏑-/⏑ - ⏑ ⏑ -/- //

gahiāgghapaṃkaaṃ via saṃjhāsalīlañjaliṃ ṇamaha. (1)

⏑ ⏑- / -⏑⏑/- - // ⏑ ⏑- / - - / ⏑ - ⏑ -/- - //

Amiaṃ pāuakavvaṃ paḍhiuṃ souṃ a je ṇa āṇanti

- - /⏑ - ⏑/- - // ⏑ - ⏑/- ⏑ ⏑ / ⏑ - - - ⏑/- //

kāmassa tattatantiṃ kuṇanti te kahaṃ ṇa lajjanti. (2)

- ⏑ ⏑/- -/ ⏑⏑ - // ⏑ - ⏑ / - - /⏑ - ⏑-/- - //

Satta satāiṃ kaivacchaleṇa koḍīa majjhaārammi

- -/⏑ ⏑ ⏑⏑/- -//- -/ - - / ⏑ - - ⏑/- //

Hāleṇa viraiāiṃ sālaṅkārāṇaṃ gāhāṇaṃ. (3)

⏑⏑ -/ ⏑ ⏑ ./ - - // ⏑ ⏑ - /- -/ ⏑ - ⏑ ⏑ ⏑/ - - //

Ua ṇiccalaṇippandā bhisiṇīpattammi rehai balāā

- ⏑ ⏑/ ⏑ ⏑ ⏑⏑ / - ⏑ ⏑//⏑- ⏑/- - / ⏑ - - ⏑ / - //

ṇimmalamaragaabhāaṇaparitthiā saṃkhasutti vva. (4)

Tāvaccia raisamae mahilāṇaṃ bibbhamā virāanti
jāva ṇa kuvalaadalasecchaāiṃ maulenti ṇaanāiṃ. (5)

Ṇohaliamappaṇo kiṃ ṇa maggase maggase kurabaassa
eaṃ tuha suhaga hasai valiāṇaṇapaṃkaaṃ jāā. (6)

Tāvajjanti asoehiṃ laḍahavaṇiāoṃ daiavirahammi
kiṃ sahai kovi kassa vi pāapahāraṃ pahuppanto. (7)

Attā taha ramaṇijjaṃ ahmaṃ gāmassa maṇḍaṇīhūaṃ
luatilavāḍisaricchaṃ sisireṇa kaaṃ bhisiṇisaṇḍaṃ. (8)

kiṃ vuasi oṇaamuhī dhavalāantesu sālichittesu
hariālamaṇḍiamuhī ṇaḍi vva saṇavāḍiā jāā. (9)

Sahi īrisivvia gaī mā ruvvasi taṃsavaliamuhaaṇḍaṃ
eāṇaṃ vālavāluṅkitantukuḍilāṇaṃ pemmāṇaṃ. (10)

Pāapaḍiassa paiṇo puṭṭhiṃ putte samāruhattammi
daḍhamaṇṇuduṇṇiāe vi hāso gharaṇīe ṇekkanto. (11)

Saccaṃ jāṇai daṭṭhuṃ sarisammi janammi jujjae rāo
marau ṇa tumaṃ bhaṇissaṃ maraṇaṃ vi salāhanijjaṃ se. (12)

Gharaṇīe mahāṇasakammalaggamasimaliieṇa hattheṇa
chittaṃ muhaṃ hasijjai candāvatthaṃ gaaṃ paiṇa. (13)

Randhaṇakammaṇiuṇie mā jūrasu rattapāḍalasuandhaṃ

muhamāruaṃ pianto dhūmāi sihī na pajjalai. (14)

Kiṃ kiṃ de paḍihāsai sahīhiṃ ia pucchiāe muddhāe
paḍhamuggaadohanīe ṇavaraṃ daiaṃ gāā diṭṭhī. (15)

Amaamaa gaaṇasehara raaṇīmuhatilaa canda de chivasu
chitto jehiṃ piaamo mamaṃ pi tehiṃ via karehiṃ. (16)

Ehii so vi pauttho ahaṃ a kuppeja so vi aṇuṇejja
ia kassa vi phalai maṇorahāṇaṃ mālā piaamammi. (17)

Duggaakuḍumbaaṭṭhī kahaṃ ṇu mae dhoieṇa soḍhavvā
dasiosarantasalileṇa uaha ruṇṇaṃ va paḍaeṇa. (18)

Kosambakisalaavaṇṇaa taṇṇaa uṇṇāmiehiṃ kaṇṇohiṃ
hiaaṭṭhiaṃ gharaṃ vaccamāṇa dhavalattaṇaṃ pāva. (19)

Aliapasuttaa viṇimīliaccha de suhaa majjha oāsaṃ
gaṇḍapariumbaṇāpulaianga ṇa puṇo cirāissaṃ. (20)

Asamattamaṇḍaṇā via vacca gharaṃ se sakouhallassa
volāviahalahalaassa putti citte ṇa laggihisi. (21)

Aarapaṇāmioṭṭhaṃ aghaḍiaṇāsaṃ asaṃhaaṇiḍālaṃ
vaṇṇaghiatuppamuhie tīe pariumbaṇaṃ bharimo. (22)

Aṇṇāsaāiṃ dentī taha surae harisaviasiakavolā
gose vi oṇaamuhī aha setti piāṃ ṇa saddahimo. (23)

⏑⏑ ⏑ ⏑/– –/⏑⏑ //⏑ – ⏑/ ⏑ ⏑–/⏑ – ⏑ –/ –– //
Piaviraho appiadaṃsaṇaṃ a garuāiṃ do vi dukkhāiṃ
–⏑ ⏑/– –/– ⏑ ⏑//–⏑ ⏑/– –/⏑ ––⏑/–//
jīe tumaṃ kārijjasi tīe ṇamo āhi jāīe. (24)

– –/ ⏑ – ⏑/– –//⏑ –⏑/ – –/ ⏑ – ⏑ ⏑ ⏑/– –//
Ekko vi kahṇasāro ṇa dei gantuṃ paāhiṇavalanto
– ⏑ ⏑/ – –/⏑ ⏑–//–⏑ ⏑/⏑⏑ –/ ⏑⏑⏑ –⏑/– //
kiṃ uṇa bāhāuliaṃ loaṇajualaṃ piaamāe. (25)

APPENDIX 2

THE OCCURRENCE OF TAMIL THEMES IN INDO-ARYAN

In the following scheme, the number before the theme indicates the first page on which discussion of that theme can be found above. The number 1 refers to pre-*Sattasaī* Indo-Aryan works, 2 to the *Sattasaī*, and 3 to classical Sanskrit; 1a means that a theme appears in the epics, 1b that it occurs in the *Buddhacarita*; 3a means that it appears in Kālidāsa, and 3b that it occurs in the *Subhāṣitsratnakośa* or other Sanskrit work written after Kālidāsa. Parentheses around a number indicate that the relation of the theme in that work to the Tamil theme is doubtful.

40	Compare dreadful objects in war to benevolent objects	3a
100	Men attack to marry a king's or hero's daughter	2 (Sa. 410)
212	Glorification of king by describing the wretched condition of his enemies	3a, 3b
212	Glorification of king by describing the widows of his enemies	3a, 3b
212	Glorification of king by describing the wretched condition of the lands of his enemies	3b

212	A bard asks a king to give gifts to him	3b
212	Contrast between a hero's cruelty and his generosity	3a, 3b
213	A king's inscrutability	3b
213	The king does not rule the earth in common	3a
214	The king is unaffected by bad omens	3b
214	*Dramatis personae* of the akam poems	2, (3a), 3b
217	Lovers rendezvous in a grain field, often as the heroine keeps birds from the crop	2
217	Lovers rendezvous at night, often in the rain	2, 3b
217	The *abhisārikā*, often in the rain	2, 3a, 3b
220	Lament of the destruction of the rendezvous place	2, 3b (Subh. 808)
221	The hero describes his beloved as beautiful but dangerous	3b
221	The heroine, who has fallen in love, is kept at home	2
225	A man must leave his wife or beloved and travel to seek money	2, 3b
226	A traveler is comforted by the thought of his beloved	2
226	A traveler does not wish to leave his beloved	2
226	Contrast between the tender nature of people and the harshness of the wilderness they must traverse or inhabit	1a, 1b, 3a
227	Description of how a girl who used to play ball must undergo austerities	3a
228	A wish that the elements may be kind to a departing daughter	3a
228	A man's heart leaves him and goes to see his beloved	(1a), 1b, 2, 3b (Subh. 478)
229	Possession of the heart of one's beloved	2
229	Hearts of lovers mix	3b
229	A traveler does not return by the promised date (usually the monsoon)	2, 3b
229	The life of a traveler's wife is in danger	2, 3b

230	The suffering of the traveler apart from his wife, often in the monsoon	2, 3a, 3b
230	The crying or dancing of peacocks described to evoke the monsoon season	1a, 2, 3a, 3b
231	The laughing of flowers in the monsoon	2, 3a, 3b
231	The sad state of the traveler's wife in spring	2, 3b
232	The heroine makes marks to count the days until her beloved's return	2, 3a, 3b
232	Pretense that the shower at hand is not the monsoon	2, 3b
233	The heroine's suffering in evening	(3a), 3b
234	The heroine's suffering at night	2, 3a, 3b
234	The hero returns during the monsoon	2, 3a, 3b
235	Description of the happy married heroine as she cooks	2
235	The mother rejoices at the happiness of her married daughter	2
236	Description of the couple's happiness with their son	2
236	The hero takes up with other women after the birth of his child	2, 3b
237	Harlots abuse the heroine	2
237	The *māninī*	1a, 2, 3a, 3b
238	Conciliation in the presence of the couple's child	2
238	The wife scolds her husband for wishing to go on a journey	2
239	The wife scolds her husband for having gone on a journey	2, 3b
239	The coyness of a new beloved	3b
240	The coyness of a new wife	2, 3a, 3b
241	The hero bathes with his wife or wives	2, 3a, 3b
241	The hero bathes with a woman with flowers in her hair	2, 3a
241	The hero bathes with a woman with a pearl necklace	3a
241	The hero bathes with women, playing on a raft	3a

242	The heroine surrounded by suitors seeks her beloved	2
242	The heroine is menstruous	2
243	The heroine cannot sleep	2, 3b
244	The messenger poem	3a, 3b
244	Messenger poem involving a journey from the South to the Himālayas	3a
246	The south (*malaya*) wind in spring	2, 3a, 3b
247	A breeze is charged with drops	3a, 3b
247	A breeze is made fragrant by the flowers with which it comes into contact	3a, 3b
248	The wind blowing through a bamboo with a hole in it makes a sound like that of a flute	3a
249	Animals listen to a girl's singing	3b
249	The heroine plays with balls or dolls or makes sand houses	3a
249	Clouds evoke generosity	3a, 3b
250	The sea giving water to clouds evokes generosity	3a
250	Clouds drink from the sea	3a, 3b
250	A bloody sword is compared to the red sky at evening	3a
250	Pearls come from the heads or tusks of elephants	3a
250	Pearls come from elephants killed or attacked by lions	3a
251	Pearls come from bamboo	3b
	Women's eyes compared to blue waterlilies	1a, 1b, 2, 3a, 3b (more common in 2 and after)
258	A woman's eyes compared to a fawn's eyes (in Tamil, always to a doe's eyes)	(1a)
260	A woman's eyes compared to a doe's eyes	2, 3a, 3b
	The eyes of a valorous man or angry woman are red	1a, 2
261	A woman's eyes are long	1a, 1b, 2, 3b
261	A woman's eyes are like arrows	2, 3a, 3b
262	The dark part of a woman's eyes are like bees	3a, 3b

262	The whites of a woman's eyes are compared to jasmine	3b
262	Bees evoke a male lover	1a, 1b, 2, 3a, 3b
263	The ruining of a garland in lovemaking	1a
263	The ruining of plants by elephants symbolizes lovemaking	1a
264	The ruining of a plant symbolizes lovemaking	1a, 1b, 2
264	A cobra's hood compared to a woman's pubis	3b
264	A woman suffering in love is compared to a ruined plant	1a, 3a, 3b
265	Ruined plants evoke the valor of a wounded or dead hero in battle	(1a)
265	A hero in battle is compared to an elephant ruining plants	3a
265	Description of falling flowers	1a, 1b, 2, 3a, 3b
266	An empty plant evokes sorrow	1a, 3a
266	Falling flowers evoke the end of love	2
266	The wind blows down flowers	3a, 3b
266	Flowers blow on a man's head	2
267	Falling flowers are compared to tears	3a
267	A shaking plantain tree is compared to a person trembling	1a
267	A lotus or waterlily shakes when hit by a fish	1a, 3a
267	The waving of a plant is compared to the motion of a woman's arms	1b, 3a
268	A beautiful woman is compared to a blossoming plant	1a, 1b
268	A moving creeper is compared to a dancing woman	3a
268	Plants intertwining are compared to lovers embracing	1b, 3a
269	The closing of flowers in evening evokes pain or loss	1b, 3b
270	The opening of flowers in the morning signifies a return of fertility	3a
270	The opening of flowers in evening signifies that the time of love is at hand	3a

270	Contrast of open flowers to closed ones	3a
270	A closed flower is like folded hands	1b
270	Bees try to enter a closing flower (in Indo-Aryan, they are caught inside)	2, 3b
271	A weak animal, often a deer, attacked by a strong animal evokes pity	1a, 3a, 3b
271	A deer or other creature afflicted by a hunter's arrow evokes pity	(1a), 1b
272	A lion (in Tamil, a tiger) defeats an elephant	1a, 2, 3a, 3b
272	Elephants that do not fear lions	3a
272	An animal with its mate evokes the happiness of the human couple	(1a), 2, 3a, 3b
273	Description of animals mating indicates a time appropriate for lovemaking	(2), 3a
273	The suffering of a person separated from his or her lover is compared to that of an animal in the same situation	1a, 1b, 2, 3a, 3b
273	A hunter (in Tamil, an animal) is unable to attack a loving animal with its mate	2, 3a
274	The efforts of the heroine to help her lover are likened to an animal's attempts to help her mate	2
274	The happy condition of an animal with its mate is contrasted to the sad condition of a person without his or her lover	3a
274	The love of a man for a woman is compared to that of a cow for her calf	1b
275	The love of a human mother separated from her child is compared to that of an animal in the same condition	1b
275	*Bhrāntimadalaṅkāra*	(1a), 2, (3a), 3b
276	A waterfall is compared to a snake	2

REFERENCES

An asterisk before the name of a book indicates that, of the various editions of the work, that edition was followed for readings and reference numbers.

The *Abhijñāna-Śākuntala* of Kālidāsa. Commentary (*Arthadyotanikā*) by Rāghavabhaṭṭa, reedited by Nārāyan-Rām Āchārya Kāvyatīrtha. 12th ed. Bombay: Nirnaya Sagar Press, 1958.

Adigal, (Prince) Ilanko. *Shilappadikāram (The Ankle Bracelet).* Translated by Alain Danielou. New York: New Directions, 1965.

Aiṅkuṟunūṟu. Commentary by P. V. Cōmacuntaraṉār. Madras: Kazhagam, 1966.

Aiṅkuṟunūṟu. Commentary by Auvai C. Turaicāmippiḷḷai. 3 vols. Annamalai: Annamalai University Press, 1957–58.

**Aiṅkuṟunūṟu Mūlamum Paḻaiyavuraiyum* (with an old commentary). Notes by U. V. Swaminathaier. 5th ed. Madras: Kapīr Accukkūṭam, 1957.

Aiyappan, A. "Social and Physical Anthropology of the Nayadis of Malabar." *Madras Government Museum Bulletin*, general section 2, 1930–37, pp. 13–85.

Akanāṉūṟu. Commentary by N. M. Vēṅkaṭacāmi Nāṭṭār and R. Vēṅkaṭācalam Piḷḷai. Madras: Kazhagam, 1965.

Allchin, Bridget, and Raymond Allchin. *The Birth of Indian Civilization: India and Pakistan before 500* B.C. Baltimore, Md.: Penguin Books, 1968.

Aparārka-Yajñavālkīya-Dharmaśāstranibandha. Poona: Ānandāśrama Press, 1903–04.

Apastambadharmasūtra. Edited by George Buhler. Bombay: Bombay Sanskrit Series, 1892–94.

Apte, Vaman Shivaram. *The Practical Sanskrit-English Dictionary.* 3 vols. Rev. ed. Poona: Prasad Prakashan, 1959.

Banerjee, N. R. *The Iron Age of India.* Delhi: Munshiram Manoharlal, 1965.

Baudhāyana Dharmasūtra. Commentary by Govindasvāmin. Mysore: Mysore Government Oriental Series, 1907.

Böhtlingk, Otto, and Rudolf Roth. *Sanskrit-Wörterbuch*. 7 vols. St. Petersburg: Kaiserliches Akademie der Wissenschaften, 1855–75.

The Buddhacarita: or, Acts of the Buddha. Edited and translated by E. H. Johnston. Calcutta: University of the Punjab (Lahore), 1935–36.

Burrow, T. *The Sanskrit Language*. London: Faber and Faber, 1955.

Burrow, T., and M. B. Emeneau. *A Dravidian Etymological Dictionary*. London: Oxford University Press, 1960.

Cāmi, P. L. *Cañka Ilakkiyattil Ceṭikoṭi Viḷakkam*. Madras: Kazhagam, 1967.

Casal, J., and G. Casal. *Site Urbain et Sites Funeraires*. Paris: Presses Universitaires de France, 1956.

Cilappatikāram. Commentary by Aṭiyārkkunallār. 7th ed. Madras: Kapīr Accukkūṭam, 1960.

Ciṟupāṇāṟṟuppaṭai. One of the ten poems of the *Pattuppāṭṭu*, q.v.

Crawley, Ernest. *The Mystic Rose*. New ed., rev. and enl. by Theodore Besterman. 2 vols. New York: Boni and Liveright, 1927.

Deleury, G. A. *The Cult of Viṭhobā*. Poona: Deccan College Postgraduate and Research Institute, 1960.

The *Dhvanyāloka* of Śri Ānandavardhanacharya. Lochana Sanskrit commentary by Śrī Abhinavagupta. Varanasi: Chowkhamba Vidyabhavan, 1965.

Edgerton, Franklin, and Eleanor Edgerton. *Kalidasa, the Cloud Messenger*. Ann Arbor: University of Michigan Press, 1964.

Eliade, Mircea. *Cosmos and History: The Myth of the Eternal Return*. Translated by Willard R. Trask. New York: Harper and Row, 1959.

———. *Patterns in Comparative Religion*. 4th ed. Cleveland and New York: Meridian Books, 1967.

———. *The Sacred and the Profane*. New York: Harcourt Brace and Co., 1959.

———. *Shamanism: Archaic Techniques of Ecstasy*. Translated by Willard R. Trask. Bolling Series 76. New York: Pantheon, 1964.

Frazer, James George. *The New Golden Bough*. Edited by Theodore H. Gaster. New York: Mentor, 1969.

The *Gāthāsaptaśatī* of Sātavāhana. Edited by K. P. Parab. Kāvya Mālā Series 21. Bombay: Nirnaya Sagar Press, 1899.

Hart, George L., III. "Woman and the Sacred in Ancient Tamilnad." *Journal of Asian Studies* 32, no. 2 (1973): 233–250.

Heidel, Alexander. *The Gilgamesh Epic and Old Testament Parallels*. Chicago: University of Chicago Press, Phoenix Books, 1953.

Index des mots de la litterature tamoule ancienne. Pondichéry: Institut Français d'Indologie, 1967–70. Vol. 1 (a–au), 1967; vol. 2 (ka–tau), 1968; vol. 3 (na–ṉa), 1970.

Ingalls, Daniel H. H. *An Anthology of Sanskrit Court Poetry: Vidyākara's "Subhāṣitaratnakośa."* Harvard Oriental Series 44. Cambridge: Harvard University Press, 1965.

———. "The *Harivaṃśa* as a Mahākāvya." *Mélanges d'Indianisme à la Mémoire de Louis Rénou*. Paris: E. de Boccard, 1968.

Jain, Jyoti Prasad. *The Jain Sources of the History of Ancient India*. Delhi: Munshiram Manoharlal, 1964.

Kailasapathy, K. *Tamil Heroic Poetry*. London: Oxford University Press, 1968.

Kalittokai. Commentary by Nacciṉārkkiṉiyar. Madras: Kazhagam, 1967.

The *Kāmasūtra* by Śrī Vātsyāyana Muni. Commentary Jayamangala of Yashodhar. Kashi Sanskrit Series 29. Benares: Chowkhamba Sanskrit Series Office, 1929.

Kamparāmāyaṇam. Madras: U. V. Swaminathaier Library, 1957—.

**Kampar Iyaṟṟiya Irāmāyaṇam* [Critical edition of the *Kamparāmāyaṇam*]. Annamalai: Annamalai University Press, 1956—.

Kane, Pandurang Vaman. *The History of Dharmaśāstra*. 5 vols. Poona: Bhandarkar Oriental Research Institute, 1930–62.

Kāvyaprakāśa of Mammaṭa. Sanskrit commentary (*Bālabodhinī*) by Vāmanāchārya Rāmabhaṭṭa Jhalakīkar. 7th ed. Poona: Bhandarkar Oriental Research Institute, 1965.

Keith, Arthur Berriedale. *A History of Sanskrit Literature*. London: Oxford University Press, 1920.

———. *The Religion and Philosophy of the Vedas and Upanishads*. Harvard Oriental Series 31 and 32. Cambridge: Harvard University Press, 1925.

———. *The Sanskrit Drama.* London: Oxford University Press, 1924.

Knorozov, Y. *Predvaritel'nye Soobshcheniya ob Issledovanii Protoindiĭskikh Tekstov.* Moscow, 1965.

Kōvintan̲, K. *Cañkat Tamil̲p Pulavar Varicai.* Vol. 2 (Paraṇar). Madras: Kazhagam, 1961.

Kumārasaṃbhava of Kālidāsa. 1–8 sargas. Commentary by Mallinātha, edited by Kāśīnātha Panduranga Parab. Bombay: Nirnaya Sagar Press, 1879.

Kur̲iñcippāṭṭu. One of the ten poems of the *Pattuppāṭṭu*, q.v.

Kur̲untokai. Commentary by U. V. Swaminathaier. 4th ed. Madras: Kapīr Accukkūṭam, 1962.

Lal, B. B. "From the Megalithic to the Harappan: Tracing Back the Graffiti on the Pottery." *Ancient India*, no. 6 (1960), pp. 1–24 (New Delhi, 1962).

Lord, Albert B. *The Singer of Tales.* Cambridge: Harvard University Press, 1964.

The Mahābhārata. Critically edited by Vishnu S. Sukthankar. Poona: Bhandarkar Oriental Research Institute, 1933–66.

Mahadevan, Iravatham. "Tamil Brahmi Inscriptions of the Sangam Age." *In Proceedings of the Second International Conference Seminar of Tamil Studies* I: 73–106. Madras: International Association of Tamil Research, 1971.

Malaipaṭukaṭām. One of the ten songs of the *Pattuppāṭṭu*, q.v.

Maṇimēkalai (with commentary). Notes by U. V. Swaminathaier. Madras: Kapīr Accukkūṭam, 1965.

The *Manusmṛti* (by Manu). Commentary by Kulluka, edited by Narayan Ram Acharya Kavyatirtha. 10th ed. Bombay: Nirnaya Sagar Press, 1946.

Maturaikkāñci. One of the ten songs of the *Pattuppāṭṭu*, q.v.

McCann, Charles. *100 Beautiful Trees of India.* Bombay: T. P. Taraporevala Sons and Co., 1959.

Mullaippāṭṭu. One of the ten songs of the *Pattuppāṭṭu*, q.v.

**Nar̲r̲iṇai Mūlamum Viḷakkavuraiyum.* Commentary by Auvai C. Turaicāmippiḷḷai. 2 vols. Madras: Aruṇā Publications, 1966, 1968.

Nar̲r̲iṇai. Commentary by A. Nārāyaṇacāmi Aiyar. Madras: Kazhagam, 1962.

Neṭunalvāṭai. One of the ten songs of the *Pattuppāṭṭu*, q.v.

Nilakantasastri, K. A. *The Cōḷas*. 2d ed. Madras: University of Madras, 1955.

———. *The Culture and History of the Tamils*. Calcutta: K. L. Mukhopadhyay, 1964.

———. *Development of Religion in South India*. Madras: Orient Longmans, 1963.

———. *A History of South India from Prehistoric Times to the Fall of Vijayanagar*. 3d ed. London: Oxford University Press, 1966.

Paripāṭal. Commentary by P. V. Cōmacuntaraṉār. Madras: Kazhagam, 1964.

**Paripāṭal*. Commentary by Parimēlaḻakar, notes by U. V. Swaminathaier. 4th ed. Madras: Kapīr Accukkūṭam, 1956.

Le Paripāṭal. Translated and annotated by François Gros. Pondichéry: Institut Français d'Indologie, 1968.

Parpola, Asko, Seppo Koskenniemi, Simo Parpola, and Pentti Aalto. *Decipherment of the Proto-Dravidian Inscriptions of the Indus Civilization*. Copenhagen: Scandanavian Institute of Asian Studies, 1969.

Patiṟṟuppattu. Commentary by Auvai C. Turaicāmippiḷḷai. Madras: Kazhagam, 1963.

**Patiṟṟuppattu Mūlamum Paḻaiya Uraiyum*. Notes by U. V. Swaminathaier. 6th ed. Madras: Kapīr Accukkūṭam, 1957.

Paṭṭiṉappālai. One of the ten songs of the *Pattuppāṭṭu*, q.v.

Pattuppāṭṭu. Commentary by P. V. Cōmacuntaraṉār. 2 vols. Madras: Kazhagam, 1966.

**Pattuppāṭṭu*. Commentary by Nacciṉārkkiṉiyar, notes by U. V. Swaminathaier. 6th ed. Madras: Kapīr Accukkūṭam, 1961.

Pattuppattu, Ten Tamil Idylls. Translated by J. V. Chelliah. Madras: Kazhagam, 1962.

Perumpāṇāṟṟuppaṭai. One of the ten songs of the *Pattuppāṭṭu*, q.v.

Pillai, Thakazhi Sivasankara. *Chemmeen*. Translated by Narayana Menon. New York: Harper, 1962.

Pillay, K. K. "Aryan Influences in Tamilaham during the Sangam Epoch." *Tamil Culture* 12, nos. 2 and 3 (1966): 159–170.

———. "Landmarks in the History of Tamilnad." *Proceedings of the Second International Conference Seminar of Tamil Studies* I:12–26. Madras: International Association of Tamil Research, 1971.

Polo, Marco. *The Travels of Marco Polo.* Edited by Manuel Komroff. New York: Garden City Publishing Co., 1930.

Pope, G. U. *The Naladiyar, or Four Hundred Quatrains in Tamil.* London: Oxford University Press, 1893.

Porunarāṟṟuppaṭai. One of the ten songs of the *Pattuppāṭṭu,* q.v.

Puṟanāṉūṟu. Commentary by Auvai C. Turaicāmippiḷḷai. 2 vols. Madras: Kazhagam, 1962, 1967.

**Puṟanāṉūṟu Mūlamum Uraiyum.* Notes by U. V. Swaminathaier. 6th ed. Madras: Kapīr Accukkūṭam, 1963.

Puṟapporuḷ Veṇpā Mālai. Commentary by Cāmuṇṭi Tēvanāyakar, notes by U. V. Swaminathaier. 11th ed. Madras: Kapīr Accukkūṭam, 1963.

*The *Raghuvaṃśa* of Kālidāsa. Commentary (*Sañjīvinī*) by Mallinātha, edited by Kasinath Pandurang Parab. 2d rev. ed. Bombay: Nirnaya Sagar Press, 1888.

The *Raghuvaṃśa* of Kālidāsa. Commentary (*Sañjīvinī*) by Mallinātha, edited and translated by Moreshwar Ramchandra Kale. Vol. 1, cantos I–VII. Bombay: Sharadakridan Press, Saka 1817 (A.D. 1895).

Ramanujan, A. K. *The Interior Landscape, Love Poems from a Classical Tamil Anthology.* Bloomington: Indiana University Press, 1967.

———. *Speaking of Siva.* Baltimore, Md.: Penguin Books, 1973.

Rāmāyaṇa. See *Vālmīki-Rāmāyaṇa.*

Sambamoorthy, P. *South Indian Music.* Book IV, 2d ed. Madras: Indian Music Publishing House, 1954.

Śatapatha-Brāhmaṇa: The White Yajurveda. Edited by Albrecht Weber. Part 2, the *Śatapatha-Brāhmaṇa.* Berlin and London: F. Dümmler, 1855.

Sharma, Ram Karan. *Elements of Poetry in the Mahābhārata.* Berkeley: University of California Press, 1964.

Singaravelu, S. *Social Life of the Tamils: The Classical Period.* Kuala Lumpur: University of Malaya, 1966.

Skanda Purāṇa. 7 vols. Bombay: Sri Venkatesvara Steam Press, Saṃvat. 1966 (A.D. 1910).

Smith, Vincent A. *The Oxford History of India.* Edited by Percival Spear. 3d ed., rev. London: Oxford University Press, 1958.

Spate, O. H. K., and A. T. A. Learmonth. *India and Pakistan: A General and Regional Geography*. 3rd ed. Bungay, England: Methnen, 1967.

Stein, Burton. "Integration of the Agrarian System of South India." *In Land Control and Social Structure in Indian History*, edited by R. E. Frykenberg, pp. 175–216. Madison: University of Wisconsin Press, 1969.

Subhāṣitaratnakośa. Compiled by Vidyākara, edited by D. D. Kosambi and V. V. Gokhale. Harvard Oriental Series 42. Cambridge: Harvard University Press, 1957.

Subrahmanian, N. *Pre-Pallavan Tamil Index*. Madras University Historical Series 23. Madras: University of Madras, 1966.

Subramoniam, V. I. *Index of Puranaanuuru*. Trivandrum: University of Kerala, 1962.

Tamil Lexicon. 6 vols. Madras: University of Madras, 1936. *Supplement*, 1938.

Thurston, Edgar T. *Castes and Tribes of Southern India*. 7 vols. Madras: Government Press, 1909.

Tirukkuṟaḷ. Commentary by Parimēlaḻakar. Madras: V. V. V. M. Kōpālakruṣṇācāryar Co., 1965.

Tirumurukāṟṟuppaṭai. One of the ten songs of the *Pattuppāṭṭu*, q.v.

Tolkāppiyam, Poruḷatikāram, Akattiṇai Iyal, Puṟattiṇai Iyal. Commentary by Nacciṉārkkiṉiyar. Madras: Kazhagam.

Tolkāppiyam, Poruḷatikāram, Ceyyuḷiyal. Commentary by Nacciṉārkkiṉiyar. Madras: Kazhagam.

Tolkāppiyam, Poruḷatikāram, Kaḷavu, Kaṟpu, Poruḷ Iyalkaḷ. Commentary by Nacciṉārkkiṉiyar. Madras: Kazhagam.

Tolkāppiyam, Poruḷatikāram. Commentary by Iḷampūraṇar. Madras: Kazhagam, 1961.

Tolkāppiyam, Poruḷatikāram, Meypāṭṭiyal, Uvamaiyiyal, Ceyyuḷiyal, Marapiyal. Commentary by Pērāciriyar. Madras: Kazhagam, 1966.

Turner, Ralph Lilley. *A Comparative Dictionary of the Indo-Aryan Languages*. London: Oxford University Press, 1962.

The Vālmīki-Rāmāyaṇa. Critically edited by G. H. Bhatt et al. Baroda: Oriental Institute, 1960—.

Vēṅkaṭacāmi, Mayilai-Cīṉi. *Maṟaintu Pōṉa Tamiḻ Nūlkaḷ*. Madras: Cānti Nūlakam, 1967.

Vikramorvaśīya of Kālidāsa. Commentary by Ranganātha. 6th ed. Bombay: Nirnaya Sagar Press, 1925.

Warder, A. K. *Introduction to Pali.* London: Pali Text Society, 1963.

———. *Pali Meter.* London: Pali Text Society, 1967.

Warren, Henry Clarke. *Buddhism in Translations.* New York: Atheneum, 1963.

Weber, Albrecht. *Das Saptaçatakam des Hāla.* Abhandlungen Für die Kunde des Morgenlandes vol. 7, no. 4. Leipzig, 1881.

———. *Ueber das Saptaçatakam des Hāla.* Abhandlungen Für die Kunde des Morgenlandes vol. 5, no. 3. Leipzig, 1870.

Westermarck, Edward. *A History of Human Marriage.* 3 vols. 5th ed., rewritten. London: Allerton Book Co., 1921.

Winternitz, M. *A History of Indian Literature.* Calcutta: University of Calcutta, 1959–63. Vol. I, pt 1, translated by S. Ketkar, 1962; vol. 1, pt. 2, translated by S. Ketkar, 1963; vol. 2, translated by S. Ketkar and H. Kohn, 1963; vol. 3, fasciculus 1, translated by H. Kohn, 1959.

Zvelebil, Kamil. *The Smile of Murugan: On Tamil Literature of South India.* Leiden: E. J. Brill, 1973.

———. "From Proto-South Dravidian to Old Tamil and Malayalam." *Proceedings of the Second International Conference Seminar of Tamil Studies* I:45–72. Madras: International Association of Tamil Research, 1971.

INDEX

Abhinavagupta, his ideas regarding suggestion, 189–190
Abhisārikā, 217–219
Afterworld: indigenous Tamil notions of, 41-43; Tamil Valhalla, 41–42; belief that spirit remains in memorial stone, 42-43; northern ideas of, 65–67; dead parents in southern land, 80. *See also* Death
Aiñkuṟunūṟu, nature and date of poems, 7–9
Akam: a Tamil poetic category, 7; characters of and their Indo-Aryan counterparts, 214–216; *tiṇais* of: *kuṟuñci*, 216–221; *pālai*, 221–229; *mullai*, 229–236; *marutam*, 236–243; *neytal*, 243–244.
Akanāṉūṟu, nature and date of poems, 8–9
Akavunaṉ, 144-145; the Akavaṉmakaḷ, 145–146
Allchins, on the Megalithic culture, 252–253
Āḻvārs: their songs a consequence of ecstatic worship, 29; their role in the prevailing of Hinduism, 72; their role in making northern and southern synthesis, 132; and the sacred nature of human love, 179; and the *Bhāgavatapurāṇa*, 279
Ānandavardhana, his theory of suggestion, 169; 188–190
Aṇaṅku. *See* Sacred power
Animals: weak animal attacked by strong evokes pity, 271; animal hit by an arrow evokes pity, 271–272; an animal with its mate is like a human couple, 272–274; a separated animal like a lonely lover, 273; a hunter cannot bring himself to attack an animal, 273–274; an animal tries to help its mate, 274; affection of an animal for its offspring, 274–275; in *bhrāntimadalaṅkāra*, 275–277. *See also* Deer, Elephant, Tiger, Cow, Monkey, Fish
Āṇṭāḷ, her sensuous description of Krishna, 180 n
Ape. *See* Monkey
Army, of four parts, 80
Arrow. *See* Weapon
Arundhatī, 59
Ascetic: avoided by people, 64; Tamil attitude towards, 70–71
Astrology: festival of Paṅkuṉi, 45–46; festival of Kārttikai, 46–47; in the Tamil anthologies, 72–78
Aśvaghoṣa. See *Buddhacarita*

Balarāma, 57
Ball, a girl's toy, 226–227
Bamboo: a source of pearls, 251–252; ruined by elephants, 265; like a woman's arms, 267–268
Bard. *See* Pāṇaṉ
Bathing: king bathes before battle, 32; one bathes after worshipping the memorial stone, 42; and pollution, 126; a woman meets her lover while bathing, 164; the hero bathes with his courtesans, 241–242. *See also* Pollution
Battle, 31–38; nature of the battlefield, 32–33. *See also* War
Bee: as sexual image, 165–166; 173–174; 262–263; tinkling of ornaments like humming of, 171, 218–219; sound of like a flute, 172, 248; bees follow woman as she goes to rendezvous, 218–219; they swarm in the evening, 234; as the subject of a messenger poem, 245; like eyes, 262; enters flower, 270
Bhāgavatapurāṇa: only really innovative post-Kālidāsan work in Sanskrit, 279; by a Tamilian who knows the Tamil Vaishnava literature, 279 n
Bhāsa, *āryā* meter in, 207
Bhrāntimadalaṅkāra, 275–277
Birds: as omens, 43–44; owl hooting in the day is a bad omen, 43; calling of a crow means that guests are coming, 43; frightened from fields by the beating of snares, 186–187; a goose is the subject of a messenger poem, 244. *See also* Heron
Brāhmī script: when introduced into

of ecstatic worship, 29; their role in the prevailing of Hinduism, 72; sacred nature of human love for, 57, 179–180
Neytal: Funeral rhythm, 84; situations under the poetic category of, 243–244; heroine cannot sleep, 243–244
Night: as time of suffering for the separated, 168, 174, 185, 234; rendezvous during, 217–220
Nilakantasastri: his opinions of northern influence in early Tamilnad, 10–12; his discussion of a Tamil poem enumerating low castes, 120–121
Northern influence in early Tamilnad, opinions of other scholars, 10–12

Ocean: likened to love, 167; night vaster than, 168; clouds take water from, 250. *See also* Water
Odyssey, journey in as initiation, 223–224
Omens: indigenous, 43–45; borrowed, 79–80; throbbing of arm in Kālidāsa, 175; hooting of owl, 193; king unaffected by bad omens, 214
Oral poetry: and the Tamil poems, 152–158; folk nature of some simple Tamil poems, 181–182; literary nature of Tamil poems, 254; oral literature drawn on for medieval Tamil Purāṇas, 280
Ornaments: woman's anklet taken off at marriage, 50; their role in controlling a woman's power, 111; ornamentation of breasts causes sacred power to stay there, 137; broken bangle like the crescent moon, 166; ornaments tinkle like humming bees, 171; earrings like lightning, 193–195; anklets silenced for rendezvous, 218–219; women wear pearl necklaces while bathing, 241–242

Paddy. *See* Grain
Pālai: situations under the poetic category of, 221–229. Nature of the wilderness, 221–222; journey a symbolic initiation, 222–225; journey is for wealth, 225–226; wife protects traveling husband, 226; traveler does not want to leave wife, 226; people lament to see couple in the wilderness, 226–227; ask that elements be kind to traveling girl, 228; hero addresses heart, 228–229; heroine fights with hero over his impending journey, 238–239
Pāli: *āryā* and other *mātrā* meters in, 206–208
Pāṇaṉ: beats *taṉṉumai* drum in battle, 31; protects wounded, 37; called low, 119–120; one of four low castes, 121; fishes, 127; creates order, 135; detailed description of, 138–140; Kōṭiyaṉs and Vayiriyaṉs subcastes of? 140–141; kept in houses of rich, 143; their oral poetry copied by Pulavaṉs, 148, 156–157; Auvaiyār not a Viṟali, 149 n; nature of Pāṇaṉs' compositions, 156–157; also found in Kerala and Orissa, 158; peacock like Viṟali entering stage, 248. *See also* Kōṭiyaṉ, Vayiriyaṉ, Music, *yāḻ*
Pandya kings: their capital, 14; their emblems, 18; their festival, 46
Paradise. *See* Afterworld
Paṟai: beaten during battle, 32; causes victory, 32; Paṟaiyaṉ one of four low castes, 120–121; Paṟaiyaṉ same as Kiṇaiyaṉ? 143; Paṟaiyaṉ found elsewhere in South India, 158. *See also* Kiṇaiyaṉ
Paraśurāma, 59
Parattai. *See* Courtesan
Patiṟṟuppattu, nature and date of poems, 8–9
Peacock: hunter's wife wears peacock feather, 190; heroine like peacock descending from mountain, 193–194; evokes monsoon, 231, 235; like Viṟali entering stage, 248
Pearl: worn by hunter's wives, 190; from elephants, 250–251; from bamboo, 251–252
Pillay: his discussion of a Tamil poem enumerating low castes, 120
Piṇḍa: use of among Tamils and Aryans, 84–86
Plant. *See* Flowers
Plantain, its shaking like a person's trembling, 267
Poet. *See* Pulavaṉ
Pollution: chickens and dogs polluting for Brahmins, 53; at least some Brah-